THE
EVERYTHING®
BEER BOOK

The Everything Series:

The Everything® After College Book
The Everything® Baby Names Book
The Everything® Bartender's Book
The Everything® Bicycle Book
The Everything® Casino Gambling Book
The Everything® Cat Book
The Everything® Christmas Book
The Everything® College Survival Book
The Everything® Dreams Book
The Everything® Etiquette Book
The Everything® Family Tree Book
The Everything® Games Book
The Everything® Get Ready for Baby Book
The Everything® Golf Book
The Everything® Home Improvement Book
The Everything® Jewish Wedding Book
The Everything® Pasta Cookbook
The Everything® Study Book
The Everything® Wedding Book
The Everything® Wedding Checklist
The Everything® Wedding Etiquette Book
The Everything® Wedding Organizer
The Everything® Wedding Vows Book
The Everything® Wine Book
The Everything® Beer Book

THE
EVERYTHING®
BEER BOOK

Everything You Need to Know to Buy and Enjoy
the Best Beers—or Even Brew Your Own

Carlo DeVito

Adams Media Corporation
HOLBROOK, MASSACHUSETTS

Special thanks to James and Lia Prendergast for their help tasting and testing; to Edward Theurkauf and Carol Robinson—homebrewers extraordinaire of Southern Pennsylvania—for sharing their favorite recipes; Robert and Julie Beth Hoover for gastronomic advice; Charles Napa; the folks at Blue Ridge Brewing Company; and to my editor, Pam Liflander, and my wife, Dominique.

An Everything® Series Book. The Everything® Series is
a registered trademark of Adams Media Corporation.

Published by Adams Media Corporation
260 Center Street, Holbrook, MA 02343

ISBN: 1-55850-843-0

Printed in the United States of America.

J   I   H   G   F   E   D   C   B   A

Library of Congress Cataloging-in-Publication Data
DeVito, Carlo.
The everything beer book / Carlo DeVito.
      p.   cm.
Includes index.
ISBN 1-55850-843-0
1. Beer. I. Title.
TP577.D485   1998
641.2'3—dc21   97-48839
                    CIP

This publication is designed to provide accurate and authoritative information with regard to the subject matter covered. It is sold with the understanding that the publisher is not engaged in rendering professional advice. If legal advice or other expert assistance is required, the services of a competent professional person should be sought.
— From a *Declaration of Principles* jointly adopted by a Committee of the American Bar Association and a Committee of Publishers and Associations

Illustrations by Barry Littmann

*This book is available at quantity discounts for bulk purchases.
For information, call 1-800-872-5627 (in Massachusetts, call 781-767-8100).*

Visit our home page at http://www.adamsmedia.com

CONTENTS

CONTENTS

CONTENTS

WHAT IS BEER?

1

CHAPTER

BOTTLED BY
ADAMS MEDIA CORPORATION

eer is what your dad drank. And you drank what he drank. And he drank what his dad drank. It was simple. Whether with dinner, after working hard outside, or while watching a football or baseball game, nothing beats the simple pleasures of an icy cold one and leaning back. Ahhh! Right?

This was not a difficult decision, and there were no different flavors. Just different manufacturers. All the beers were more or less the same, and the world of beer was a relatively safe one. Few choices make for fewer mistakes.

Since the 1970s, there have been a few domestic beer kings: Coors, Miller, Anheuser-Busch, Budweiser, Schlitz, and a small host of other regional beers. And of course, for the high-rolling crowd, there was that bitter-tasting stuff like Heineken, Becks, St. Pauli Girl, and Amstel Light. And then beer started getting complicated. First there was the beer with the lime in it. What was that all about? Since when did Mexico export beer to the United States? And then there were these microbrews that were some pretty good beers, like Sam Adams and Pete's Wicked. What was the world coming to?

As soon as I saw there was raspberry beer, I had to find out what was going on. Well, I'll let you in on a little secret: raspberry beer has been around for centuries. I learned after long study that beer was going back to its roots. But in order to explain it, you must start at the beginning.

Beer is one of the most important beverages ever concocted by man. It was used by the first established cultures to denote civility and distinction. Once used to baptize children, beer has always been attributed with both mystical and medicinal powers, and today is one of the most powerful and competitive industries in the world. Oh, yes, and it's fun to drink.

So what is beer? Beer is a brewed beverage, which means that before bottling it has to be heated or cooked. Beer is a beverage made from various combinations of these basic ingredients: barley, wheat, or some other grain; water; yeast; and hops. There are many types of beers because there are many combinations of these ingredients, and there are many ways to brew and finish a beer.

Ale and beer: alcoholic fermented beverages prepared from grain and flavored with hops. The predominant grain is malted barley. Specially prepared corn and rice are also used.

—THE ENCYCLOPEDIA AMERICANA

THE EPIC OF GILGAMESH

This document alone is responsible in large part for what we know of ancient Sumeria and of beer. It is the first, full-length epic poem of a nation. The Sumerians considered themselves the first of the great civilized nations. *The Epic of Gilgamesh* follows primitive man to his higher state of being, as a civilized man.

Gilgamesh, the hero of the poem, goes through a series of events that prove his cunning, strength, and ability to champion all that is good in society. In one section, a challenger confronts Gilgamesh, and invites him to battle. Gilgamesh agrees. As a gift, Gilgamesh sends a prostitute to his challenger

There are ales, lagers, porters, and stouts and even a raspberry beer from Belgium called framboise. But all beers distinguish themselves by being carbonated, to some extent or other. What distinguishes beer from wine is that wine is made from grapes and is not brewed. Beer is different from whiskey in that whiskey is made from the same ingredients as beer, but it is distilled much further than beer. Whiskey also has no carbonation and is usually of significantly higher alcoholic content than beer.

Beer was originally brewed in the home for individual or communal consumption. Beer has tended to be more popular in those parts of the world where grain is most easily grown. Though connoisseurs of fine wines, champagnes, brandies, cognacs, and other distilled spirits have at times turned their noses up at beer, considering it the beverage of the common people, this has hardly been the case throughout history. Beer has always been one of the most popular and most requested beverages since it first came into existence.

In Europe, the love of beer has never wavered. In countries like England, Ireland, Germany, Belgium, and the Netherlands, beer has always been a world unto itself. From the lightest beers in color and taste, to the strongest ales, to the sweetest dessert beers, theirs has been a world of purposeful preservation and enjoyment. In Europe, each country has its signature beers, and even towns are world renown because of their beers.

In America, beer is experiencing a renaissance. Somewhere between the late 1960s and the early 1980s, there were just a few large manufacturers brewing some very pale beers, and only a few small brewers survived the toughest of times. American beer drinkers started turning to European beers in the late 1980s, forcing the beer industry to re-examine itself. Some entrepreneurs opened what are now popularly called microbreweries or brewpubs. Some of them sold contract beers, which were special recipes brewed by larger brewers. Regardless, American beer drinkers' interests heightened, and the beer industry is now experiencing a huge boom.

SUMERIA AND THE BIRTH OF BEER

Scientists and academicians have been arguing over the birth of beer. The first recorded description of beer in words or artifacts suggests the brewing of beer dates back between 6,000 and 9,000 years ago.

The first beers were brewed somewhere between the Tigris and Euphrates Rivers in what is now Iran. It is no coincidence that this is the same fertile crescent thought to be the cradle of civilization. There are stone tablets dating back to the Kingdom of the Sumeria, which detail a grain known then as "emmer," and how it is supposed to be milled. Emmer was an early grain used to make beer. There are even ancient texts that show how grain fields were judged by how much beer it is thought they might produce.

Still, no one really knows for sure how the first beer was made. We do know that early peoples first moved from hunters to gatherers when they decided to grow wheat and other ancient grains—all ingredients in early beer. It has been supposed by some anthropologists that humans first began to harvest grains to bake bread. However, other artifacts have been discovered that tell us that maybe grain was harvested to make beer first. Other scholars claim that bread was created first, and then was soaked with water and left somewhere, eventually producing a liquid akin to beer. This theory might hold true, as we know that some of the first recipes for beer were made with bread instead of milled barley or other grains.

Regardless, the first beer was probably an accident. Ground grains or a bit of bread were left out in the rain, a few days in the sun, and voila!

Ancient texts do document the growing popularity of beer in Sumeria, but it must be noted that many other civilizations began to understand the unique qualities of beer in and around this time. Some found it out similarly by trial and error, while others had the finished product brought to them through trade and commerce. But wherever man was, be it Africa, Asia, the Americas, Europe, or the Middle East, the great civilizations of their day all created some kind of brew that could technically be called beer. In the Americas they made beer with corn, in Asia with rice, in

(continued)

for seven days. She invites the challenger to taste beer and the other pleasures of civilized man. "He drank seven goblets of beer. His spirit was loosened. He became hilarious. His heart was glad and his face shone." In this way, the challenger became civilized, and felt no need to defeat Gilgamesh. The primitive man had seen the light, so to speak, and was accepted into the community.

More important, *The Epic of Gilgamesh* mentions beer in many places and gives us a real sense of how important beer was in the Sumerian culture. In the poem, beer was quoted to be the drink of the gods.

Africa with millet and sorghum. If there was grain for bread, there was grain for beer.

The properties of this new drink did not go unnoticed by the ancients. Soon, the Sumerians were able to perfect this process, and the art of brewing beer was preserved for all humankind. We know that by the year 3,000 B.C. there were priests who brewed beer to ensure that it was superior enough to please the gods. The priests guarded their recipes, and not all men and women were invited to partake of beer's mysteries.

The first makers of beer were women. And the first gods of beer were women as well. Ninkasi, the goddess of plenty, and Ama-Gestin, the Earth-Mother, were two of the most revered gods of the ancient Sumerians, and were also thought to be the protectors and providers of beer. Another goddess, Siduri, the protector of breweries and beer shops, was also popular. However, a priestess who brewed beer was not allowed to drink the beverage outside of religious ceremonies. Even so, as beer became less a religious drink and more a popular beverage to be consumed, the first bar owners were also in fact women. These women were called Sabtiem.

Sumerian literature is full of stories about beer. Texts from ancient times relate that Sumerians would flock to beer establishments called Bit Sikari when their days' work was done. All social classes were allowed. Patrons sipped the brew straight from the vat, through long pieces of straw. You would stand or sit near the vat and place the end of the straw beneath the foam and into the mixture. Ancient Sumerians thought that beer had medicinal purposes, so beer became a very important cure-all. It is well known that many of these shops used the images of naked or buxom women to entice customers to sample their beers. They used signs with images or had pottery with such drawings engraved on them.

THE BABYLONIANS AND BEER

The Babylonians followed as the rulers of the Sumerians in the Middle East. During this time, beer was in its crudest stages. It was fermented and served in the same pots. It still had to be drunk through a reed. It was always cloudy and rarely filtered. The Babylonians, however, had increased the kinds of beer they brewed. They brewed sixteen different beers from either emmer or barley. Another four different beers were brewed from a mixture of grains.

The Babylonians made two great contributions to the history of beer. The first was the Code of Hammurabi. This was the code of law in ancient Babylonia, and it mentioned beer extensively. While beer was a well documented item in Babylonia, nowhere was it more fervently mentioned than in the Code of Hammurabi. At this time, beer was still considered somewhat mystical, and a brewer could not accept silver or gold for her work, but only barley in return for her product. The acceptance of money by a Sabtiem for her beer was thought to sully the holiness of the transaction. In the Code, those who overcharged for beer were sentenced to death by drowning. And those Sabtiem who harbored criminals, or who harbored those who plotted crimes and were not reported by the bar owners, were also executed.

The Code of Hammurabi also established a daily ration of beer based on social strata. High-ranking civil leaders, priests, and priestesses were allowed five liters of beer per day, which was the most allowed by law. The next highest was three liters per day for the rest of the civil workers and administrators, and the average worker received two liters.

The second most important contribution of the Babylonians was to pass on their knowledge to the Egyptians. They did this through the export of ales.

SUMERIAN BREW CHOICES

There were many types of Sumerian beer. The finest and most premium beer was called Kassagasaan. There was a red beer known as Kassig. And there were two quality black beers: Kassi (black beer) and Kassag (fine black beer).

To celebrate their tenth anniversary, the brewmasters at Anchor Brewing Company in San Francisco, California, followed the recipes for these beers as they were translated by Dr. Solomon H. Katz of the University of Pennsylvania. The result was reportedly very bubbly and had the aromas of fruit.

A MEDIEVAL DINNER

In medieval times, buttered bread and beer were a meal unto themselves. Many a serf was happy to slather his or her bread with rancid butter and count his or her blessings as they bit down into dinner. Things were slightly different then. Butter was not the nice little homogenized stick or pat that we use today. Butter back then was a collection of vegetable fats and meat drippings from numerous cooking occasions that were mixed and then seasoned with herbs. This mixture was then stored in barrels underground for anywhere from six months to two years. These barrels

BEER IN EGYPT

The Egyptians revered beer more than any other civilization. Children were baptized in beer. Workers could be paid in beer. Beer even went into the tombs of the dead to help in their passage to the next world. Even taxes could be paid in beer. One of the highest ranking positions in Egypt was that of the Chief Beer Inspector. And of course, the higher up in society you were, the better the beer you drank. Royal family, high-ranking officials, and warriors all drank the best beer. Regular workers drank the lowest or most common beer. An oft-quoted motto from ancient Egypt was: Happy is the man whose mouth is filled with beer.

One of the Egyptians' significant contributions to beer was their addition of date sugar to the brewing process. The date sugar reduced the chances of the beer spoiling too quickly and made it possible to store beer. Along with the lengthening of the beer's life, Egypt was one of the first civilizations to create commercial breweries. If you could store beer, you could make huge quantities and sell it cheaper. While it was not uncommon for a household to brew its own beer, it was also not uncommon for professional brewers to have giant clay pots or jars—larger than the average man—in which beer was stored. The beers could only last a few days in the most ideal of circumstances.

The Egyptians made their beer from half-baked bread that was forced through a strainer, mixed with water, and then stored in the earth. Egyptians brewed strong beers called Zythium (grain brewed with cumin, ginger, and juniper), and regular-strength beers named Busa. Egyptian beer was typically a lager made with dates, ginger, and honey, used separately as well as in mixtures. Egyptian beers tended to be sweet. The Egyptians were also the first to create alcohol-free beer. The temple priestesses would brew beer and then bring it to the temple and boil it, releasing the spirit of the alcohol to the gods to please them. The resulting beer was alcohol-free, and was sold to the populace to help support the temple.

The beer that was offered up was to honor the goddess Hathor. The legend of Hathor is similar to that of Noah. Re, the chief of all Egyptian gods, was not happy with Egypt, and he sent Hathor to discipline mankind for three days. After the first day, the streets ran with rivers of blood. Re was afraid that there might be no one left to worship him, so he threw barley and dates into the rivers. Hathor drank from the rivers until they subsided, then fell into a deep sleep for the next two days, sparing the lives of the remaining Egyptians. Thus, the priests would appease Hathor with their beer in order that they might be spared more bloodshed and destruction. Eventually, she became known as the Queen of Drunkenness.

EUROPE, BEER, AND THE MIDDLE AGES

During the great empires of the Greeks and Romans the art of brewing did not die, but it did not flourish either. Beer was made from grains. Wine was made from grapes. Grapes did not grow as well in the Middle East as they did in the southern European climes of Greece, Rome, and Gaul. Thus, it is not surprising that wine became the more popular drink in these realms, as it was more easily made than beer. Wine was elevated to the level beer enjoyed in other cultures. It had its own gods, the most famous of which was Bacchus.

But beer was drunk and brewing was kept alive, especially in the northern plains of Europe, known today as Germany and Belgium. The history of beer in Germany dates back as far as 800 B.C. Grains were easier to grow in these climes than grapes, so beer was naturally preferred. Beer was widely mentioned in the epic poems of these regions. In Nordic legend, a giant horn of ale that would never empty awaits in the afterlife for those who die in battle. In the Nordic regions it was popular to put garlic into one's beer, to ward off all harm or evil spirits.

(continued)

were usually sunk in peat bogs since they were cool areas. This was done so that the butter might ferment and age properly.

Beer of that time was made in a somewhat different fashion than it is today. The wort was made and cooled in the open air so that wild, airborne yeasts might land and begin the fermentation process. If a barrel of beer went bad it was blamed on the "Brew Witches."

Beer and buttered bread became the backbone of the medieval diet and were thought at the time to be a wholly substantial and indeed nutritious meal.

No children without sex;
no drunkenness without beer.

—ANCIENT SUMERIAN
PROVERB

While brewing had earlier been the domain of women, that changed in Europe in the Middle Ages. With the establishment of monasteries throughout Europe, monks needed a beverage that was nutritious, as their meals tended to be quite meager. Beer and bread were their main means of sustenance. It is also important to note that beer was allowed during times of fasting. It was the monks who first added hops to beer and gave us many of the modern refinements that have resulted in the product we are most familiar with today.

Eventually, the monks began to sell their beers to the inhabitants of the nearest towns, earning money for the church or for the monastery itself. These beers eventually became renowned and drew much business to the town. Trying to catch onto a good thing, local townspeople began brewing beer. Beer was going through another golden age. It was then that the nobility and administrators of these areas began levying taxes on beer brewed by commercial beer makers. Because the monasteries were religious and therefore exempt, these were eventually shut down by ducal decree. This left only the municipal brewhouses, who paid the tax and were very profitable. The brewmasters from these municipal houses eventually formed a Brewer's Guild. By the 1300s, beer was the most popular beverage of Northern Europe, England, and Ireland.

BEER
Ingredients —

COMMERCIAL BEER AND THE GERMAN BEER PURITY LAW

Before the use of hops, Europeans used various herbs, roots, berries, and even flowers to flavor their beers. The most frequently used flavoring for beer was called grut—an individualized mixture of herbs which gave each brewery its own flavor. Grut licenses were issued, guaranteeing that a special flavoring was unique to that brewery and that no one else could brew that same beer. Many brewers used wildly different things to ensure that their beer was unique. Some ingredients were downright hallucinogenic.

For all the good beer that was brewed in the Middle Ages, there were some accidents as well. Brewing at this time was still not an exact science, and with each brewery trying to outdo one another, some mistakes became hazardous to the drinkers' health—even causing death. These sometimes fatal mistakes were blamed on "brew witches." Brew witches were thought of as ethereal spirits, but were often the brewmaster or whomever the brewmaster blamed. The last brew witch was burned at the stake in 1591. Fortunately, it was around this time that hops became an accepted ingredient in beer, leading to more stable brews and less health hazards.

The first hops were introduced around A.D. 800. Hildegarde, a Benedictine nun who was an abbess in Rupertsberg (now Mainz, Germany), was the first to record the use of hops in brewing. Up until that time, the hop plant had been used to preserve and tan leather, was used in the manufacture of shampoos, and was also known as a popular sedative. Hildegarde discovered that hops gave beer a longer life and a more reliable finished product.

Even into the early 1400s, the use of hops in ale sometimes resulted in riots, and it took a sovereign writ in 1436 to quell the public disapproval of such use. Brewers of "hopping beers" had to be protected by sheriffs in London. It was not until the 1500s that hopping was accepted as a part of brewing. Hops added flavor, and more important, gave beer a longer shelf life. In short, the beer was better in quality and clearer.

In 1516, Duke Wilhelm IV of Bavaria issued the Reinheitsgebot, or the German Beer Purity Law. This established that water, malted barley or wheat, hops, and yeast were the only ingredients that could be found in beer. This ensured a homogenous product. Not only was the duke interested in protecting consumers' rights, he was interested in improving the national standard so that beer could be reliably exported, and if so, then taxed. The duke was really much more interested in money than he was in beer as a commodity. Let's face it, the duke only drank the best beer anyway. He wasn't interested in the consistency of his own personal beer as much as concerned about growing an industry for export and making money from it. However, it became the basis from which all beer is made today, and in Germany it is still a law that Germans hold near and dear to their hearts.

While all of the German breweries pay great attention to the laws concerning beers served within the German border, beers being exported do not have to pass these strict regulations. The most recent case under which someone was prosecuted and convicted under the Reinheitsgebot was in 1986.

DIFFERENT VARIETIES OF BEER

2

CHAPTER

BOTTLED BY
ADAMS MEDIA CORPORATION

ALES AND LAGERS

There are two main categories of beer: ales and lagers. Ales are among the oldest beers in the world, and predate lagers by several thousand years. The Sumerians and Egyptians drank mostly ales, whereas lagers date only from the mid-nineteenth century. In fact, it was not until lager came along that ale had to be identified as anything but beer.

Ales are fermented warm and made with a top-fermenting yeast—a yeast that rises to the top of the brew mixture during fermentation. Ales are generally stronger and more assertive in taste than lagers because of their relatively fast and warm fermentation, as opposed to the slower, colder lagering process. In many pubs throughout Europe, and especially in England, ales are served at room temperature.

Lager, from the German word *lagern*, literally means to store. Lagers are made with a bottom- or cold-fermenting yeast that sinks to the bottom of the brew mixture during fermentation. A lager traditionally needs to age for a period of up to several months to complete the fermentation, whereas ales can be complete in as little as seven to ten days. Because of their longer fermentation process, lagers are generally smoother, crisper, and more subtle in taste than ales. Lagers are always served cold.

The following is a description of some of the common beer styles.

Alt or Altbier

Altbier is one of the oldest beers in the world. Some people have mistaken alt for meaning ale, but in fact it means old. This is not an aged beer, but a beer whose tradition is long and heralded. It is called old because it is brewed in an old style, with a single-celled, top-fermenting yeast. Alt beers are traditionally brewed warm with top-fermenting yeasts, like an ale, but are stored cold, like a lager. So is it an ale or a lager? Alt is brewed like an ale so it is considered an ale.

Alts tend to be well-hopped beers, so they tend to be a little bitter in taste. Alts also tend to range from light rust to dark copper in color. These beers are well known for being brewed in

Dusseldorf, Germany. There are also strong alt-brewing traditions in Dortmund and Munster.

Barley Wine

This is an often misunderstood beer. Barley wine is an ale—it is not wine at all. Also known as strong ale (in Belgium), this is the most potent beer made. This strong barley-brewed ale is called barley wine because its alcohol content is so high (barley wine's alcohol level often ranges from eight to fourteen percent, which is more similar to the alcohol level of wines than that of beer). It packs quite a punch. In fact, barley wines contain the highest alcohol content of any beers and taste more like liqueurs than beers.

The best of the barley wines are not only strong, but are flavorful and well bodied with a strong taste of malt. The worst of these beers are nothing more than exercises in how high of an alcohol content one can get in a beer. No matter how strong the hopping, the fruity flavors and aromas of a barley wine will tend to show through. Barley wines tend to be dark and rich, and leave a long-lasting aftertaste that warms the throat—hence the name "winter warmer." Many beer connoisseurs consider barley wine a dessert beer. It is not to be drunk with the same gusto as a pilsner or a wheat beer; rather, it is to be sipped and savored as a gourmand experience.

Belgian Ales

Depending on the country you are in, ordering a Belgian ale could bring you many different things. Inside Belgium, ordering an ale is likely to bring you something close to an English ale—only spicier. Outside of Belgium, it is common to group any number of top-fermented beers produced in Belgium under this category, and ordering a Belgian ale is likely to bring you anything from a Flemish brown ale (Liefmans), Belgian red ale (Rodenbach), or golden ale (Duvel), to a saison (Saison Dupont) or Trappist (Chimay, Orval) beer.

A Flemish brown ale has nothing in common with its English counterpart. A Flemish brown ale is reddish or rust colored, and is brewed from a complex mixture of grains and yeasts. After a two-stage fermentation, it is aged in barrels for a period of time.

Trappist beers are beers brewed in the Trappist tradition. The Trappist dubbel tends to be darker and drier than the trippel, which tends to be lighter and sweeter. Saison is a spicy beer that can range anywhere from a copper to bright orange color.

Without question, the greatest invention in the history of mankind is beer. Oh, I grant you that the wheel was also a fine invention, but the wheel does not go nearly as well with pizza.

—DAVE BARRY

Bitter

Bitters are some of the most popular beers in England, and aren't that bitter at all. When the English first started brewing beer with hops, the taste was drier than the ales that had predated them. The name "bitter" was given to the drier taste, and thus was bitter born. Bitter beers are usually golden or amber in color and range from mild to very flavorful. These beers taste somewhat like a pale ale, and are not as bitter as an India Pale Ale. This is a very pedestrian (in the best sense of the word) beer in England—in local pubs it is not uncommon to hear the request, "Give me a pint of your best bitter."

There are several different grades of bitters, usually ranked by their gravity. Bitter is the lowest or most ordinary of these beers and is followed by special bitter and extra special bitter. The extra special bitter has a little higher alcohol content and a more complex flavor than the bitter and special bitter. In England, bitter is still drawn from wooden casks and pumped by hand.

Bock and Doppelbock

Bocks are strong lagers brewed with twice as much malt as a traditional lager. Bocks are clean and crisp due to a lengthy, cold maturation. Most often brewed for seasonal consumption during the winter or early spring, some bocks are strong enough to be consumed with dessert.

Doppelbocks are stronger than bocks, though not twice as strong as their name implies (*doppel* is German for double). Perhaps the most well-known and imitated doppelbock is the

Paulaner Salvator. In honor of this beer, many brewers offer a doppelbock with the -ator ending, such as Spaten Optimator, Hacker-Pschorr Animator, and Ayinger Celebrator.

Brown Ale

Like bitters, brown ales are brewed for popular consumption. These are not gourmet beers. Brown ale is a good beer to drink when you're going to be down at the pub for a long time. Brown ales come mostly from Northern England, are dark, and have an alcohol level somewhere between four and five percent.

The deep, dark color of these beers comes from using chocolate (dark-roasted) malts. These beers are very much like pale ales, with a little less hops and a little more malt. Brown ales are easy to drink and are good for beginners as well as for those who have tasted their share of beer. For those with a discerning palate, well-crafted brown ales should have some caramel overtones, and have both a nutty and fruity flavor without being sweet. Some brown ales are flavored with brown sugar or molasses. A good brown ale is not very strong, but neither is it weak or watery. This is a flavorful ale. American versions of brown ale tend to have a somewhat drier finish than that of their English forebears and are typically called nut brown or honey brown ales.

Canadian Ale

Traditional Canadian ale is hard to come by these days. Many of the commercial brewers that make this style of beer are not doing justice to the fine tradition of Canadian brewing. The most commercial are fizzy and weak. The legendary ales of Canada were first brewed at the turn of the century. Several microbrewers have attempted to revive this style recently. Like altbier, Canadian ale is brewed warm with top-fermenting yeasts, then stored cold like a lager.

Canadian ales should be golden in color, with some bitterness. There should be some body to this beer—even a creaminess, which is why they are also known as cream ales. There should also be a very strong taste of grain and spice, but not overwhelmingly so. Canadian ale should be very crisp and pronounced in flavor.

Dark (or Dunkel) Lager

Before the golden pilsner (lager) became prevalent, there were dark lagers, or in Germany, Dunkels. These beers have the crispness associated with lagers, but offer a spicier malt and lighter hop taste. The original dark lagers of Munich were dark brown, and many dark lagers are offered in the United States as Bavarian or Munich-style lagers.

Dortmunder Export/Helles

These German lagers are making a well-deserved comeback among microbrewers. Both are noted for their tasty, balanced flavors. Dortmunder Exports are less hoppy but fuller in body than pilsners, and you'll find beers of this style labeled as Dortmunder, Export, or with both names together. A Helles (German for clear or light-colored) is lighter than a Dortmunder, and is less hoppy and more malty than a pilsner.

India Pale Ale

This name is a throwback to the days of the British Empire when the British Army occupied India. Because pale ales were popular back home, many brewers tried to supply them to their compatriots overseas. However, many of these beers lost their flavor on the long journey from England. Turbulence on the journey, drastic changes in temperature, and the long time between bottling and consumption all played a part in the disintegration of body and flavor.

In order to counteract this, an English brewer named Hodgson crafted a very strong pale ale. A combination of higher alcoholic content and more hops proved to have enough stamina to withstand the journey, and India Pale Ale was born. In England it is also known as IPA. Because the beer was stored in oak casks, the beer would pick up this flavor in transit. Some brewers today still store it in oak casks, and drinkers should still be able to taste the oak in the beer.

In keeping with its original intent, India Pale Ale is usually higher in alcoholic content than regular pale ales, containing about 5–7.5

percent alcohol by volume. They are golden in color and are bitter. These are strong, clean beers that leave a dry aftertaste.

Kölschbier

This is another of the classic German ales, and is very popular in Germany in the summer. Kölsch (pronounced "kelsch") is golden in color and should have some fruitiness to it. While it is very refreshing, you should taste some bitterness. Because this is not a filtered beer, the finish is somewhat cloudy.

The name kölsch is derived from Köln, Germany (better known as Cologne). In order for a beer to be named Kölschbier, it must be brewed by members of the Köln Brewer's Union. Much like the names 'Champagne' or 'Bordeaux' in the wine world, the Kölschbier name is protected and controlled, and may not be used by anyone not belonging to, or approved by, the union.

True to the history of beer throughout time, many Germans swear by Kölschbier's medicinal powers. It is said to be an excellent curative for digestive problems.

Lambic

Lambics are a type of wheat beer that is fermented with wild yeasts. Commonly associated with the area just south of Brussels (possibly getting their name from the town of Lembeek), Belgium, lambics are now being tried in other parts of the world. Gueuze is a blend of old and young lambics in which a second fermentation is induced when the young lambic is introduced into the old. Faro is a lambic sweetened with rock candy.

Lambics are also used as a basis for some, but not all, fruit beers, and are labeled as such by Belgian producers. A kriek lambic is a lambic that is made with cherries, while a framboise (or frambozen) lambic is made with raspberries. Outside of Belgium, you might find fruit beers in general labeled as lambics. For example, the Samuel Adams Cranberry Lambic is a cranberry fruit beer but does not use a lambic as its base.

Pale Ale

Usually a dry-hopped ale, the term pale is used loosely in this grouping of beers. Ales underwent a series of changes, especially in the Middle Ages. As beers became darker and darker and evolved into porters and stouts, practically anything brewed that wasn't a darker beer was labeled a pale ale. Pale ales range in color from light golden to amber and rusty copper. Body and color range tremendously. American pale ales tend to be lighter than their English counterparts.

Pale ale came into its own in the eighteenth century, when hopping became more or less a consistent if not perfected brewing technique. The English used several different types of hops, including Brewer's Gold, Galena, Kent Goldings, and Northern Brewer. These types of hops impart a unique bitterness and aroma to the beers.

Pilsner

Originating in the Bohemian (today's Czech Republic) town of Plzen (Pilsen) and later in Budweis, pilsners were the first lagers that were clear and golden. Early popularized by Budweiser and its imitators in the United States, pilsners are the most widely produced beers in the world. This style of beer is characterized by its balanced, dry, hoppy taste. It is designed to be a simple, refreshing drink. The mass-produced versions are brewed with adjuncts such as corn and rice, but the classic versions—defined by a flowery, dry finish—have never gone out of style in continental Europe and are being revived by microbrewers in the United States.

Porter

The first thing to know about porter is that it was brewed before stout. Like stouts,

WHEAT BEER
Australia

PILSNER
Czechoslovakia

BOCK BEER
Germany

DRY STOUT
Ireland

STRONG ALE
England

DARK LAGER
Denmark

PALE ALE
Canada

porters can range from dark brown to almost black. Generally speaking, porters are the sweeter of the two, and have less alcohol by content. There should be a real sense of the grain in the taste. The weakest porters are somewhat watery but very drinkable—a darker version of a brown ale. These are excellent for a long night of sipping; the roasted flavors should shine through. Some have a fruity or chocolate taste to them.

Drinking a pint or two of this at a pub can be a meal, and a nutritious one at that. In fact, porter is named for the porters of Victoria Station in London, who made a meal out of this heavy, dark brew. Originally, there was no such single brew as a porter. It was a combination of beers mixed at the pub as directed by the customer. But one brewmaster crafted an ale that came close to this concoction, called it porter, and the name stuck. There is little real difference today between stouts and porters.

Many beer experts agree that the porter had all but died in its country of origin and was only recently saved by American microbrewers. The truth is that the English have never forgotten porter, and have been brewing the lesser gravity and alcohol version for years.

Scottish Ale (Scotch Ale or Scots Ale)

The first thing that strikes you when buying this beer is that it is graded by shillings. This is reminiscent of a time when the British government taxed beer by its gravity: the heavier and stronger the beer, the higher the tax. When ordering a Scotch ale in an authentic Scottish pub, do not order beer by asking for a heavy, light, or named beer; order it by its rating: "Give me an 80 shilling."

Below are the ratings:

Scottish Light	60 shilling
Scottish Heavy	70 shilling
Scottish Export	80 shilling
Scotch Ale	90 to 120 shilling

These are very flavorful beers, but some find them very overpowering, especially the 90 to 120 shilling brews. Scotch ales are usually darker than English ales and tend to be marginally stronger in alcohol content. The malt is also much more prevalent. They are so malty, you may even smell it. There is little hops to taste, but these ales do tend to be somewhat sweet. This is a beer that will keep you warm on a cold night.

Stout

Stout came after porter and was originally called stout porter. It has traditionally been a stronger version of porter, often darker than porter, if that's possible, with strong coffee or burnt caramel flavors. In discussing stouts, it is more accurate to speak of the stout family of beers, for there are various kinds of stout such as dry stout, imperial stout, oatmeal stout, and sweet stout.

Stout beer is not for the beginner. In many instances it is not for the discerning beer yeoman, especially the Russian imperial stout. Stout is an acquired taste. Its rich flavor and heavy gravity is not for downing on a hot, humid day. No one ever quenched a hot thirst drinking a stout—you'd probably choke on it after mowing the lawn in July. It is an acquired taste for a mature palate. It is for sipping and savoring.

Sweet stout is an ale that has strong overtones of fruit flavors, especially plum, and is brewed with chocolate malt. It is one of the best known stouts, owing to the fact that it contains lactose (milk sugar), which gives it a sweet, smooth taste. It is also recommended in England for its medicinal properties. This is a beer of low alcoholic content. This style is also known as English stout, and is of the greatest gravity in this group.

Dry stout is also known as Irish stout, and its well-known manufacturer is Guinness. These stouts tend to have a maltier, roasted flavor and are usually greater than the sweet or oatmeal stouts in alcoholic content. Dry stout gets its distinctive flavor from the use of unmalted roasted barley.

Oatmeal stout is actually brewed with oatmeal, and that flavor comes out along with coffee and burnt toffee overtones. This tends to be a very smooth, dark beer with a great amount of body, but is not necessarily high in alcoholic content.

Imperial stout was originally brewed as a very strong stout for the pre-revolutionary czar of Russia, a fan of this English-style beer. Because a typical English stout did not travel well, losing much of its flavor on the journey from England to Moscow or St. Petersburg, brewers catering to the czar loaded their brews with hops. This fortified the beer with a bitter flavor and great body that lasted, making it the strongest of the stout family. This heady brew is known in some parts of the world as either Russian stout or Russian imperial stout.

Trappist

The name Trappist refers to the place where this beer is brewed, not how it is made. Trappist beers are ales that have been brewed in abbeys for hundreds of years. By law there are only six Trappist breweries in the world that can sell Trappist beer. One is in the Netherlands, and five are in Belgium.

The real secrets of these beers are the top-fermenting yeasts used to brew them. The abbeys have cultivated these yeasts for the last four or five centuries, and they are quite unique and difficult to duplicate outside of their particular abbey of origin. It's what gives these beers such a special place in the beer-brewing world.

Most Trappist beers are very strong, ranging from six to thirteen percent alcohol by volume. These beers are bottle-conditioned and tend to be sweet, as some of the abbeys use sugar to brew their beer. The colors range from golden to dark brown. They are all beers of high gravity. Several of the abbeys have given different designations to their beers, ranking them like the Scottish ales. The categories are single, dubbel, and trippel. Trippel is the strongest of the three and is usually bitter and paler than the others. The single is the mildest of these beers, and was in centuries past brewed for the monks themselves. The dubbel is usually darker and a little stronger than the single.

Some beers may be labeled as abbey (also abbaye or abdij) beers to honor holy orders that used to produce beer, or because they are licensed from existing abbeys. These may or may not follow in the Trappist tradition.

Vienna-style (Amber, Märzen/Oktoberfest)

Known for their reddish or amber color, these lagers have a low to medium bitterness and a sweet, malty taste and aroma. Traditionally brewed in March (März) for Oktoberfest, the Vienna-style has been popularized around the world.

Wassail (also called Yule Ale, Mulled Ale, Winter Warmer, and Holiday Ale or Beer)

Wassail is a toast in Old English meaning to be in good health. *Waes hael* means literally to be whole or be hale. Wassail beer is the fragrant, spiced ale that was served in the Middle Ages during the holiday season, the time we think of today as being roughly from Thanksgiving to New Year's. Wassail was the toasting beverage of many a medieval household. A host would have said "Waes hael" as he offered you a cup of yuletide libation. More often than not, guests would partake of the wassail bowl and then, with their hosts, go out caroling, or wassailing, as it was known.

Most often wassail was a strong ale that was warmed with spices, sugars, and fruits. The fruits would be those native to the area (it has been conjectured that crab apples were a favorite), and the spices would be ginger, clove, nutmeg, or any other exotic spice that could be found at the time. Today, wassail is similarly a strong ale warmed on the stove with mulling spices and fruits of the chef's selection, usually apples, pears, plums, or oranges, and has the same stimulating and warming effect on guests in the darker, colder months of the year.

Wheat Beers (Weizenbier or Weissbier)

While Europeans, especially Germans, have been drinking wheat beers for hundreds of years, they are only now becoming popular in America. Traditionally served during the summer, they are now all-year beers. The mash of this beer has wheat in it, ranging from twenty to sixty percent, which gives the beer a unique flavor. Some brewers use malt or unmalted wheat as well. Some recipes use an even mix of malted wheat and malted barley. The beers themselves range from four to six percent alcohol.

SEASON'S GREETINGS
WASSAIL (AKA WELCOME ALE)

4 large cored apples
8 pats butter
2 quarts apple cider
2 bottles Scotch ale
5 whole cloves
2 teaspoons nutmeg
1 small can frozen orange juice concentrate
1 cup dark brown sugar
extra sugar
extra cinnamon

Preheat oven to 375°F. Take cored apples and cut them in half. Cut through the center of the apple. The resultant halves should look like oddly shaped doughnuts. Place in baking dish. On top of each apple-half, place one pat of butter, and then sprinkle generously with sugar and cinnamon. Bake for 20 minutes.

In a large pot, add cider, beer, nutmeg, and cloves. Cook on low heat. Add frozen juice concentrate and brown sugar. Stirring constantly, cook on low heat for 10–15 minutes. Pour contents into serving bowl. Then take the baked apples and float them in the bowl.

Berliner Weisse is an extremely sour, pale beer that is brewed with lactose (milk sugars). It is brewed in Berlin and popular in northern Germany. It is very cloudy with sediment and has low alcoholic content, usually three percent or less. Sometimes it is served with fruit syrups (most often woodruff and raspberry), so that the patron may retard some of the sourness to his or her own liking. A wheat beer is often served with a slice of lemon in it. To order a fruit syrup you would say "wit schuss."

Weizen means wheat, and *weiss* means white in German. These are both wheat beers popular in southern Germany. A hefeweizen is a beer that has been treated with yeast. These beers are light and refreshing, and should have no bitterness at all. There should be little taste of hops. The aroma should always be fruity and spicy. A wheat beer should be no darker than medium gold in color, highly carbonated, slightly cloudy, and somewhat sour. It is a beer that stretches across two categories, as it is an ale that is served cold, like a lager.

There are variations on these beers, including dunkelweizen, a dark version of wheat beer that has a roasted flavor to it, and weizenbock, a lager brewed with wheat.

Witbier (Bière Blanche)

Witbier is a wheat beer unique to Belgium that has been brewed with forty-five to fifty percent wheat. It is very light in color, a discernible yellow, and cloudy—so much so that it looks almost white. The cloudiness and effervescence comes from being treated with yeast. Sediment is almost always present.

The town of Hoegaarden, Belgium, originated this style. It is brewed with different spices, including orange rind and coriander, which are added to give it its wonderful flavor and aroma. If you are in a French-speaking town, order this beer by calling it "bière blanche"; if you are in a Dutch-speaking town, order it as "witbier."

SPECIALTY BEERS

The following beers defy categorization for one reason or another. These are known as specialty beers. Some experts disagree and force these into one area or another. To each his own. This catch-all category holds some excellent beers, regardless.

Fruit Beers

The two most famous versions of fruit beers come from the Senne Valley in Belgium. Kriek is a lambic beer brewed with cherries. It is reddish in color with a sweet/sour taste. Framboise is a lambic made with raspberries and is slightly reminiscent of Chambord, but not as intense. The color is amber tinged with a slight purple color.

Fruit beers can be made from wheat beer, ales, or lagers. Long a tradition in American brewing, they are gaining in popularity around the world. Many brewpubs and microbreweries create a fruit beer by adding fruit (or extract) to their basic pilsner or wheat beer. Honey is a popular flavor, particularly with a wheat beer, but it is not too hard to find beers flavored with cherry, apricot, pumpkin, raspberry, maple syrup, and even chili.

Steam Beer

Steam beer, also known as California common or small beer, is the most difficult beer to ascribe to one side of the ledger: ale or lager. A steam beer uses both top- and bottom-fermenting yeasts. The resulting beer is a unique hybrid of ale and lager. It is clear and crisp like a lager, yet full-bodied as an ale, with a great maltiness about it. It should also have a real hoppiness about it, like a lager, and should finish dry. It should be amber to copper colored.

This is a beer that has been brewed down through the ages, most notably by the English and the Germans. As the heated mixture fermented, it would hiss, and thus the Germans called it *dampfbier*, or steambeer. While it was not incredibly popular in Europe, it became a huge favorite in America around the turn of the century on the west coast, especially in San Francisco, California. Popular legend has it that when the casks were finally opened in California, they hissed loudly, and thus the name "steam beer" came to be associated with it.

Steam beer is a trademarked term, and can only be sold under that name by the Anchor Steam Beer Company of San Francisco, California. This small brewery reinvented this special process and revived a wonderful American tradition. The brewery is well known for its large, shallow brewing kettles.

Some experts explain that California common beer was more a child of necessity than a mother of invention. When the first brewers went to California, they were woefully short on supplies and tried to make lagers without being able to store or serve them cold. It served brewers well that they could use the new German yeast, popular for lagers, but they needed to boil the mixture to kill off any bacteria. These beers were also highly hopped to prevent spoiling.

Black and Tan

Also known as a half-and-half, this style isn't really a style at all. Black and tan, while it is brewed and bottled as a single style today in the United States, was not originally developed like other beers. Black and tan is a mixture of two different beers: a light lager or ale, and a dark beer such as a porter or stout. The mixture in the British Isles is much debated. Some are absolute in their belief that the black and tan is a mixture of stout and light-bodied ale. Others are just as sure that it is a mixture of porter and lager. Most certainly the renditions we are treated to today are based on the porter and lager mixtures popular in the United States after the great waves of Irish and German immigrants arrived in the mid to late nineteenth century.

This is a beverage that has all the flavor characteristics of both beers. It has the roastiness of a porter or stout, with its flavorful chocolate and caramel overtones, and it has the more light-bodied, refreshing qualities of a pilsner, a dry finish with enough hops to give it some kick.

WHAT IS LIGHT BEER?

Light beer is usually a lager in a pilsner style. It has a light, hoppy taste with an alcohol level that can range from 2.7 to 4 percent. In America, it is usually known as a beer with lower calories and a lower alcohol content, but there is no rule or law in America stating the minimum or maximum calorie content for a light beer. The beers range in their reduced-calorie intake with the lowest at less than 100 calories per bottle. In Canada, the "light" in a beer refers solely to alcoholic content.

Light beers are made in two different ways. One method is to simply water down the beer. After brewing and clearing, etc., the beer is ready for bottling. It is then watered down, injected with extra carbonation, and bottled. The better beers are brewed with enzymes that convert the dextrin or carbohydrates to sugars. These beers, too, are sometimes watered down.

The most popular beers of this type include Coors Light, which was first brewed in 1979, followed by Miller Light in 1985, and Bud Light in 1987. Another popular imported light is Amstel Light, imported by the Heineken USA Group. The lightest of these beers calorie-wise is Miller Lite, coming in at ninety-six calories.

Light beer took off in America when Miller Lite joined the fray in 1985. The highlight of their aggressive marketing campaign was ads that featured famous sports personalities arguing over the beer's two attributes: less filling or tastes great. The campaign was one of the most successful in advertising history. It made drinking this less potent brew acceptable to the American male—the American market's biggest beer consumer. Not only were reduced calories a benefit, but the ads' positioning attempted to dispel the idea that light beers were less desirable because of their watered-down taste.

These beers tend to be lightly colored, clear, and clean. They must be served as cold as possible to hide their lack of taste. At worst, they are watery, tasteless wastes of time that serious beer drinkers ignore with good reason. However, there are some microbrewers that have taken up the challenge of brewing quality light beers.

BETTER LIGHT BEERS

Here are some of the better light beers. Asterisks indicate the best of this list.

- Boston Shiplight**
- Harpoon Light**
- August Schell Light Beer
- Berghoff Light Beer
- Cave Creek Chili Light
- Champion Red Light Beer
- Dixie Light Beer
- Flying Aces Light Beer
- Henry Winehard Private Reserve Light Beer
- New Orleans Best
- Old Depot Light Beer
- Point Light
- Rolling Rock Light Beer
- Wiedemann Light

THE NOT-SO-SOFT DRINK

There have been many attempts by the biggest brewers to expand their product lines (non-alcoholic beers, ice beers, dry beers, light beers, near beers, light-light beers), but the most unforgettable was Anheuser-Busch's non-alcoholic beverage called Chelsea. Chelsea was introduced in 1978 and was a soda marketed as "the adult soft drink." It wasn't as sweet as conventional sodas, and carried fewer calories. It was a mix of fruit flavors and seltzer water. However, what differentiated it from other sodas was that this beverage, when poured into a glass, had a head that made it look like beer. It was even packaged to look like a bottle of beer, including the labeling.

NON-ALCOHOLIC BEER

Perhaps you've heard, seen, or read something about non-alcoholic beers at one point or another and wondered: What the heck is non-alcoholic beer? And why would I drink it? Non-alcoholic beers are for those who can't have alcohol but miss the taste of beer. People not drinking alcohol for health, dietary, or other reasons—for example, heavy-equipment operators, pregnant women, designated drivers—can still enjoy the taste of beer with a non-alcoholic brew.

Non-alcoholic beer, or "near beer" as it is sometimes called, is beer that has been brewed and reheated and boiled after it is ready for bottling so that the alcohol is burned off. It is then bottled, injected with inert gas, and capped. Non-alcoholic or near beer may only have an alcohol level of 0.65 percent by volume. While near beers have only recently come into demand, they were invented centuries ago by the Egyptians. The beers were brewed for the gods, then boiled so that the fumes might rise up to intoxicate and please the gods. The resulting beer, free of alcohol, was sold for public consumption.

Like light beers, near beers tend to be watered down to reduce alcohol levels. Often, taste is sacrificed. They tend to be light golden colored and very clear. Some are gassier than others in an attempt to make up in fizz what they lack in taste. Many of these beers, save a rare few, are brewed by mass-market breweries.

Listed below are some non-alcoholic beers worth tasting. These beers should always be served icy cold. It is no surprise that the best of these brews are from Germany, and that these German counterparts stand up as beers, not just as non-alcoholic beverages.

The Best but Hard to Find*

- Clausthaler Bier
- Clausthaler Herbfrisches Schankbier
- Harke Beck Non-Alcoholic Malt Beverage
- St. Pauli Girl N.A. Non-Alcoholic

Other Good Near Beers

- Birell Non-Alcoholic Malt Beverage
- Bitburger Drive Alkoholfrei
- Coors Cutter Non-Alcoholic Beer
- Old Style Royal Amber Non-Alcoholic Malt Beverage
- Pro Non-Alcoholic Beer
- Utica Club Non-Alcoholic

You Won't Gag Drinking These

- Brigade Non-Alcoholic Malt Beverage
- Buckler Non-Alcoholic Brew
- Dab Kraft-Perle Cereal Beverage
- Genesse Non-Alcoholic Beer
- Jones Amber Style Non-Alcoholic Brew
- Old Milwaukee Non-Alcoholic
- Schlitz Non-Alcoholic Malt Beverage
- Sharp's Non-Alcoholic Beer

You May Gag on These

- Busch Non-Alcoholic Beer
- Falstaff Non-Alcoholic Malt Beverage
- Hamm's Non-Alcoholic Malt Beverage
- Kingsbury Brew Near Beer
- Kingsbury Red Non-Alcoholic Brew
- Metbrau Near Beer
- Molson Excel Non-Alcoholic Beer
- O'Doul's Non-Alcoholic Brew
- Pabst Premium Quality Non-Alcoholic Malt Beverage
- Schmidt Select Near Beer
- St. Christopher Non-Alcoholic Beer

* All of the best near beers mentioned in this category are brewed in strict accordance with the German Beer Purity Law of 1516.

(continued)

Outraged citizens, from senators to nurses' associations, were up in arms. They were sure that Anheuser-Busch, and the entire brewing industry, were attempting to turn their children on to what was obviously a drink intended to look like beer, thereby turning unsuspecting children toward a life of alcoholism.

With public opinion against them, Anheuser-Busch canned the line, so to speak, and attempted to reposition their product. It died an ugly death. "No one, of course," wrote Philip Van Munching in *Beer Blast*, "found irony in the fact that the brewers of Budweiser had been slapped down for trying to give drinkers a socially acceptable substitute for beer."

WHAT'S ZIMA?

If you haven't heard of Zima, let alone tasted it, and you're under thirty, you must have been living under a rock for the last five years. But some people drink it and still don't know what it is. As Richard A. Melcher wrote in *Business Week* magazine, "Zima was defined almost entirely by what it was not: it was not a beer, it was not a wine cooler, and without even a color."

Most beer books and most beer experts refuse to even acknowledge the existence of Zima. As Marty Nachel wrote: "Zorry, it'z not beer." However, it is a malt-based beverage and is sold in the beer section. It is brewed, by a brewer, and is a malt beverage. So, if it walks like a duck, talks like a duck. . . . But there is one thing it definitely has against it—it doesn't taste like beer at all!

Zima was the brain child of an executive committee at Coors Brewing Company of Golden, Colorado. The number three beer brewer in America in 1990 and 1991, Coors was trying to find a way to stimulate sales without concocting a beverage that would cut into their current ten percent market share. They did not want another beer, and they did not want a wine cooler. But they did want something that was related to their core brands. They were not the only brewer then considering selling a clear malt beverage. Miller Brewing Company was also testing a similar product, Qube.

While Miller bowed out of the competition early, unsatisfied with its product, Coors tested their brew using focus groups to target the young Generation X audience. This was the market they felt was interested in something new. Their ad campaign in late 1993 and early 1994 was one of the largest the beer-brewing industry had ever seen, and Zima became a hit. Zima had garnered a surprising 1.1 percent of the entire beer market, selling one million barrels in 1994.

All of this doesn't tell us what it is. Zima is a malt-based beverage that is brewed somewhat like beer. Instead of a hops and barley taste, it offers citrus flavors. And of course, it's clear instead of yellow to golden in color. Some people drink it straight like a beer or alone in a glass, while others pour it over ice.

Zima Clear Malt

This beverage has no real body when compared to most beers. There is no head when poured. Absolutely clear in color, this beverage is lightly carbonated and almost citrusy in flavor. It has lemon, lime, and grapefruit overtones. This very light brew leaves little aftertaste.

Zima Gold

In an effort to stimulate sales, Coors also introduced Zima Gold. Zima Gold is golden in color, like a pilsner, with no hops or barley flavors at all. The feeling is very much like an old version of ginger beer, though not quite as peppery. Zima Gold is somewhat sweet. Lots of spices are abundant, almost like a mulled beer, with cinnamon, clove, and lots of ginger.

BIRCH BEER, ROOT BEER, GINGER BEER, AND SARSAPARILLA

There are other beverages on the market today that are called beers and ales. Products like birch beer, root beer, sarsaparilla, ginger beer, and ginger ale used to be related to the beer industry. Many of these started out as brewed, alcoholic beverages and only later found their largest audience in the soft drink industry. Their history and current state of popularity sheds new light on some very old brewing practices.

Birch Beer, Root Beer, and Sarsaparilla

At one time birch beer and root beer were brewed and made with yeast. So they were very much a part of the beer world. They were also offered as a non-alcoholic alternative to beer. As in the real beer industry, there has recently been a proliferation of birch and root beer microbrewers, and homebrewing these beverages has become a hugely popular hobby.

While today's modern versions of birch beer and root beer overlap quite often, birch beer and root beer used to be very different drinks. The problem in trying to find a standardized distinction is that these drinks were brewed in different ways in every town around the country. Root beer and birch beer were homemade treats brewed in the kitchen, the backyard, or the barn, and farms and hamlets had their own favorite recipes. One town's root beer might be another town's birch beer. Birch bark, juniper, wintergreen, hops, vanilla, sarsaparilla, sassafras, ginger, licorice, spikenard, and other herbs and grasses were used to make these drinks. All were brewed with yeast at one stage or another.

Birch beer was "a nonmalt, slow-fermenting potent brew originally made from black birch sap, twigs, and honey," states the *Encyclopedia of Beer*, edited by Christine P. Rhodes. To make a wide-ranging comparison, birch beer is to root beer what ale is to lager. Birch beer is older, is less carbonated, and has lots of body. Root beer is usually more carbonated, sweeter, and smoother. The true distinction between birch beer and root beer should rely on several taste factors. First, birch beer should taste less sweet than root beer. Birch beer should have more bite and leave you with a drier palate.This is due to the combination of birch bark and wintergreen. Conversely, root beer should be sweeter, creamier, and smoother than birch beer. Like real beers, both birch and root beers run the gambit from foamy, frothy heads, to less carbonated beverages with little head.

The popular form of root beer we know today dates as far back as 1870, when a Philadelphia pharmacist named Charles Hires began selling the concoction. Much like Coca-Cola, it was sold as both a refreshing beverage as well as a medicinal cure-all. Hires' root beer was a brewed concoction whose ingredients included berries, roots, and other herbs. Hires' beverage became an overnight sensation at the 1876 Philadelphia World's Fair.

In the 1960s the FDA banned the use of sassafras, a key birch beer/root beer ingredient, as a carcinogen. Now wintergreen and a new, non-carcinogenic extract of sassafras are used.

Sarsaparilla is a name few people can identify as a separate beverage with any real discernible taste or brewing differences. Some of today's current manufacturers of sarsaparilla swear that sarsaparilla and root beer are not the same. Sarsaparilla is a popular folk name, and it has been suggested that the name was given to it so that it could be served in bars as the non-alcoholic beer of nineteenth-century America. Mostly it was served to children and ladies in bars and restaurants. In England, a wine flavored with sarsaparilla, known simply as Sarsaparilla, was popular among ladies of the Victorian era.

Another popular variation of the drink we popularly know as birch beer, white birch beer, is currently being brewed by the Frederick Brewing Company, maker of Blue Ridge beers. Their birch beer is exceptional and well worth searching out. White birch beer is a clear, colorless birch beer that was very popular in the Mid Atlantic and Northeast states for many years. A quality beverage, it is made from all natural ingredients. If you can't find it, call them at (301) 694-7899.

Ginger Beer and Ginger Ale

Ginger beer was an ale brewed with ginger. Ancient brewers used ginger and other spices to counterbalance the malt in the days before the use of hops became popular. The flavor and bouquet are immediately recognizable. Its alcohol level is usually around two percent by volume. This is a potent brew, even as a soft drink, whose flavor you will never forget. It's difficult to find a true ginger beer.

There is also a soft drink known as ginger beer. These "beers" are sweet, dry, and peppery, but carry a full dose of ginger. It is hard to imagine anyone sitting down and drinking a six-pack of this stuff, but you should taste it at least once in your life. Ginger beer, the soft drink, became popular in England in the late 1700s and throughout the 1800s as a result of the spice trade. Like root beer, ginger beer became a popular, non-alcoholic substitute for real beer.

BEST BEERS THAT BECAME SOFT DRINKS

Best Birch Beers
- Blue Ridge Birch Beer (white birch beer)
- Briar's Birch Beer
- Mystic Seaport Birch Beer

Best Root Beers
- Sioux Sarsaparilla
- Briar's Sarsaparilla
- Stewart's Root Beer

Best Ginger Beers
- Stewart's Old Fashioned Ginger Beer
- Olde Tyme Ginger Beer

Non-alcoholic ginger beer is made with water, sugar, lemon rinds, ground ginger, and brewer's yeast.

A very popular drink in some parts of the world is a Moscow Mule. One shot of vodka and one shot of lime juice are shaken with ice and poured into a ginger beer. Many bars may substitute ginger ale, but ask for ginger beer if it is available. It is interesting to note that the drink was originally made with alcoholic ginger beer, very much like a Boilermaker. Another drink is a Dark and Stormy: a shot of dark rum poured into a highball glass containing 4 oz. of ginger beer and a lime wedge. The non-alcoholic version of a Black and Tan is made by pouring 6 oz. of ginger ale into 6 oz. of ginger beer.

Ginger ale, a true soft drink, is made from carbonated water with caramel coloring and some flavoring added, usually a syrup containing ginger, sugar, and other flavoring. The Messers. Schweppes and Co. first served ginger ale at the 1870 World Exposition. In a short amount of time the drink became the most popular of the fair.

HOW TO TASTE BEER

3

CHAPTER

BOTTLED BY
ADAMS MEDIA CORPORATION

Appreciating beer is no different than appreciating anything else—like cars, sports, or even food. The more you know about anything, the more discerning you become. As a baby, maybe your favorite food was pureed plums. Then you're in kindergarten, and you're tasting real foods—macaroni and cheese, peanut butter and jelly, chicken, roast beef, hot dogs, hamburgers. You're moving up. Then you get to junior high and high school. Mom and dad can take you to a restaurant with them now. Now you taste other, more complicated foods. Maybe you have lobster or lobster bisque. You try grilled pork chops with chutney, pasta primavera, or Chinese food. Maybe you have sushi or Indian food. You start to get a better understanding of the cuisine, and as you do, your tastes develop. You know after a few mouthfuls whether you're going to like a particular style of cooking or never try it again.

That is what tasting beer is like. If you've been drinking only a small handful of beers for most of your life, then it's time to consider going out into the big, wide world and doing a little research and taste-testing. You wouldn't want to eat at McDonald's, Burger King, or Wendy's every night for the rest of your life, neither should you want to drink the same beer forever. Consider yourself ready to take the next step and try something else. Go for it!

Most people hate the taste of beer—to begin with. It is, however, a prejudice that many have been able to overcome.

—WINSTON CHURCHILL

HOW *NOT* TO JUDGE A BEER

There are the right and wrong ways to judge new beers. As you attempt to taste each new beer, remember that it must be tasted in its own context. Here are some examples.

Color

Never, ever judge a beer by its color. A beer is not strong or weak based on its color. The darker beers are not always the strongest and the lighter the weakest. Dark beers are not more flavorful than lighter beers. There are plenty of light beers that are extremely flavorful—like wheat beer. Some stouts and porters are the same color, but they don't taste alike at all.

Strength

Just because a beer is strong by its alcoholic content does not mean it is a better beer. You should never judge beer by its alcoholic content—only by its taste. Taste is everything with beer. If you're looking for alcohol, try some distilled whiskies. If you're looking for flavor, body, aroma—an experience—then beer is what you want.

Clarity

Clarity is great in conversation and on your television screen. Clarity is not a necessity in beer. Some of the world's best beers are completely opaque. On the other hand, some of the world's best beers are clear. The strongest beers are not all opaque and are not always clear. Clarity has nothing to do with how good a beer tastes, or whether it has gone bad. The only time clarity matters is when a pilsner or lager is cloudy. Smell it carefully. Has it gone bad? Check the other bottles to see if the body is consistent with the others. No lager should be cloudy. Other than that, clarity is a clear issue: some of the best beers are cloudy; some of the best beers are not cloudy. Leave your preconceptions at the door.

Chugging vs. Sipping

As you taste new lagers and ales—that is just what you want to do—taste, the objective is not to try to drink an entire yard of beer for the new world's record. Take a mouthful, let it rest in your mouth some, and then swallow. Some beers are meant to be drunk in copious amounts. Wheat beer goes down easy, if you don't mind the sour taste, and is incredibly refreshing. You could down several on a hot afternoon without even blinking. However, framboise is not something to be drinking a six-pack of on a Saturday night. Each beer has its own pace.

While sipping or drinking at a moderate pace is truly required by some beers, chugging is never necessary. If you're not tasting, you're not savoring and enjoying. Beer is meant to be had with a meal or with friends or, preferably, both. It is meant to be drunk at a leisurely pace.

Serving Temperature

Just as different wines are served at different temperatures, so are beers. As we already discovered, many beers in Europe are served slightly below room temperature, and many are served at room temperature. This may seem unpleasant, but the simple truth is that by keeping some beers too cold, you kill some of the flavors in the beer. Also, the gases in the beverage tend not to free up as well as when beer is warmer; hence, in a really cold beer you tend to digest more of the gases before they've had a chance to release—especially if you're drinking from a bottle.

Traditional American breweries adopted the lager/pilsner tradition of brewing and drinking cold beer and have now blanketed the entire world with it. Beer was marketed in America to be consumed at icy cold temperatures. Drinking beer cold not only hides the good flavors, it hides the imperfections. Americans drink beer ice cold because we've been trained to drink it cold. We may have tasted a lot of different beers, but drinking a lot of different beers when you don't know what you're looking for is like driving James Bond's car and not knowing where any of the cool buttons are—you might pull off some funky things but you're more likely to blow yourself up.

The proper serving temperature varies from beer to beer. The following temperature guideline is for you to use when considering what temperature to serve your next round of beer.

BEST TEMPERATURES TO SERVE BEER

European and American lagers, cream ales, steam beers, Kölsch, and wheat beers.	The coldest: 43–48°F (7–9°C)
Belgian ales, bitters, brown ales, Scotch ales, pale ales, red beers, and rauchbier	A little warmer: 45–54°F (8–12°C)
Stouts, porters, lambics	British cellar temperature: 55°F (13°C)
Barley wines, altbiers, TripleBock, Trappist ales	Room temperature or slightly lower
Wassail or mulled ale	Warmed

TOP TEN PARTY SECRETS:

1. Separate the food and drinks. This creates movement or "party flow."
2. Invite guests with different interests—who wants a room full of manicurists or doctors?
3. As the host, try to control your alcohol intake; otherwise, you run the risk of missing out on all the fun.
4. Avoid finger foods that leave something in your hand.
5. Buy top-shelf liquor: your friends are worth it.
6. Theme drinks are a fun idea, but don't count on everyone liking them. Make sure to have enough alternatives, both alcoholic and non-alcoholic.

THE FIVE SENSES

There are five things you should keep in mind when tasting a beer for the first time. These are what I call the five senses: sound, sight, smell, taste, and common sense. Just like when you're about to hit a tee-shot, or how you look both ways before you cross the street, keep these things in mind each time you taste a new beer.

Sound

The first thing to keep in mind is to listen to the beer. Whenever you pop or twist off a beer bottle top, you hear a lot, though you usually don't think about it. Next time, pay attention. When you twisted or pried off the cap, did the beer make a loud hissing sound, almost like a pop? This is a well-carbonated beer. Did it let out a low, quick hiss? This is a sign of a faint hint of carbonation. The first thing you'll notice when tasting different types of beers from different parts of the world is that all beers are not carbonated to the same degree. Just because your beer didn't let out a loud noise doesn't mean it is defective. Porters and stouts especially are not highly carbonated, so they are not going to be loud.

The other thing you can hear is the body. As you're pouring the beer into the glass, you can actually hear the body of a beer. Does it pour quickly with little sound, or does it have a certain thickness that makes it sound like you're emptying an oil can? Stouts, porters, and more full-bodied beers will do this. Noticing these things is all part of building up the excitement in tasting a new beer.

Seeing

Seeing a new beer for the first time is an interesting event. I can still remember tasting my first framboise, thinking as I poured it, What the heck is this stuff? It was a dark beer with an almost

(continued)

7. Buy plastic cups rather than paper. All paper cups will eventually drip.
8. Have the makings of a pot of coffee ready.
9. End the party on a high note. Your guests will leave while they are having a good time, and they'll remember it as a successful party.
10. Clean up immediately after everyone leaves. Even though you're tired, it's still better than waking up to the mess in the morning.

purplish tint. I wasn't so much turned off as in complete confusion. I could see it definitely had body. I could see as it splashed around the inside of the glass what colors were in it, and whether a head developed or not.

When I drank the beer, I could see how the beer slid on the glass and what kind of residue it left. And when I had drunk half-way down the glass, I could see the quality of the Belgian lace. ("Belgian lace" occurs when the foams from the head of the beer—no matter how slight—leave their mark on the inside of the glass. Good Belgian lace is consistent, with few large gaps. It should look like a thousand little snowflakes on the inside of your glass.)

Seeing a beer reveals mostly the product's clarity. Remember, many of the European ales come from recipes that originated hundreds of years ago. Many of these beers are not clear, unlike the lager tradition of clear, cold beer that we Americans are more familiar with. Stouts, porters, and lambics are opaque. Bottle-fermented beers have sediment in the bottles (check the label to make sure the beer was bottle-conditioned when you see sediment in a bottle). All lagers are clear. Clarity should not be judged against other beers. Clarity should be judged only against other beers of that same style. All beers, regardless of what you are drinking, should be judged against the ideal finished product of that style.

Color is another interesting guide to a beer. As you become more and more familiar with different styles, you will see a wide range of colors, from the pale, cloudy yellow of a wheat beer to the dark, coffee color of a black stout. As you taste different brands within the same style, you will be able to compare the color and finish of each beer. All of these points should help you determine the quality of the beer you're drinking.

Smelling

Try smelling a Budweiser that's as cold as you keep it in your refrigerator. Is there any smell? Why does that matter? Because if you can't smell, you can't taste. Why is it you don't taste so well when you have a cold? Studies have proven that people who can't smell can't taste, so much so that tuna fish has been mistaken for vanilla frosting!

Just like the smell of bacon sizzling on the grill or brownies baking in the oven can perfume a whole room and drive you mad with desire, the smell of a beer can set you up for the experience of drinking. If you do it right, and if you do it often enough, you will smell many wonderful things in the beers you try. Try a pumpkin-brewed beer. The first thing to hit is its aroma. It's full of the smells of clove and cinnamon, not to mention fresh pumpkin. With a framboise, you can smell the raspberries right away. The same is true of all quality beers, whether porters, stouts, lagers, or ales.

Malt and hops are two prevalent beer ingredients. Malt smells can range from a fruity sweetness to rich and caramely. Hops have a more herbal, perfumy smell. Sometimes hops give off the smell of grass or pine. Compare what your nose tells you with the ingredients included on the label. The more you smell your beer, the more you get out of tasting it.

It's important to not become frustrated in the beginning. When you first start experimenting with beers, you won't know what you're smelling and it will seem a giant waste of time. It is not a waste of time. The more you do it, the more you will understand. When it doesn't work in the beginning, keep doing it. You'll eventually discover a whole new world in your beer.

Getting Skunked

This is a well-known problem, recently made popular by Budweiser in its "freshness date" advertising campaign. The problem is that beers are like vampires—they don't like light. When beer has been exposed to too much light or been stored too long, it develops a certain unmistakable smell. Some distributors are willing to take back bad beer, especially if you're a good customer, but most are not. Regardless, you shouldn't drink beer that smells rancid. If you get unlucky and end up with beer like this, you've been skunked. No reason to punish yourself, just move on.

Tasting

Follow this scenario each and every time. Take a mouthful of beer and let it sit a full five to six seconds. Swish it around some. It's not mouthwash, so don't do a one-two-three and swallow. Let it roll around your mouth. Make sure all the parts of your tongue are exposed to it. Make sure you taste the sour, the bitter, and the sweet, then swallow.

You will begin to pick out the tastes, just as you can tell when your food is too salty or peppery. Hops and malt are the salt and pepper of the beer world. They're in everything to varying degrees, and between reading about and tasting different beers, you'll notice their influences more and more. When your taste buds can distinguish the hops and malt flavors right away, they'll move onto picking out the more subtle flavors: the butterscotches, fruits, or chocolates.

Common Sense

This should be your favorite "sense" to use. You've listened to beer, seen it, smelled it, and then tasted it, and now there is only one more thing to do—make up your mind! Did you like it or not? It's that simple.

If you didn't like the taste but the beer wasn't immediately repulsive, smell it again and take another sip. Taste all the flavors that you are smelling. If it still tastes bad, then don't sweat it. You didn't like it. Some beers that may require a more mature beer palate are wheat beer, rauchbier, and lambic beer. No matter how cool it is to be sitting there drinking porter, if you don't like it, don't drink it. However, if you don't like the beer, don't call the bartender over and complain that you got a bad beer. Tasting beer requires patience and responsibility.

With these five senses tuned, anyone can become an expert beer taster. It's not so much about knowledge as it is about finding good beer and sharing it with friends and loved ones.

SWEET AND SOUR

Malt and hops are the two most prevalent smells in beer, but sweet and sour are perhaps the two easiest smells to discern. Generally, if you have a sour lager, you've been skunked, and can probably smell it. However, some beers are supposed to be sour-tasting. Wheat beer is preeminent among them. The sourness of wheat beer comes from lactose, or milk sugars, which also add to the finish of this extraordinarily thirst-quenching beer. Many beer drinkers either accentuate the sourness with a slice of lemon, or play against it by adding a raspberry syrup. In some places both are used.

If, on the other hand, you taste some sweetness, then there are only a few ways in which this could be occurring. First, you could be drinking a faro beer. Faro beer, one of the most famous

A TASTING GLOSSARY

As you read more and more beer reviews you will come across a unique terminology used to describe the sensations of smell and taste. This technical vocabulary is not unlike that used by wine experts. This glossary is a valuable tool for the novice or intermediate to figure out what somebody might be saying, and is a great refresher (so to speak) for the expert.

Acidic or Acetone

Usually means that corn has been used as an adjunct. This is often a sign that the mash had some kind of bacteria problem.

Aftertaste

The flavor sensations left in your mouth after you have tasted a beer that allow you to taste the finish of the beer and assess its true measure. Best accomplished by slowly swishing the beer around in your mouth, exposing it to all of your taste buds, then swallowing.

Aggressive

A powerful flavor that may not necessarily overwhelm the beer, but definitely defines it.

Astringent

As in wines, this is a very dry sensation that makes your mouth pucker. Contrary to popular taste, this is not a bad thing and is done on purpose.

Aroma

How a beer smells, sometimes referred to as "the nose."

Banana

The taste or smell of banana means there is a good chance that there is a small amount of banana or pear oil in the beer. The

banana flavor or overtone should only appear because it was intended by the brewer; otherwise there might be something wrong with your beer. This goes for most fruit flavors.

Bitter

Usually the indication of a very strong hops. Malt beverages are very rarely bitter, but if so, you're better off sending them back.

Body

The body of the beer refers to whether it is weak or light-bodied, medium-bodied, or full-bodied. Body refers to the consistency and flavor of a beer. Beers may be dark but flavorless and so lack body. A very flavorful pilsner might be considered to be full-bodied. The term is mostly relevant when comparing beers of the same style made by different brewers.

Butter, Buttery, or Butterscotch

Diacetyl gives butter its flavor and is used to mellow out the taste of many harsher flavors. Diacetyl occurs during certain brewing processes. Butter is good in some European ales; butterscotch is bad.

Cabbagey or Catty

Another term for skunked beer. Throw it out.

Caramel

Usually the result of using a kilned malt, malt that is roasted or baked, to produce a dark, rich color and taste.

Cheese

A slight aroma or taste of cheese could indicate the use of a strong hops. The flavor of cheese in a beer can also indicate that there is amyl alcohol in the beer which has oxidized. Send it back.

Chocolate or Chocolaty

This is usually the result in dark beers of a chocolate malt, a very dark malt kilned to a very dark color.

(continued)

Belgian ales, has hard sugar added to it in the finishing process. Another sweet beer, lambics, are brewed with fruit extracts and syrups, and produce some of the most heavenly beers known to man.

There is another kind of sweetness that is not as easily detected and is most prevalent in the mass-produced beers. In compliance with the German Beer Purity Law of 1516, adjuncts are forbidden. Many of the American beer manufacturers use adjuncts like corn and rice, forbidden under the German Beer Purity Law of 1516, to sweeten the beer and take some of the bitterness away. They do this so their product appeals to the widest possible audience, because it is thought that the bitterness might turn away younger drinkers.

Citrus

Smelling or tasting of a citrus fruit, particularly lemon. Usually the indication of a very strong hops.

Clove

Usually present in holiday and special once-a-year brews such as wassail and mulled beer. Also a distinctive taste in wheat beers from Germany (weizen and hefe-weizen).

Cloying

When a beer is so sweet, sour, or bitter that it becomes overwhelming and unenjoyable.

Coffee and Toffee-ish, -like, etc.

Usually indicates the presence of a kilned malt.

Complex

A beer is considered complex when there are many layers of tastes happening all at once, including malt, hops, and other flavors that have been brewed into it.

Corn

If there is the flavor of corn, it usually means there is corn in the mash. However, if the taste of corn is overpowering, then there was something that went wrong during fermentation. Dimethyl sulfide is the result.

Crisp

Clear and highly carbonated with a dry aftertaste. A crisp beer will shock the palate, have a fullness of taste, and a fully discernible finish.

Finish

The same as aftertaste.

Floral

Indicates the presence of strong hops.

Fruity

Usually the result of esters, the organic compounds that form in beer. Slight taste of apple (as opposed to green apple), banana, or sometimes nutty flavors.

Ginger

A spice used in some special seasonal brews including pumpkin, wassail, and mulled beer. Also used in the brewing of ginger beer.

Grassy

Indicates a strong presence of hops.

Gravity

This has to do with the body of the beer. Light beers have less gravity than heavier, full-bodied beers. Gravity of a beer can and is measured by professionals. This system is based on the beer's weight relationship to water.

Green Apple

A taste that is a result of different alcohols produced from a bad fermentation, when the temperature was too high. This taste does appear in some of the sweeter beers and in some wheat beers, and in these cases it is purposefully present. Any lager or other ale that exhibits this flavor should probably be sent back.

Herbal

Indicates the use of hops.

Honey

This is a taste you will sometimes find in beer. It is what it is. Some beers are made with honey—the amount of honey that is acceptable to the individual drinker. Most of these beers tend to be on the darker side, with a certain sweetness to them. These beers tend to be popular with those who are not fans of bitter beers.

Leather (or Leathery), Paper, Cardboard

Some Trappist beers have a leathery taste that is part of that beer's tradition. However, a pilsner that tastes leathery is definitely stale.

Beer is proof that God loves us and wants us to be happy.

—BENJAMIN FRANKLIN

Malty or Maltiness

Usually indicates there was a very distinctive malt or that there was little or no hopping. Hopping gives beer its bitter taste. Those beers without adjuncts (corn or rice) will seem especially malty compared to a typical mass-produced beer.

Medicinal

If a beer smells or tastes like rubbing alcohol or your doctor's office, then it has gone bad.

Metallic

This is not a beer named for a rock group. If it tastes of aluminum or tin or any other kind of metal, don't even think twice—send it back.

Mild

A very lightly hopped beer. A description that has its root in England, owing to the fact that hops were not used in England for many centuries. People who like highly hopped beers tend to think of many UK beers as mild, although many now are not.

Milk

Like green apple, this taste occurs naturally in some beers where it is a prominent feature. The most notable case is wheat beer, where a milk taste indicates the presence of lactic acids or sugars. A lager that has a milky taste or is cloudy has gone bad.

Moldy or Musky

If it smells like it's been sitting in a damp basement, it probably has. A beer smells moldy because it has some kind of bacterial problem.

Mouthfeel

Mouthfeel is how the beer is perceived and feels in the mouth. Describes the range, in terms of body, from light or weak to full-bodied.

Nutty

A nutty taste is the result of an excellent malt and is a wonderful treat. This taste does not exist because you are having peanuts with your beer.

Perfumy

Indicates a strong presence of hops.

Piney

Usually indicates the use of strong hops.

Range

These ranges are not official, but merely provide a guideline to help you assess a particular beer.

Taste: weak–mild–moderate–strong–powerful
Flavor: sweet–mild–bitter
Color: black–brown–red–amber–golden–pale
Bouquet: hoppy–mild–malty

Roasty

Usually indicates the use of a kilned malt.

Salty

If any beer tastes salty, send it back. It's usually a good sign that the brewery used too much salt.

Slurry

Unsettled sediment floating around in the beer.

Skunky

A beer that has been exposed to light for a long period of time. Also known as light-struck.

Smoky

This term is especially associated with rauchbier, or smoked beer. Smokiness is added by malting the grain over an open fire.

Soapiness

A hint of soap or soapiness means a beer has gone bad. Usually the result of fatty acids present in the beer that gives it a waxy or soapy taste.

Sour or Tart

Sourness or tartness in anything other than wheat beer is a bad sign. A lager should never be tart, unless it is a lemon beer.

Spicy

Spiciness indicates the presence of strong hops or the use of different spices in the brewing process. Ginger beer, pumpkin beer, wassail, and mulled beer are labeled spicy because they all have many spices in them.

Toasty

Usually indicates the use of a kilned malt.

Vanilla

The aroma or taste of vanilla comes from the brewing process. Vanilla is sometimes added to beers as well.

Wood or Woodiness

Some beers, such as the best pale ales, are stored in wooden kegs to age for a specific period of time and can pick up a slight woody or oaky taste from the barrel. In a lager, a woody taste means the beer has been exposed to oxygen and may be a sign that the beer is bad.

ORGANIZING A TASTING

There are no hard-and-fast rules when having a beer tasting, but there are things you should keep in mind when you're thinking of inviting friends and family over to explore some beers. You need to know what the beer you're going to be tasting is, what it's attempting to achieve—or emulate—and you need to follow some of the basic rules already discussed. Remember to buy enough for each person to taste. A tasting is to help you learn more about beer, not to ruin your liver. If it's just you and a few friends, and you are considering only a few beers, you might each want to have your own bottle. However, as the scale of the tasting widens, you might want to bring down those quantities. For example, if the crowd is made up of six or seven people, you might want to offer half a glass to each, especially if the menu of tasted beers is a long one, say ten styles. The more beers there are to taste, the less you want to consume. The idea is to taste the beer, not get drunk. And of course, the more people, the more expensive it is to keep pouring them all that beer.

A Vertical Tasting

There are two types of beer tastings: vertical and style. In wine, a vertical tasting refers to drinking a number of vintages of the same style wine; i.e., a Cabernet Sauvignon from various years by the same producer. So if you were having a vertical tasting, you'd purchase Cabernet Sauvignon solely from John Doe's winery and you would buy it in different years (1976, 1980, 1986, 1990, etc.). At the tasting, you'd taste each one in ascending order, drinking the oldest (and hopefully the best) wines first.

It's a little different in a beer tasting. A vertical tasting in beer is a sample of each of the varieties produced by a brewer.

When doing a vertical tasting of a brewery, you must obey two rules if you want to get anything out of the occasion. The first rule is to start with the lightest beer and end with the darkest beer. The second rule is to go from the lightest in alcohol content to the strongest. These rules do not always coincide, but more often than not they should be kept in mind. The reason for this? Dark beers are usually more flavorful, more powerful in their tastes. If you drank from darkest to lightest, your taste buds would miss out on a lot of very delicate nuances in the lighter beers. The very heavy tastes of chocolate malts and roasted flavors would bombard your taste buds so that when you got to a pilsner you would not be able to sense some of the very fine floral scents and flavors. And of course, you start with the lesser alcoholic beer so you won't be smashed by the time you get to the barley wine. If you started off a tasting with barley wine, again, your taste buds would be shot by the time you got to the wheat beer.

For a vertical tasting at home, it's safest to take a well-known brewer that produces a wide range of very different styles such as Samuel Adams, Pete's Wicked, Sierra Nevada, or even Miller. Don't pick five lagers since that's not going to expand your taste buds. Let's take Samuel Adams. They produce a large range of beers, and their beers are available throughout the country, so you won't have to go to too much trouble or expense to get a selection of their styles. Here are the styles you could choose from, most of which are available from your local beer distributor:

- Summer Wheat
- Cherry Wheat
- Dark Wheat
- Hefeweizen
- Golden Pilsner
- Boston Lager
- Octoberfest
- Stock Ale

- Scotch Ale
- Winter Lager
- Double Bock Dark Lager
- Triple Bock
- Brown Ale
- Cream Stout
- Honey Porter
- Cranberry Lambic

This list is rather long and too much for one tasting, but it should give you an idea of what the order of the tasting should be. From this list, an excellent first-time tasting would be:

- Summer Wheat Beer—Wheat beers are light and of the ale family.
- Hefeweizen—A bottle-conditioned beer.
- Cranberry Lambic—Light and refreshing, like a wheat.
- Boston Lager—A very solid commercial lager.
- Scotch Ale—A stronger beer, with a more potent, up-front taste.
- Brown Ale—One brown ale for taste and subtlety.
- Cream Stout—This is dessert. Thick, rich, creamy. Like a milkshake.
- Triple Bock—One of the best American beers today, almost like sherry. A definite sipping beer.

While this select list is manageable, it means you're going to have one, big, day-long event. These beers cannot be swilled down in an hour's time and fully appreciated. If you're going to do a tasting, limit yourself to no more than six to eight beers. After that, your taste buds, no matter how mature, will begin to dull.

Another tasting menu might be strictly ales:

- Pale Ale—pale to golden cloudy beer
- India Pale Ale—usually a little darker with a much stronger taste
- Scotch Ale—even a little more bitter and stronger
- Bitter—a beer with plenty of hops
- Brown Ale—an amber to brown cloudy beer, very full-flavored, less carbonation
- Porter—little carbonation, but heavier still than brown ale
- Stout—little carbonation, creamy, thick

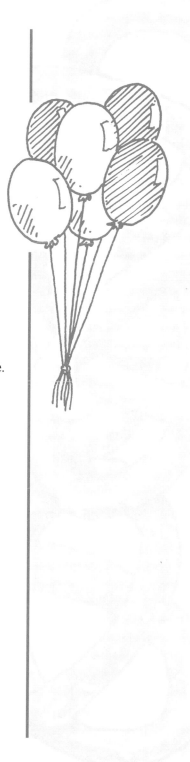

Ye Olde
PUB
Est. 1824

WHAT TO EAT DURING A TASTING

A true aficionado has bits of bread and sometimes cheese between tastings, and often connoisseurs wash their mouths out between sampling each beer. While at home with friends, you may not want to have people spitting their beer and water out. Have your guests take small sips of beer and offer water, bread, cheese, and crackers between beers to cleanse the taste buds before the next beer.

Some cheese to consider are stilton, cheddar, and bleu. These cheeses are sharp and will cleanse the mouth of any beer taste, heightening the taste sensation of the next beer. Pretzels and potato chips are good too.

Here's a good wheat beer tasting:

- Wheat Beer—basic wheat beer served with a little lemon, and if you're ambitious, raspberry syrup
- Hefeweissen—bottle-conditioned wheat beer
- Weissen—brewed with unmalted wheat; serve with lemon
- Berliner Weisse—same as Weissen
- White Beer—a light bottle-conditioned beer

Or you could do dessert beers:

- Gueuze—a mixture of young and old lambic beers
- Kriek—a lambic beer brewed with cherries and cherry juices
- Framboise—a lambic beer brewed with raspberries and raspberry juices
- Faro—a lambic beer finished with rock candy

Or a stout and porter menu:

- Porter—a very dark, full-bodied beer
- Stout—a very dark, even chocolaty beer, full-bodied and creamy
- Russian imperial stout—see above, but stronger in taste and alcohol content
- Barley wine—the strongest of all beers; not really a stout or porter, but a perfect nightcap to the evening, much like the others

A Style Tasting

A style tasting is exactly what it says it is—tasting one particular style. In the wine industry this is called a varietal tasting because you are drinking only that one style of wine. In a style or varietal tasting, like beers should be compared. Don't start tasting porters and then throw in a stout, as it will seem out of place. This is basically a taste test. You buy the same style by several different manufacturers. As with any other type of tasting, start with the lightest beers and work your way up after that. These types of tastings can be a learning experience about beer and a taste test to see how alert and mature your taste buds are.

In these kinds of tastings, whenever possible, try to include a beer from one of the major producers. This will give you a better understanding of what they are doing to make that style of beer more salable to the widest possible audience. Style tastings bring out the good and bad in beers.

Here's a sample of a pilsner tasting:

- Budweiser
- Pilsner Urquell
- Dock Street Bohemian Pilsner
- Saranac Golden Pilsner Beer
- Heineken
- Becks

Here's a suggested tasting of brown ales. The three beers with asterisks are popular European original brown ales and should be included in any brown ale tasting that you are organizing. Taste the European versions first to know what the standards are before you start tasting their American counterparts. Pick three or four others from the remainder of the list to round out the tasting. The list is large, but some of these beers have only a regional distribution.

- Samuel Smith's Nut Brown Ale*
- Newcastle Brown Ale*
- Coresendonk Monk's Brown Ale*
- Breckenridge Ballpark Brown Ale
- Downtown Brown Light Brown Ale
- Oldenburg's Holy Grail Nut Brown Ale
- Yellow Rose Hancho Grande Brown Ale
- Smuttynose Old Brown Dog Ale
- Oregon Trail Brown Ale
- McNeill's Professor Brewhead's Brown Ale
- Saint Arnold Brown Ale
- Yegua Creek's Sara's Brown Ale
- Marthasville Sweet Georgia Brown Ale
- Oasis Tut Brown Ale
- Griffon Brown Ale

(continued)

The main thing to remember is to keep it safe. Beer is an alcoholic beverage and you don't want to send your loved ones home a bit tipsy after a tasting. Make sure you serve plenty of food after the tasting is over. It's best to schedule a tasting on a Saturday, anytime from noon to evening, so that people have a day to recuperate.

Things to Remember:

- Drink lots of water
- Hear, see, listen, smell, taste
- It's supposed to be fun, not stuffy. Enjoy!

SURVIVING A HANGOVER

There is nothing worse than that end-of-the-world, my-head-is-going-to-explode kind of feeling often associated with hangovers. One prevailing theory about hangovers is that dehydration is the culprit because, as the body processes liquor, it uses up a great deal of water. Another hypothesis describes a hangover as a minor withdrawal episode from an addictive substance. Of course, at the time, you couldn't care less, you just want to feel better—no matter what.

Here are several remedies after you've already made the fatal mistake of tasting too much. None of them will make the room suddenly stop spinning, or will stop the little men with golf shoes from walking around inside your stomach, but they should put you into stable condition, eventually.

- No matter how much you feel like you're going to throw up, drink a glass of orange juice and two aspirins before you go to bed. If you don't like aspirin, use Advil or Tylenol. It sounds impossible, and it won't stop all the pain instantly, but this works. A glass of water would suffice if orange juice at the time seems too grotesque. You will wake up feeling much, much better.
- The fashionable remedy is the Bloody Mary. A little tomato juice, a little vodka, some Tabasco, salt and pepper, and some lemon, and you're good to go. If you've got a little horseradish, it's even better. Grit your teeth and drink it.
- The Palm variety remedies use orange juice and booze. Some prefer the Palm Springs version, which is the Mimosa—your favorite Florida orange juice and champagne.

Otherwise, you might want the Palm Beach variety—a screwdriver, or orange juice with a little vodka.

- Coffee and grappa, anyone? Or maybe an Irish coffee with those pancakes?
- How about a Scotch milk punch? Mix 2 oz. of Scotch and 6 oz. of milk, and add one teaspoon of sugar and a sprinkle of nutmeg. Stir very well. Some people have this stuff on the breakfast table after a big night to pour into their morning coffee. Whatever works.
- How about a little hair of the dog—5 oz. of tomato juice and 4 oz. of beer with a little salt and pepper, lemon juice, and Tabasco.
- This is the toughest-man-in-the-world remedy. Mix two raw eggs in a blender with 8 oz. of tomato juice, a tsp. of lemon juice, salt, pepper, and Worcestershire sauce. And then slam it down.

BEER CONTAINERS

4

CHAPTER

BOTTLED BY
ADAMS MEDIA CORPORATION

Before the bottling and canning of beers, beers were either served on the premises of the brewer or sold in large quantity by the bucket. The Sumerians and the Egyptians served right from the brewing kettles with long straws. To drink beer in this manner you would take your straw and poke it into the frothy brew in the brewing kettle until it went down into the actual beer.

The next advancement came when the later Egyptians and other later civilizations started serving beer in vessels usually made of clay to meet the needs of those who wanted to bring beer home (if they were not brewing it there already). The bottle did not come until long afterward.

The heart which grief hath cankered
Hath an unfailing remedy— the Tankard.

—C.S. CALVERLEY
BRITISH POET

THE HISTORY OF THE BOTTLE

The first recorded bottling of beer was said to have been accomplished in the mid-1500s by the dean of St. Paul's at the Westminster School in England, Alexander Newell. Newell was said to have had two passions in life: beer and angling. It was his love of angling that forced him to devise the idea of bottling his favorite brews to bring with him as he fished. His story is told in Fuller's *Worthies of England*. "While Newell was catching of fishes, Bishop Bonner was catching of Newell, and would certainly have sent him to shambles, had not a good London merchant conveyed him away upon the seas." (In other words, Newell was caught drinking by the bishop, who could have sent him to jail.)

But Newell returned to England after several years and returned to beer and angling. It was during one of his fishing trips that Newell remembered he had left a bottle on the bank of the Thames the fateful day he had earlier left England. He searched for it, thirsting, but was not sure of what he would find. Then, glory of all glories, there it was. As Fuller reports, "he found no bottle, but a gun, such was the sound of the opening thereof." The pop of the bottle surprised Newell. He was not sure if it was any good, but one careful sip told him he was onto something.

While Newell's unsuspecting invention was glad news to beer fans all over England, he was probably not the first inventor of this type of beer packaging. However, he is the first to be recorded doing so. Of course, this opened up new avenues for beer lovers.

Louis Pasteur

Possibly the last person you'd expect to find a biography of in a beer book, the famous French chemist Louis Pasteur (1822–95) was one of the most influential beer experts in the world. Wrote Walter Sykes, one of the great scientists and brewers in history, "More to him (Pasteur) than to any other man living or dead do we owe much of our present knowledge of that difficult, maybe even mysterious process carried on by the agency of living organisms *viz.* fermentation."

Pasteur had written a book on brewing called *Studies on Fermentation—The Diseases of Beer, Their Causes, and the Means of Preventing Them*, researched and written between 1857 and 1868. This book was meant to help the French brewing industry surpass the German and English stronghold on that beverage. But the French brewers paid it little mind, and the German and English obviously read it cover to cover because they turned many of his findings into practical improvements. In fact, modern brewing only happened because of Pasteur.

Pasteur invented pasteurization, a word we're all familiar with even if we don't know what it means. Pasteur found that food decays swiftly due to living organisms within the food. Pasteurization is a process designed to preserve food by superheating it first, followed by flash-freezing. Pasteur refined his invention working with beer, superheating the beer and then flash-cooling it and bottling it. This killed off the active yeasts in the bottle, enabling the beer to stay fresher longer.

There are two types of pasteurization that are quite popular today. The first is to boil and cool the beer in the bottle in which it is going to be stored. This method is known as tunnel pasteurization and is the cheapest, easiest way to do it. However, the machines that do this are incredibly huge and take up much room in a brewery. The machines heat the beer in the bottle, after which the bottles are capped and cooled down.

A second method, the flash method, achieves the same end but in different steps and with different machines. In the flash method, beer is piped through the various stages. It is superheated, twice, and cooled as the pipes flow between heating and cooling chambers. Thus a continuous flow of beer can be piped and pasteurized. The only problem with this method is that the bottles, kegs, and other beer containers that are designated to store beer have to be sterilized. This requires special cleaning and superheating. Both methods are still very popular today.

It is also important to note that Pasteur's book assisted other scientists to develop a thesis on the fermentation process and the role that yeasts play in it. His treatise also isolated and identified numerous yeast strains. His work helped lay the foundation for the lager beers that would soon become the favorite beers of the world.

Pasteur's theories were not wasted on American brewers either. Adolphus Busch became known by 1875 as "The King of Bottled Beer." Busch used this title to expand his business substantially. Both Schlitz and Pabst breweries used strains of yeast that Pasteur had identified in his experiments. Without Louis Pasteur's scientific research on behalf of the French brewing industry, the modern beer industry would not have happened.

Bottle Conditioning

Bottle-conditioned beer is beer that undergoes a final fermentation or maturation after it is bottled. Unlike bottling, no one has really ever laid claim to the great tradition of bottle-conditioned beer. We do know, however, that it started sometime in that same century, the 1500s. For the most part, sugars, yeasts, and spices may have been added to the beer before it was finally capped. Many times beer was stored in bottles or jars, capped, and then stored in the ground. Since many people homebrewed and didn't have a place to store the beer, burying it became a very popular mode of storage. The earliest recorded recipes called for nutmeg and sugar to be added to the basic ingredients, and then for the entire concoction to be buried in sand. The idea was to guard against bottle explosions, and the added pressure of the weight of the ground on the cork helped it from coming undone.

Vintners had bottle-conditioned wines long before anyone thought to do it with beer. The process used by winemakers was called *méthode champenoise*, which is the way the best champagnes are still made. First the wine is made, then stored in casks for aging and maturing. When it is time to be bottled, a small amount of yeast and sugar are added to create the carbonation that champagne is well known for. The first makers of bottle-conditioned beer must have been well aware of this time-tested tradition.

Today, brewers add sugar and yeast to beer, but they don't bury it. Active yeasts are sometimes added to beer that is still fermenting to make sure the distribution of these yeasts is assured before bottling. Many beer connoisseurs collect bottle-conditioned beer and store it laying down, as a wine collector would store wine, because the conditioning process that takes place in the bottle is said to continue for up to five years. While this type of beer production has slowed down to a trickle of the entire beer market, it is a tradition that is alive and well. With the growing popularity of international beers, there is a new interest in these beers.

TYPES OF BOTTLES

There are as many types of bottles as there are breweries, but most bottles are differentiated by two primary characteristics: their capacity and their color. Beer bottles come in three distinctive colors: brown, green, and clear. Brown and green glass were originally used to

keep the beer from souring due to exposure to light. For beers that are specially fermented, clear glass can be used. The color of the glass is not a sign of a better beer, and there is no one type of regularly fermented beer that can or can't be stored in either brown or green glass. Samuel Smith's Taddy Porter and Miller High Life—both specially fermented—are bottled in clear glass, while Heineken and Rolling Rock are bottled in green glass, and Budweiser and Duvel come in a brown bottle.

A rule of thumb to keep in mind is that the darker the glass, the better the beer is kept. Clear glass doesn't block out any light and beer can be burned by light (also known as light-struck or skunky). Green glass lets in less light than clear, but the best color is brown or amber because it lets in the least light of all the different colored glass.

The other thing one should know is that beer in a bottle, no matter the color of the glass, will eventually go stale. While you can stem the tide of oxidation, you cannot stop it. Refrigeration will help you keep your beer longer. The important thing is to check the air space at the top of the bottle neck, between the liquid and the bottle cap—called the "ullage." A lot of ullage means that the beer probably won't keep well. If it has little ullage, your chances of holding on to it for a while without it going bad will be better.

Big Mouth

The most famous of this type of bottle is the Mickey's Big Mouth. Many soft drink manufacturers used this style long before any brewer decided to use it. These are not usually large-capacity bottles. They range from twelve to sixteen ounces. Their distinguishing feature is the extra-wide neck, which supposedly makes for easier (and faster) drinking.

Flexi-Cap or Grolsch Bottle

This is a bottle with a rubber stopper cork that is attached to the bottle by a metal hinge. The most popular beer to use this is Grölsch beer.

UNIQUE BOTTLE-CONDITIONED BEERS

Chapeau Gueuze Lambic
bottle-conditioned fruit beer, one of the world's best beers

Saison Dupont
bottle-conditioned Belgian saison is a very special brew

OTHER EXCELLENT BOTTLE-CONDITIONED BEERS READILY AVAILABLE

Witkap-Pater Abbey Singel Ale
bottle-conditioned Belgian

Chimay Ale—Premiere
bottle-conditioned Belgian

LaMaudite Beer on Lees
brewed by Unibroue, Canada

Jug

Usually a half-gallon container sold by microbreweries or brew-pubs. Several brewers retail their beers in earthenware jugs. This is a marketing angle, as there is no real advantage (or disadvantage) to bottling beer in a jug. The only problem with a jug is that once you open it, you have to drink the entire contents within forty-eight hours or the beer will lose its carbonation and go flat.

Long Neck

No, this isn't a member of the clam family. These are usually sixteen-ounce bottles, known for their long necks. In America, where beer is most often drunk straight from the bottle, these are thought to be the best bottles to drink from because the drinker can hold the beer by the bottle neck and not hold the body of the beer. This way the beer is not heated by the drinker's hands.

Quart

Quart bottles are not unique to either America or Europe. These bottles come in all shapes and sizes. They can be as plain or as ornate as possible. Like a jug, once you open the bottle and drink some of it, if you try to store it for more than a couple of days, depending on how much is missing from the bottle, the beer may go flat. It holds thirty-two ounces.

Stubby or Nip

These are usually four- or five-ounce beer bottles. They are normally the same circumference as their larger brethren, but are substantially shorter. Stubbies are proof that you don't have to drink a lot of beer to enjoy it.

CANS

As is usually the case, necessity is indeed the mother of invention. During World War II the army needed a way to cheaply and safely transport beer. Much like the British in India, this led to a revolutionary breakthrough in beer: the can was born. The can was lightweight, cheap, and less prone to breakage. There were breweries selling beer in a can before the war, but it was not a popular idea and didn't catch on. The first brewery in America to offer canned beer was the Gottfried Krueger Brewing Company. They offered their Krueger Cream Ale for the first time on January 24, 1935.

It wasn't until servicemen returned from the war, having drunk beer from cans on the front, that canned beer became more accepted. Another contributing factor was that cans were cheaper. This began many of the beer wars of the post–World War II boom years. As the world's greatest economy boomed, the beer industry, still staggering from the Prohibition era, now suddenly had to contend with price wars, and large brewers with canning facilities benefited greatly from them. Interestingly, at this time beer was canned with no easy-lift opening tab. You had to puncture the can with a can opener, much like opening a can of vegetables. The first easy-open lift-tab was used by the Pittsburgh Brewing Company in 1962. In the early 1950s the Coors Brewing Company became the first company to use an aluminum can.

With the invention of the liner that separates the beer from the metal, the six-pack became one of the staples of American beer brewing. It beat the alternatives—most of which were heavier, more expensive bottles—or buying a jug or pail of beer at the local bar or brewery. With aluminum, the six-pack became even lighter and the manufacturing cost even cheaper. Like bottles, cans come in different sizes and styles:

Stubby or Nip

Like the bottled version of this name, these are four- or five-ounce beer cans that are shorter than normal cans.

12 oz.

These are the cans of six-pack fame, held together by a plastic series of rings around the top.

Tall Boy

Usually about sixteen ounces, these are comparable to the long necks of the bottling world. A tall boy is just a bigger beer.

Beer Ball

For those who don't want to buy a case or a keg. Smaller than a case, but the convenience of a keg. Ranges from a half gallon to one gallon of beer.

Cans vs. Bottles

How many microbreweries can their beers rather than bottle them? There are only a few contract brews that can their beers because contract brews are made at big breweries. Most micro-brewers can't afford the equipment necessary to can beer. It is also accepted that bottled beer simply tastes better than canned beer. Don't let any "beer" salesman tell you otherwise.

The only time beer is ever supposed to come into contact with metal is during the brewing process. Metal leaves a funky taste and smell. Bottles are odorless and leave no aftertaste as a result of contact. Bottles are better, but does this mean you really shouldn't be drinking beer from a can? If a canned beer is your favorite lawn-mower beer, then who cares? But if it's a new beer you're trying to taste for the first time, buy bottles and pour the beer into a glass to experience it. If you like it, you can always drink it from the bottle (or can) later, but you should experience each new beer in a glass first. If you have to choose between a can or a bottle, always drink from a bottle.

TAPPING INTO BARRELS, CASKS, AND KEGS

Barrels, casks, and kegs are all used to store beer at some point in the production or consumption process. Their only difference is in how much they store. A barrel, whether wood or metal, by U.S. government standards has to contain 31$\frac{1}{2}$ gallons or 117 liters. In England, an Imperial Barrel contains 36 gallons. Kegs store either 15$\frac{1}{2}$ or 7$\frac{3}{4}$ gallons. Casks are not tied to any specific volume.

A Brief History

The term cask dates back to the Roman Empire as early as the fourth century. A cask was a large vessel made of hewn wood pieces, long and thin, which stood upright in order to form the sides. Each of these carefully cut pieces was called a stave. The classic cask or barrel swelled in the middle and tapered somewhat at both the top and bottom. This middle section was called the belly or the bulge. This shape is achieved by carefully crafting each stave so that it is at its widest in the middle and narrow at the ends. When the sides are all put together, the bulge is formed. These pieces of wood are made to fit together snugly. After the pieces are fitted together, large metal hoops are fitted very tightly around the barrel to keep the staves in place. These hoops are very tight and force the staves into a tighter fit. Some techniques called for red-hot metal hoops, so that when the metal cooled it might contract and make the seal on the cask that much tighter. In this fashion, a barrel is made watertight. These bands also help to cure any minor problems of ill fit, as the pressure on the staves is great.

Up until the late industrial revolution, the making of a barrel or cask was considered almost an artform. The name of this craft is cooperage and the person who takes up this vocation is called a cooper. There are several different types of cooperage. The one type we are most concerned with is wet or tight cooperage. Wet

COLLECTING

Collecting bottles and cans is one of the biggest segments of the breweriana movement. There are entire museums and Websites with odes to these marvels of packaging and marketing. Some of the best clubs or associations and exchanges are run by American Breweriana (their address and phone number can be found in Chapter 12).

cooperage is the art of making watertight barrels, so called because you are storing something wet, and the staves have to be fitted tightly so the barrel does not leak. Another type is dry or slack cooperage. These terms refer to the fact that they are used to store dry things and can be somewhat slack in their makeup. And then there is white cooperage. White cooperage refers to the art of making buckets and pails.

Whether for beer or for wine, the best casks or barrels are made from oak. The flavors imparted to an alcoholic beverage by oak cannot be duplicated. The French oak casks are superior because of their construction and the flavor the wood imparts to the stored beverage, whether wine or beer. Other good woods are German and Polish oak. Most European woods are better for aging fine beers and wines because they don't contain the tannins so prevalent in American wood. The pieces may be hewn, but the wood has to be thoroughly dry before the actual making of the barrel to ensure that the barrel will not leak and will not warp when it dries. For centuries casks were mounted (made) only in the summer. The casks that are still made with wood are dried commercially. Today most barrels and kegs are made of metal.

Cask Conditioning and Beer Service from Wood

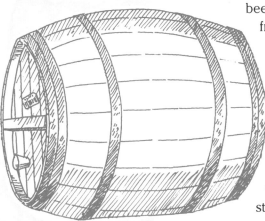

The cask is still used in England to store and serve unfiltered beers. More than half of all beer sales in England come from hand-pumped beer from casks. This is a centuries-old tradition. The beers served from these casks are also conditioned in them with approximately thirty million active yeast cells per ounce.

For cask-conditioned beers, the beer is brewed and then placed in a wooden cask after finishing. Usually a sugar syrup and a clarifying agent are added to the cask before sealing. The clarifying agent causes the yeasts to settle at the bottom of the cask after they are done fermenting. It is at this stage that many beers are cask-conditioned differently.

Different ingredients are added at this stage to affect the flavor of the beer. After a cask has been delivered to a pub or bar, a second cask fermentation takes place. By creating a small leakage of gases at the top of the keg, a pub or bar owner or operator might be able to best control the taste and integrity of the beverage. This is a tricky operation. Not enough gas escapes and the beer will have a funky taste. Too much gas escaping results in a flat beer—room-temperature swill.

Before the hand pump and inert gases were used, casks were fitted with two holes. One hole was placed on one of the flat-sided ends, or tops, and another somewhere along the circumference of the belly. Both were stopped with large corks. When it came time to serve the beer in a pub or alehouse, the cask was placed on its side in a cradle created for just such a purpose. The hole along the belly of the barrel was rotated toward the top, and the cork was extracted. The other hole, on one of the flat ends, was the place where the spigot was pounded into the keg. The hole in the top of the keg enabled an uninterrupted flow of ale.

Today, the few large brewers who practice barrel- or cask-conditioning do so using a different method called gekrast. This method originated in Vienna. Today's brewers have substituted new, still-fermenting beer for the sugar and yeast of olden times. Secondly, they use much stronger barrels, since today's brewers want a more highly carbonated beer. These casks must be able to withstand 50 psi (pounds of pressure per square inch) and are coated with a kind of resin or pitch so that the beer doesn't get too woody. The English use a lighter resin than the Germans and Czechs because the English tend not to age their beer as long as some continental brewers. These casks need no airhole on top. The cask is put onto the bar, standing upright, and a spigot is pounded into the side toward the lowest end of the barrel's side. The pressure of the beer inside ensures a prompt flow of beer. Serving beer from a cask is called "beer service from wood" in England.

While this type of service seems quaint and romantic, it is fading away. Wooden casks are slowly being replaced by glass or stainless steel fermenters, and many kegs or casks in English and continental pubs have been replaced with metal replicas. These new replicas look like wooden casks on the outside but are metal, covered in faux-wooden packaging.

Heavy Metal and How to Use It: *Keg Party!*

Today, most kegs are metal. They are metal barrels, heavier than a tank, and about as romantic a contraption as the inside of a washing machine. They are galvanized, reinforced, and steam cleaned, then sterilized and reused.

Today's keg is a convenient and easy way to serve beer to a large group of people. Aside from all of the crushed and half-filled plastic cups, a keg does avoid a certain amount of obvious litter. Depending on the amount of people, a keg is a very practical situation for a private social or relaxing business function.

How many people are you serving? This is the most important criteria for choosing to serve from a keg. In the United States, the keg comes in two popular sizes: half-keg and quarter-keg. The half-keg is approximately $15\frac{1}{2}$ gallons and serves about 160–170 twelve-ounce beers (give or take with spillage, head, etc.). The quarter-keg is approximately $7\frac{3}{4}$ gallons and serves approximately 75–85 twelve-ounce beers. Imported beers sometimes come in different-sized kegs. The large kegs hold a couple of gallons more, and the smaller kegs are generally within the same ballpark by about less than a gallon one way or another.

There are two types of kegs popularly used in the United States. These are the Sankey and the Hof-Stevens kegs. The Hof-Stevens keg is more in the traditional shape of a barrel, with a classic corked hole (usually with a plastic top). This system requires that the tap be screwed tightly onto the keg. If it's not tight enough, gas will escape and the beer will go flat. It is important to note that with this system there is the possibility of being sprayed with beer as you attempt to screw on the tap. One of the best ways of avoiding tap problems with the Hof-Stevens system is to make sure the tap is thoroughly clean before you attempt to affix it to the keg.

The second type of keg is the Sankey keg. These are more cylindrical containers and are popular with Budweiser, Miller, and

Coors. Often the tap and hose are already attached when they are delivered. If not, make sure you get the right tap for the right keg. Confirm this with your delivery man or when you pick up your keg. Beer distributors and other keg renters may require a deposit fee for the keg and the tap, as these are expensive and there are plenty of people who don't want to return them. Keep them in good order, don't lose anything, and you'll get your money back.

Regardless of how old you are and how strong and macho you are, it is not wise to lift and transport a loaded keg by yourself. They are heavy and awkward. Many beer professionals are more than happy to deliver the keg to its exact location, especially for a little monetary enticement. Too many would-be weight lifters have strained their backs, or worse, gotten hernias, trying to lift these large, earth-hugging objects.

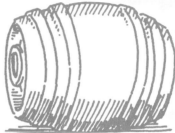

The first thing you want to do, before the beer gets to your home, is to take your nicest garbage can and clean it out thoroughly. Or go out and buy a new one. Make sure there are no leaks in the can. Have the delivery person place the keg in the clean garbage can, then fill the remainder of the can up with ice and some water. This will keep your beer cold and tasting great for the duration of the event. Large kegs in half-sized metal tubs filled with ice and water also work well. Bath tubs are also an excellent place to store a keg with water and ice to keep the beer cold and fresh for your guests.

To start the tap going, you're going to have to pump. The pump, much like a bicycle pump, builds up air pressure and forces beer up the spigot and out of the keg. It is important to pump to get the pressure going and then, as time goes on, to keep the beer flowing. Don't pump too much or too often, or your tap is going to be foam city and you'll only be able to serve foam instead of beer.

It's important to note that in the beginning you will get mostly foam, and the first few beers will be quite heady. If this continues to be a problem, try filling up several pitchers or containers first. However, if you haven't gone berserk with the pump, this stage will pass and your beer service will be easy and fun.

BEER GLASSES AND SERVICE

5

CHAPTER

BOTTLED BY
ADAMS MEDIA CORPORATION

There are no exceptions when you're seriously tasting a new style of beer for the first time, whether it's wheat beer, lambic, Pilsner Urquell, Scotch ale, porter, or a stout, YOU MUST DRINK IT FROM A GLASS! Why? The biggest reason is taste. Taste begins with being able to see, hear, and smell a beer before sipping. This is the most exciting part of the tasting process.

By pouring beer into a glass, you get to experience the beer. You get to see its color and clarity, how it swirls around the glass, and the fullness of the body. You can hear it blop-blop-blop into the glass and smell the aromas that rise from the frothy broth. Examine the head and, after taking the first sip, look at the residue known as Belgian lace. Pouring a new beer is a ceremony that may seem archaic, but it forces one to stop, examine, and experience.

Pouring a beer has practical effects, as well. When you pour the beer some of the gases are released. This is good. It helps the aroma so you can smell it better. It also breaks down some of the carbonation so that you don't ingest more gases than you have to. It gives the beer a chance to build a head, and gives you a chance to experience the body of the beer.

How important are glasses? In the very long history of beer brewing, man has invented specific glasses for certain beers, much like the wine industry has evolved a different glass for every wine. The glass by itself is of such huge importance to the Belgians that it is not uncommon for a first-time visitor to Belgium to be surprised when informed that they must order a different beer because all of the glasses for that particular beer are currently used up.

Certain glasses encourage certain things and accentuate features the brewers and creators of these beers are trying to get across—such as a pilsner glass. It is long and tall, which shows the feature pilsner became fashionable for—its clarity. The pilsner glass is also narrow and tall to accentuate the carbonation—the same way a champagne flute accentuates the carbonation better than a shallow, wide-mouthed glass. By reducing the area of beverage exposed to the open air, the beer will not lose its effervescence so quickly. The more area of liquid exposed to air, the faster it dissipates. While you do want some of the initial gases to escape, you don't want the beer to go flat. It is also important that most lagers build a nice head, and the narrow glass helps to accentuate the head. And lastly, because the glass is narrow, it is easier to smell the aromas; the funnel-like shape focuses those smells.

TYPES OF GLASSES

ALTBIER GLASS

An altbier glass is a rather unimpressive glass. It is small and almost perfectly cylindrical with no flaring in either direction. It does not look like anything more than a small glass.

BEER FLUTE

These glasses tend to resemble champagne flutes except much more pedestrian-looking and larger. Flutes range from small to large and are often mistaken for wine glasses. A wide base and a narrow stem support a bowl that is narrow at the bottom, wide in the middle, and narrow at the top.

BERLINNER WEISSE GOBLET

The most famous of all the goblets, the Berliner Weisse goblet is a pretty, very wide-mouthed glass with ornate scalloped sides. The bowl is not deep and sits atop a sturdy stem and base. Berliner Weisse is the famous "white" wheat beer known for its effervescence, cloudy appearance, and tart flavor.

BOOT (AKA STIEFEL)

The boot is a popular drinking vessel that gets passed around to each person in a group. These are very big in colleges and college towns. For anyone who has never seen a boot, it is aptly named. Usually made of glass or plastic, an experienced drinker is always wary of tilting the boot when one gets toward the foot of the boot. If the boot is not turned just right, pressure builds up in the foot. When the air gets to the foot, it releases the liquid in a gush, usually dousing the unsuspecting participant.

DIMPLED PINT MUG

The dimpled mug was for the longest time an institution in English pubs. A thick, sturdy mug, it usually has thumb-sized dimples all around it. It is short and squat with a relatively wide bowl. These ubiquitous mugs were replaced during the last 50 to 100 years by the standard pint.

GUEUZE

A gueuze glass looks like someone took an altbier glass and squeezed it ever so gently. Its slight hourglass shape looks more misshapen than planned.

HALBE

Halbe is German for half, and the halbe glass holds a half liter of beer. It is a very plain glass mug with a glass handle.

KÖLSCH BEER GLASS

This looks like a Tom Collins glass and is the traditional vessel for serving a kölsch beer in Cologne, Germany.

KRUG

A heavy glass mug. Not nearly as ornate as the English dimpled. Usually very large and sturdy so it can take a beating.

KWAK GLASS

Kwak is a Belgian brewer that makes a dark, rich beer. They have created their own glass, which looks like an aleyard with a large bowl atop the long skinny portion of the yard. It stands only about a foot high and needs a wooden frame to hold it upright.

MASSKRUG (MASS)

This large, liter-sized glass beer mug is popular during Oktoberfest in Munich, Germany. The heaviest and biggest of all glass mugs, these glasses can be nine to ten inches tall and weigh as much as three pounds!

MIDDY

A small Australian beer glass of no distinctive design that holds anywhere from seven to ten ounces.

NONIC "BULGE" OR THE ENGLISH PUB GLASS

This cousin of the pint glass is a very simple kind of pint glass, except for the bulge that appears about half an inch from the rim of the glass. This bulge is also known as a sleeve. Like the standard pint, it also comes in an Imperial size. English pub glasses sometimes have a slight curvature in the body, but only slightly so.

ORVAL'S GOBLET

Named after the famed abbey that produces one of the finest Trappist beers in the world. The monastery dates back to the eleventh century. It was at that time, legend has it, that a beautiful noblewoman lost her gold ring in the lake near the monastery. Praying for the ring's return, she swore that she would build a church or monastery on the very spot. No sooner said, a beautiful trout sprang from the water and returned the ring to her. This scene is depicted on the brewery's label.

In the twelfth century, the abbey became well known for its pharmaceutical mastery. Its ale was renowned for its medicinal powers as well as for its taste as a popular beverage. The glass from Orval has a wide base with a short stem and a large, round bowl with a mouth no bigger than the circumference of the bowl.

PESCARA PILSNER

Shaped like a traditional pilsner glass, the Pescara is narrower and sits atop a base and stem.

PILSNER

The pilsner glass is narrow, slightly cylindrical, and tall. Usually more narrow at the bottom and wider at the mouth, the traditional pilsner elegantly flares out somewhat to a slightly wider mouth. Great for wheat beers as well as pilsners.

PINT GLASS (AKA STANDARD)

There are three different pint glasses.

STANDARD PINT GLASS

A straight lined glass that is very simple; narrow at the bottom and only slightly wider at the top. Holds sixteen ounces. You've seen them everywhere.

IMPERIAL PINT

Same design as the standard, only bigger. Holds twenty ounces.

ENGLISH PUB GLASS

See Nonic "bulge," above.

PONY

This is a small glass that hails from Australia and holds four or five ounces. It looks like a cordial glass and is used to serve strong ales.

RIEDEL VINUM BEER

Riedel is one of the world's premier glass and crystal makers, and the Vinum beer glass is beautiful. It is a little heftier in weight and size than a tall white wine glass. A wide bowl that narrows as it rises and sits nice and high on a tall, narrow stem, this is an exquisite piece and is especially suitable for lagers.

RIEDEL VINUM GOURMET

The Vinum Gourmet has a short stem that supports a bowl that is wide at the bottom and narrow at the mouth. It looks like an elongated brandy snifter. The narrow mouth atop the wider bowl helps to focus the aroma. This glass is excellent for ales, porters, and stouts.

SCHNELLE

A taller, thinner cousin of the stein. Usually made of earthenware, with a hinged lid.

STEIN

An earthenware vessel invented during the notorious outbreak of bubonic plague in Europe (fourteenth century) to keep flies and other possible disease-carrying insects and germs out of beer. Became very popular in Germany and took on a life of its own.

THISTLE

The Belgians, who are responsible for at least half the beer glasses in existence today, also created the thistle, the most unique of all beer glasses. A large, round, fat bowl sits on a foot and a thick stem. Near the top of the bowl, the glass begins to curve in, as if it were about to become a sphere. Then it turns suddenly outward, creating the effect of a crown sitting on top of a head. It looks like a thistle. This glass is not always easy to get and was created to optimize the aroma of beer. It is strongly associated with Scottish ale. It is reported that Scottish soldiers became enamored with the glass during World War I.

TULIP

This is a wonderfully graceful glass that also has its practical side. Because of the way the glass is shaped, one can drink the beer and get a little bit of the foam at the same time. Strong ales are usually served in tulip glasses, and the creamy head helps to mellow out and enhance the flavor of the beer. Sitting atop a sturdy foot and short, thick stem, sits a bowl, tapered toward the top, that resembles a tulip. Just before the rim, the glass is pinched in, creating a flaring out at the rim.

TUMBLER (SCHOONER)

Usually a twelve-ounce glass with little distinction, a tumbler looks like a Tom Collins, but not quite so tall and narrow and with a little bowing to it. A schooner is the fifteen-ounce version of this glass.

WEIZEA OR WEIZEN

This wheat beer glass has a narrow base, with a large to semi-large bowl about halfway up the glass. These are big glasses that hold eighteen to twenty ounces.

WILLIBECKER

Looks very much like a tumbler, with a narrow base, a flared-out midsection, and a very slightly tapered mouth.

YARD-OF-ALE (YARD, ALEYARD, OR COACHMAN'S HORN)

The yard is another drinking vessel popular with college students. This long tube-like glass vessel with a small bowl at the bottom holds about a quart of beer. It is called a yard because the glass is approximately thirty-six inches tall. Much like the boot, the pressure at the bottom builds until air releases the beer in the ball. It also comes in half yards.

The yard was reportedly originated by an innkeeper in Belgium who was known to sell beverages to drivers who could not otherwise be served. Due to the Napoleonic Code, a driver whose carriage contained nobles could not descend from the carriage. The tall beaker was easily passed up to the thirsty driver where it was quickly imbibed. So much for drinking and driving regulations under Napoleonic Code.

FROZEN MUGS

It's time to put your frosted mugs in the same closet with your pet rock and mood ring. Frozen mugs are out.

There are several good reasons for this. In the history of European beer, no country has ever featured frozen mugs. Lager was invented to be stored cold . . . that's what lager means. But the first brewers of lager didn't have refrigeration, per se. They stored the casks of beer in caves dug into the sides of mountains. They served lagers chilled, but not icy cold. You're just muting the tastes if you serve beer icy cold.

Another thing to remember when serving from frozen mugs is that ice forms on the inside of your frosty mug. By freezing your mugs, all you're doing is diluting the body and the flavor of the beer.

WHICH GLASSES SHOULD YOU OWN?

When it comes to classic beer glasses, there are no two better containers to own than the pint and pilsner glasses. Every beer fan starting off should have four of each. Why four? Because it's more fun to taste with someone else than to do it alone. You can usually purchase these glasses separately; however, they are also sold in sets of four as well.

Every aficionado needs a place to start, and these two classics have features that will serve you well. As you become more and more knowledgeable about beer, you might want to add different style glasses to your collection. But however deep your fascination goes into this secret world of water, hops, barley, and yeast, these two sets of glasses will always stand you in good stead and will forever be the most serviceable of any of the other vessels from which you can drink.

We've already discussed the benefits of the pilsner glass. Why the pint? Most ales around the world are served in a pint glass, especially in Britain and Ireland, the true home of the pint. But why is it a classic? Rule number one of any glass is that it should hold the contents of one regular bottle of beer. No matter what glass it is, pint, pilsner, or otherwise, it should take the full contents of the bottle.

The pint is also excellent for one of the same reasons for which a pilsner is popular—it affords an excellent view of the beer in the glass. You can see much better than in any other beer glass what exactly it is that you are drinking. Another thing that's important to note is that ales tend not to be as highly carbonated as lagers and pilsners in specific. So the pint does not have to be tall and cylindrical, as opposed to wider and more open. And because there is not as much escaping gas, helping the aroma to rise, it gives you a bigger area from which to smell your beer.

What is wrong with a mug or another type of glass? Many mugs, and a Berliner Weisse-style glass, are made so that the glass will not afford you a clear look at the beer you are drinking. Beer flutes would be fine, but these glasses tend to be small and do not hold very much beer. Thistle and duvet-style glasses are very nice but not always easily accessible to the general consumer. A yard, horn, or boot is not for the serious beer taster, though they have their place with the right crowd.

HOW TO CARE FOR YOUR NEW GLASSES

Rules for keeping your new glasses clean.

1. Don't put your glasses in the dishwasher. Many dishwashing detergents leave all kinds of films for clearer rinsing and faster drying. They also leave a residual taste and aroma that will ruin your experience for sure. Wine drinkers don't put their special glasses in the dishwasher, either. This leads us to rule number two.
2. Always wash your glasses by hand and use hot water and as little soap as possible.
3. Never towel dry your glasses. You might as well put them in the dishwasher. Let them dry on a rack. Air drying is very important. Dishtowels leave lint and odors that they have picked up.
4. Store them in a clean, dry place. Use a place that doesn't get too many odors.

The idea is to avoid having your glasses pick up any unpleasant smells or tastes that could ruin your drinking experience. If you don't think any of this matters, do a test run. Wash one glass by hand and one in the dishwasher. When they are both dry, stick your nose as deep as you can into each glass. When you are trying a new beer and you really want to experience it to its fullest potential, then you'll want to do everything possible to make sure that the tasting is a success.

HOW TO POUR

While pouring might seem a minor concern, it is in fact very important. Don't pick up any hints on how to pour beer from beer commercials. Many beer ads show beer being poured from a foot away from the glass, and the beer goes splashing around and a head (which implies body) immediately appears. Apple juice would do the same thing at those heights.

With lager and light- to medium-colored ales, pour right down the middle of the glass, aiming the stream at the bottom of the glass, but not from several feet away; instead, just from the top of the glass. Once a head develops, tilt the glass so that the head does not get overly large. The important thing to remember about pouring a head is that it shouldn't be higher than two fingers. That's the international measuring stick.

Lawnmower beers tend to build a large head quickly, but since most of these beers have little body, the head dissipates quickly. Make sure when you're pouring not to pour too big a head or you'll have to wait for the head to go down before you can pour the rest of the beer and drink it. Wheat beers are very much the same.

Bottle-conditioned beers require a different strategy. Because many bottle-fermented beers have sediment, you should remember not to pour out the last ounce or two. This sediment is yeast and can cause not only flatulence, but serious digestive problems due to excessive gas. It is highly recommended that as a first-timer you do not drink these settled yeasts.

MORE ON STEINS

The word *stein* comes from a German word for stone or stoneware, from which early drinking vessels were made. Today we think of a stein as a large mug with a handle and hinged lid. Stein collectors (and there are many of them), identify the hinged lid as the difference between the mug and the stein. A mug without a handle is called a beaker.

The hinged lid was a result of the bubonic plague. Drinkers did not want flies or other insects that might be carrying the deadly disease to infect their water or beer. So sometime in the fifteenth or sixteenth century a hinged lid was attached, and that is how the stein has been known ever since. While the stein had its more practical uses during the plague and its functional uses have become obsolete, the stein has continued to be popular. Many different types of steins are known to us today, and they have all become more ornate over time. A stein says something about its owner. The stein is a statement of individuality, and has become an objet d'art that is very much in demand by collectors.

There are no hard-and-fast rules about what constitutes a stein besides the basic mug with a hinged top. Over the centuries steins have been made out of everything that is not water soluble, including pottery, glass, a substance known as faience, precious metals, and wood. Stein Collectors International, a collecting and auction society, has some rare examples made from leather, ivory, ostrich eggs, and horns. The most common classifications of steins are: Early Stoneware, Faience, Glass, Pewter, Porcelain, Relief and Painted Stoneware, Mettlach, Regimental or Military, Occupational, and Character steins.

Early Stoneware

Many of the oldest steins came from the Westerwald region of Germany where the Rhein and Mosel Rivers meet. This was a great pottery center in Germany. The earliest steins were made of stoneware and date back to the fifteenth century. Stoneware requires clay and timber (for fire), so many of the first steins came from factories that made stoneware to begin with. Like other pottery, steins were shaped on a potter's wheel and baked at very high temperatures in potter's ovens, called kilns. And like other pottery, sometimes a glaze was applied for decorative use. The glaze also reduced the porousness of the vessel.

The steins from the Westerwald region have a purplish color—with a gray or blue tint—and a clear salt glaze. Their lids were generally made with pewter. Later steins had thumb lifts to make the lid easier to open while drinking. Often the bodies of the steins were either

HOW TO FIND OUT MORE ABOUT STEINS

Stein Collectors International

This site is an excellent source of information, including bulletin boards and responsive members. For collectors and aficionados as well as for novices.

Glenna Scheer
Executive Director
281 Shore Drive, Unit E
Burr Ridge, IL 60521
http://paterson.k12.nj.us/
~steins/

Der Stein Haus

This is an exceptional Website with plenty of photos and other graphics, as well as presentations of small private collections.

http://www.net-gate.com/
~fkossen/steinhaus.html

painted or carried inscriptions. Some of the later more ornate steins had a base made of pewter to protect the pottery from chipping. Steins are still being made in the same way in this region today and are considered of the highest quality. Many collectors prefer them.

Faience

Faience (or phaience) was Europe's answer to fine Chinese porcelain. This cheaper and locally made pottery was lighter and finer than stoneware, and dates from the mid-seventeenth century. Because porcelain and faience were much softer materials than earthenware and tended to chip more easily, these steins had pewter or other metal bases to protect the steins from breaking. These steins were difficult to produce and were very ornate. In fact, this marked a trend in stein decoration, as faience steins began the long tradition of decorative artwork that has continued to make the stein so popular. According to Stein Collectors International, "painted designs included animals, architectural scenes, birds, crests, figural scenes, verses, etc." Many steins from this era can be found in museums in Germany and around the world.

Glass

While some glass steins date from the fifteenth century, the greatest production occurred much around the same time as faience. Steins from the eighteenth and nineteenth centuries were usually blown glass with engravings and pewter hinged lids. These glass steins came in an array of vibrant colors, including ruby red, gold, cobalt blue, and emerald green. Some glass was painted over and very much resembled faience. Enameled steins followed soon afterward. In the later part of the nineteenth century, inlaid glass mugs were also made that were very fine and expensive.

Pewter

Pewter is a metal alloy that dates back to the Bronze Age. Steins made of pewter date back to the sixteenth century. Pewter is largely tin mixed with various other metals in specific amounts. With steins being made of cheaper and newer materials in the late 1700s and early 1800s, the desire for pewter steins died down. However, in the late 1800s there was a renewed interest in pewter steins. These pewter steins tended to be simple but perfect, and not cheap. Their workmanship was usually very high in quality. Much of the final shaping, polishing, stamping, and engraving were all done by hand, and were carefully inspected by their manufacturers, as well as by discerning consumers. Many craftsmen used the thumb lift as a means of artistic expression, and many of these same artisans left their touchmarks somewhere on the steins to identify their individuality.

Porcelain

Porcelain dates back to ancient China, but the first porcelain steins date back to eighteenth-century Germany. Porcelain is made from kaolin (also referred to as china clay), is fired at much higher temperatures than stoneware, and tends to be much more delicate. It is finer, whiter, and much more easily prone to chip. Porcelain steins tend to be very ornate. Many also have very intricate inlaid lids. The most notable of these kinds of steins were made in the Meissen factory in Germany. Later on, manufacturers began using transfer decorations that made hand painting minimal. Lithophanes were also added to many of these steins. By varying the thickness of the porcelain, manufacturers could include scenes that were not visible unless the porcelain was held up to the light. This was a very popular effect and has become an important aspect in collecting this type of stein.

Earthenware

Earthenware pottery does not require the high, intense heat of porcelain or stoneware; however, it remains more porous when it stands alone. Thus, many of the steins made of earthenware are covered in a thick glaze that makes it a suitable vessel and easier to decorate. Because it was cheaper to produce and very malleable, it was mass produced. Many relief pottery designs were used. The steins found in shops and flea markets all around the world are most commonly made of earthenware. This type of material gave birth to many different types of steins, most popular of which is the character stein. Other types of steins that came from this type of material were brewery steins and sports steins. Some collectors look for steins manufactured by Diesinger (D.R.G.M.), Gertz Hauber & Reuther (HR), Thewalt, and Martz & Remy. Collectors particularly prize works by such renown stein artisans as Franz Ringer and Karl Beuler. Ringer first worked for Villeroy & Boch, but later worked for the equally well-known stein manufacturer Reinhold Merkelbach.

Mettlach

Renowned manufacturer Villeroy & Boch began making steins around 1840 in the small town of Mettlach in Germany's Saarland. Between 1880 and 1910, Villeroy & Boch created some of the most famous steins ever produced. None were more famous than their chromolith steins. Their coal-fired kilns produced a much more uniform stoneware. Many of the secrets of this fine stoneware process were lost in a fire in the early twenties. According to International Collectors these included "hand-painted, mosaic, tapestry, print-under-glaze (PUG) and relief items, sometimes incorporating more than one technique. V & B used an extensive marking system that included the old tower (castle) trademark, the year of production, form number, size number, etc." While the secrets of this golden age are lost, Villeroy & Boch continues to make steins in limited production that are of high quality but nowhere close to those of the golden period.

Regimental or Military Steins

Regimental or military steins are some of the most detailed and fascinating of all the steins. When Germany became a world power, most men were required to enlist for three years of military service. As they neared the end of their training or their enlistment, many men bought steins commemorating their military career or experience. These were not very expensive steins, and were made from almost any kind of material: porcelain, glass, stoneware, or pottery. But each stein did have very specific markings, making it uniquely individual. Many steins of this type not only held a serviceman's time of enlistment, but his regiment and status.

The body of the stein might have a number of different things on it. Some had famous battle scenes closely identified with that regiment. Some had a list of recruits from the time of the individual's enlistment. Some steins had several battle scenes. Many had the regimental colors and/or insignia. The finial on the lid was decorated with a cannon, a horse and rider, or something else commemorating his enlistment. Also unique was the thumb lift. Like the finial, it was used to tell something about the individual. A Bavarian or a Hessen had a lion on his. Prussians' steins had eagles for thumb lifts. A griffin identified a man from Baden.

Occupational Steins

Rather than categorized by the type of materials from which they are made, occupational steins, like regimental or military steins, are characterized by their subject. Dating from the early nineteenth century until about the late 1920s and 1930s, many are made of porcelain. The designs and scenes illustrate different trades. The types of trades more plentiful than not were directly related to the numbers of workers plying their trades in those years.

Character Steins

Like regimental or occupational steins, character steins were known for their inspiration rather than the materials from which they were made. Many were made of pottery. More often than not, according to Der Stein Haus, a stein collector's collective, "character steins are interesting because they commemorate the renown and the comic personality, animals of all kind," as well as well-known characters from religion, history, or literature. The devil, a replica of a human skull, and other of these types of motifs were very popular in this type of stein. Mettlach, as well as places like Mustershutz, Mayer, Wessels, and Bohne were well-known manufacturers of this type of stein.

OTHER STEINS

Among other classification of steins, one of the most popular is the art nouveau stein. Many of these were made of stoneware and earthenware, and were notable for their design. These were made mostly in the Westerwald area of Germany by a small core of artisans. Many were exported to the United States; however, there are a small number of large private collections in Germany. Many were produced by Reinhold Merkelbach. Merkelback steins often had the artisans mark on them. One of the most renowned designers of art nouveau steins was Henry Clemens van de Velde.

Another popular type of stein celebrates a city or region. Such steins celebrate myths and legends like the Munich Monk, the Munich Maid, and the Twin Towers of Munich.

THE WORLD TOUR

6

CHAPTER

BOTTLED BY
ADAMS MEDIA CORPORATION

BEERS AROUND THE WORLD

There are many wonderful beers brewed all over the world. For the beer enthusiast, the following beers truly demand your attention. That is not to say that beers that do not appear on this list do not deserve to be tasted. Try these to your heart's content and enjoy. (The following beers are listed by country.)

Belguim

Cantillon Kriek Lambic
Cantillon Framboise Rose' de Gambrinus
Cantillon Grand Cru
Brasserie Cantillon
Gheudestraat 56, Anderlecht
1070 Brussels
Belgium

Listening to Belgians argue over the best lambics is like listening to Dubliners argue over Irish stouts. Belgium has supported the entire lambic industry for more than two centuries, but these tremendous beers are finally getting the worldwide notoriety they deserve. One of the best brewers of lambics is Brasserie Cantillon.

The Cantillon family came from Lambeck, began selling lambic beers in 1900, and later settled in Brussels. The brewery is still run by the same family. Their beers are more sour than Lindemans'. The Kriek Lambic is a red beer with a very sharp, sour cherry taste. The Rose' de Gambrinus is a reddish orange beer that tastes of sour raspberries. The Grand Cru is a vintage lambic beer. All are of exceptional quality and taste. These are sipping, dessert beers. You are not going to have these with a steak or hot dog. These beers are best served in brandy snifters or wide-open glasses so that you can enjoy their nose.

Chapeau Gueuze Lambic
Brouwerij de Troch
20 Lange Straat
B-1741
Wambeek
Belgium

Lambic beers for many are an acquired taste. This gueuze is one of the finest examples of a gueuze beer you will ever taste. This

This would be a good time for a beer.

—FRANKLIN DELANO ROOSEVELT

is a delicate and fine after-dinner or late evening drink that is meant to be savored. Definitely for more developed taste buds.

Premier Chimay Peres Trappistes
Cinq Cents Chimay Peres Trappistes
Grand Reserve Chimay Peres Trappistes
Abbaye de Notre-Dame de Scourmont
6483 Forges
Belgium

The name is pronounced "she-MAY." These are delicious beers that are succulent and fun to drink. All are excellent examples of bottle-conditioned beers. These Trappist beers, made by monks, are of a style in-and-of-themselves. The three styles mean red, white, and blue. Premier is red; Cinq Cents is white; and the Grand Reserve is blue.

Duvel Belgian Beer
Brouwerij Moortgat
Breendonkdorp 58
2870 Breendonk-Puurs
Belgium

Duvel is a unique experience. It is even more fun to drink from a Duvel glass. This wonderful strong pale ale has few peers. What makes this beer so special is that it undergoes three fermentations. The first two fermentations, one hot and one cold, are followed by bottle conditioning before shipping.

Hoegaarden Original White Ale
Brouwerij De Kluis
46 Stoopkens Straat
3320 Hoegaarden
Belgium

Hoegaarden has for many years been one of the best brewers of wheat beers in the world. Formerly run by Pierre Celis, who now runs Celis Brewery, this old-time brewery burned down in 1985. Many had lost hope that it would be able to survive such devastation. It has flourished, and a grateful public has continued to support this exceptional brewery.

Kwak

Brouwerij Bosteels
Kerkstr 92
B-9255 Buggenhout
Dendermonde
Belgium

While beerdom is known for its many glasses, none is more famous than the story of the yard of beer. A Belgian innkeeper by the name of Pauwel Kwak made a strong orange beer that became famous throughout Europe, and his inn was along a much-traveled trade route. However, Napoleonic Law restricted him from selling his beer to the coachmen who were weary from their hectic schedules on the post road. The law stated that while a nobleman was in the carriage, a coachman could not get down from the coach to have a drink. Therefore, Kwak decided to circumvent the law by offering the beer in a glass we know today as the yard-of-ale glass. With this glass, a driver did not have to dismount to have a drink, and the glass fit the coachman's stirrup. This beer is a strange brew, hard to describe. An amber ale, it is powerful and flavorful with an almost herbal essence.

Lindemans Framboise Lambic
Lindemans Kriek Lambic

Brouwerij Lindemans
257 Lenniksebaan
1712 Vlezenbeek
Belgium

Lindemans has been making beer for generations. Your beer education is not complete without having tasted the lambics from Lindemans. Calling these incredibly delicious beverages beers seems almost silly. It's like calling champagne wine; it doesn't do it justice. These ales are brewed with natural fruit juices and extracts that the brewery makes. The final product is pink (kriek) or purple (framboise). Both are very delicate drinks to be sipped and savored. This, like gueuze, requires a little understanding and experience. This is for the sophisticated beer drinker. No guzzling!

Orval Trappist Ale

Brasserie D'Orval S.A.
6823 Villers-Devant-Orval
Belgium

The emblem of this brewery is a fish with a ring in its mouth jumping out of water. The story of Orval is one of the strangest and most fascinating of all the brewery histories in the world. It is said that the duchess of Tuscany came to visit the monks of a particular abbey in 1076. Upon losing her favorite gold ring in the lake near the abbey, the duchess prayed that her ring might be returned. Just after her prayer, a fish jumped out of the lake and returned the gold ring to her. She was so astonished that she exclaimed, "This is truly a val d'or!" or a valley of gold. Orval means "golden valley."

Brewed with many different kinds of barley malts, this pale ale is fermented three times, including a bottle fermentation. Sugar is used during the course of fermentation, but the beer is not sweet. Orval is also known for its wonderful thick-stemmed glass. The small bowl of this glass opens widest at the rim so that one can enjoy the very aromatic qualities of the beer.

Rodenbach Grand Cru Belgian Red Ale

Brouwerij Rodenbach
133-141 Spanje Straat
8800 Roeselare
Belgium

The Rodenbach brewery was founded in 1820. If you like red beers, then you will love Rodenbach beers. These are the red beers that all other red-beer brewers try to emulate. Among the Rodenbach beers, the Grand Cru is acknowledged worldwide as the best red beer produced anywhere. Brewed from four malts and five yeasts, and aged for two years in unlined twenty-foot-high oak casks, this is one of the best crafted brews ever made. This beer is brewed with care and tradition, and both show through from the first smell.

These beers are sour, which is the classic Flanders tradition. Reddish in color, this beer is also known as "The Burgundy of

Belgium." It is smooth with a good nose and a very big taste that includes some sourness (from its lactic flavors) and tannins. There are also some caramely flavors, as well as a big nose and hint of cherry.

Saison Dupont

Brasserie DuPont
5 Rue Basse
7904 Tourpes-Leuze
Hainaut, Wallonia
Belgium

The first thing you will notice when you open the bottle is a little bulb of head that immediately plops out of the bottle. That is just the first hint of how enticing this beer actually is. With its big, creamy head—thick like foam, like a sort of whipped cream—Saison offers a drinking experience that is unique. A yeasty ale, there is almost a sourness to it, but it is not sweet. It is an exceptional brew with citrus overtones.

The DuPont brewery dates back to 1850 and has been run by the DuPont family since 1920. This establishment uses incredibly old traditions to craft a beer few can match. It is worth every hardship endurable to taste this beer.

Westmalle Tripel Trappistenbier

Abdij Der Trappisten Van Westmalle
Antwerpsesteenweg 496
2390 Malle
Belgium

This bottle-conditioned beer is one of the few beers that can be cellared for up to two years. Monks from the La Trappe monastery founded Our Lady of the Sacred Heart Abbey in 1794. This abbey, located in Westmalle, did not produce its first beer until 1836. By the late 1800s the beer had found its way into the hearts of the Flemish laymen. Still a monastery, the brewery has been renovated several times in order to keep up with technology and the growing demand. A bitter hop taste and gold in color, their tripel is one of the best in the world.

Witkap-Pater Abbey Singel Ale
Brouwerij Slaghmuylder
Denderhoutembaan 2
8-9400 Ninove
Belgium

This is the only brewery allowed to use the "trappiste" appellation that is not actually an abbey. The Slaghmuylder Brewery is located in Flanders. It is still run by members or descendants of the Slaghmuylder family, 134 years after its founding. The original brewer was Emmanuel Slaghmuylder.

Witkap means "white head," which probably refers to the lovely white head on a glass of this excellent old ale. This is a golden, clean, creamy, refreshing beer with some fruity and vanilla flavors. It has almost a wheat beer flavor. After brewing, the beer is clarified by centrifuge to remove all particles, and then bottled with sugar and yeast for bottle conditioning. It is very complex and absolutely delicious.

Canada

Blanche De Chambly
Maudite
La Fin Du Monde
Raftman
La Gaillarde
Unibroue
Quebec, Canada

These are some of the most wonderful Trappist-style ales you will ever taste that are not made in Belgium. Most popular are Maudite, La Fin Du Monde, and Raftman. These are world-class-caliber beers and can be laid down for up to two years. On many of their labels you will see the phrase "on lees." This means it was bottle-fermented. Truly a European-style beer and one of the best beers made in the world.

Granville Anniversary Amber
Granville Island Bock
Granville Pale Ale
Granville Island Brewing Company
Vancouver, Canada

All of these beers are very nice, new beers being brewed by a Pacific Northwest brewer. Founded in 1984 by Mitch Taylor, Granville brews its beers in accordance with the Reinheitsgebot. The Bock and the Pale Ale are good, but the Anniversary Amber is very tasty.

Original Red Cap Ale
Brick Brewing Company
Ontario, Canada
Founded in 1984 during the microbrewery revolution in North America, Original Red Cap Ale became an immediate hit for this small Ontario microbrewer. A unique ale.

St. Ambrose Pale Ale
St. Ambrose Oatmeal Stout
La Brasserie McAulsan
Quebec, Canada

Founded in 1989 by Peter McAulsan, these beers have catapulted to immediate international fame. The St. Ambrose Pale Ale is golden-reddish in color, and is bitter with overtones of citrus. The St. Ambrose Oatmeal Stout is black and has excellent mouthfeel; roasty and somewhat sweet. These are two very tasty beers.

Czech Republic

Budweiser Budvar
Karoliny Svelte 4
370-21 Ceske Budejovice-Budweis
Czech Republic
You will have to go to Europe to taste this exceptional pilsner beer but it deserves inclusion anyway. Much more robust and full-bodied than its American namesake, trademark infringement (this brewery was founded after the American Budweiser brewery) keeps this wonderful beer out of the United States. If you go abroad, drink it and enjoy.

Pilsner Urquell
Plzensky Prazdroj
30497 Plzen
Czech Republic
This is the granddaddy of the entire American mass-producing beer industry. Even the microbrewers have their interpretations of this exceptional beer that changed the course of beer history. Remember, urquell means "original."

England

Boddington's Pub Ale Draft
Boddington's Breweries, Ltd.
Manchester, England M60 3WB

This is an experience you have to try. This is the only recommended beer sold solely in a can. Boddington's Pub Ale Draft is a light, golden, hazy ale that is mellow and only slightly carbonated. It has lemony, citrusy flavors and a bitter hops taste, but it is an experience that is too much fun.

This is the one beer that, even though it's sold in a can, you should *never* drink from the can. The idea of this beer is to give a hand-pumped-from-a-keg kind of feel. The hand-pulled method usually adds slight carbonation. As the beer is pulled through the keg it produces a creamy head and a little gassiness in the beer itself. The Boddington's can is rigged with something the brewer calls its Draughtflow™ System. "By releasing millions of tiny bubbles when opened, Draughtflow™ cans give you the creamy head and authentic fresh taste of a Boddington's pub ale." In other words, you have to start pouring this as soon as you open it. Wait for the beer to settle after pouring. When it comes out, it is a white mass. Then the bubbles begin to rise and the beer begins to separate. The first thing you'll notice is that the head is incredible. The head on this beer is white, fresh, and creamy and tastes like whipped cream or crème fraîche. The head is thick, like frosting, and will not dissipate for a while. An exceptional invention and experience, try it—you will definitely like it.

Marston's Pedigree Bitter

Marston, Thompson & Evershed
The Brewery
Shobnall Road
Burton-on-Trent
Staffordshire DE14 28W
England

One of the few clear ales made in Europe using the old Burton Union System, Marston's Pedigree Bitter is one of the most intriguing beers you will ever drink. While the Burton System is costly, Marston's Pedigree Bitter has been brewed the same way since 1834. A golden amber in color, the beer develops a creamy head and has good carbonation. This is a hoppy beer at its best.

Samuel Smith's Oatmeal Stout
Samuel Smith's The Famous Taddy Porter
Samuel Smith's Imperial Stout

Samuel Smith Old Brewery
Tadcaster
North Yorkshire LS24 9DSB
England

Samuel Smith is to the beer industry what Mouton or Lafite is to the wine industry—a hallowed name. Founded in 1758, Samuel Smith Old Brewery, in Yorkshire, England, is still privately owned and run. The beer is still made in the same brewery, in Tadcaster, as it has been for the last three centuries. The brewery itself is the oldest in Yorkshire, which is home to many brewing companies, including Courage and Bass. Samuel Smith does not make a mediocre beer. They make excellent beers, and having to choose among them is a painful experience. Their beers were even celebrated by Charles Dickens in his classic, *A Tale of Two Cities*. All of Samuel Smith's beers are made in the Yorkshire squares, a unique and old-time brewing system only they use.

The first thing you will notice when you pour The Famous Taddy Porter is that the bottle is not black—it's the beer! You will also notice the body. The nose will catch your attention right away, and the head will rise nice and creamy. Many say that Taddy Porter gets its unique taste from the open vats, lined with slabs of granite pulled from local quarries, in which it is brewed. No porter on Earth compares. To drink this is an experience that is unique and unforgettable. This isn't cheap beer in the United States, but you will not be disappointed.

The Smith brewery only recently brought back their Imperial Stout. Full-bodied, with complex flavors and aromas, this is a potent brew. Imperial Stout was originally brewed for Catherine the Great and, subsequently, the Russian czars. It was brewed very strong so that it would last the long journey and still be potent and flavorful long after it got to the czar's palace.

This beer is dark with an almost purplish color, and it has some chocolate overtones, as well as a roastiness. First brewed again by Smith's in 1980 at the request of their American importer, Imperial Stout, it became immediately the Imperial Stout to beat. For an extra kick, taste this beer in a brandy glass so that you can experience it to the fullest.

Oatmeal Stout has a touch of red. This beer has no bite, but lots of flavor with a fruity nose and taste. This is not a sweet beer, but something incredibly different. It's also very malty. Only Samuel Smith could make three similar beers that do not taste anything alike but are of exceptional quality.

Theakston Old Peculier

T & R Theakston Ltd.
Wellgarth, Masham
Ripon, N. Yorkshire
HG4 4DX
England

Old Peculier gets its name from the old Norman French saying that means "the old particular ale," referring to an ale of olden times. Old Peculier is one of the oddest beers produced and is a beer of no particular style, save its own. Old Peculier has been made in Masham, in Yorkshire, since 1827 when it was founded by Robert Theakston. Theakston owned and operated a series of brewpubs that served his various brews. As his small empire grew, so too did the demand for his strange ale. Eventually, he founded a brewery, and his beer is still brewed there today.

Theakston is one of the few remaining breweries that still employs a cooper and a cooper's apprentice. Together they build barrels, as well as refit and refurbish old ones. These huge kegs are the famous final step in the brewing of the strange and wonderful beer. The beer is brewed with numerous barleys and yeasts, as well as several different sugars. After brewing, it is then stored in wooden barrels.

The final product is a dark, roasty, fruity, and complex beer that finishes surprisingly dry. It is reminiscent of a plum pudding beer with caramel and chocolate overtones. Truly one of the most fascinating beers you will ever drink.

France

3 Monts
Grande Reserve
Bierre De Noel (Flander's Winter Ale in U.S.,
Canada, and UK)
Brasserie St. Sylvestre
Sylvestre-Cappel, France

These three ales are some of the best old-time ales you will ever have. Named for three hills in the Flanders region, this farmhouse brewery dates back to 1918, and it is still in the same family. A reddish/copper color, the Bierre De Noel is excellent, as are the 3 Monts and 3 Monts Grande Reserve. The Grande Reserve has an alcohol content of 7.5 percent. This microbrewery makes quality hand-crafted beers.

Germany

Diebels Alt
Privatbrauerei Diebels
Brauerei-Diebels-Strasse 1
47661 Issum
Germany

One of the finest examples of an alt beer produced in the world. There are many fond imitators in the United States; however, this beer is more complex and subtle than any of them.

Einbecker Ur-Bock Dunkel
Einbecker Brauhaus
Papen Strasse 4-7
3352 Einbeck
Lower Saxony
Germany

The tradition of brewing dates back more than 700 years in the city of Einbeck, Germany, where this exceptional beer is made. Einbecker Brauhaus, which brews Ur-Bock Dunkel, is the culmination of this heritage. Over the centuries, all of the hundreds of brewhouses in Einbeck have been gathered into one manufacturer, the only maker of this excellent beer. While their pils is only adequate, their Ur-Bock Dunkel is one of the great beer experiences of a lifetime.

Reichelbrau Eisbock
Kulmbacher Reichelbrau A.G.
Postfach 1860
8650 Kulmbach
Germany

This ice beer is one of the preeminent beers of its type. After brewing, the beer is frozen for sixteen days and the ice removed. After that it is aged in oak casks for eight weeks and then bottled. This Franconian beer is thought of as a dessert beer because of its high alcohol content. It is meant to be sipped, but it is not sweet. It is very dark and rich with a thick body and strong nose. You can't help but taste the malt. One of the best beers you will ever taste.

Salvator
Paulaner-Salvator-Thomas-Brau
Hochstrasse 75
8000 Munchen 95
Germany

This is the original doppel-bock beer—and still the undisputed king of that style. Everything that has come after—many with the -*ator* at the end of the name—have been flattering, but pale imitations. The Paulaner brewery dates back to 1631, when the monks of St. Paul were brewing these same beers. The name Salvator means "savior," and it comes from the fact that the monks used to brew this particular style for the Lenten season to sustain them through the fasting periods. They began selling their beer as a means of raising money for their abbey in the late 1700s, and by the early 1800s they were a secular business. This dark, strong beer (7.5 percent alcohol by volume) is also big on taste and long on flavor. The aftertaste will stay with you for a while. This is one of the tastiest beers you will ever have.

Schlenkerla Rauchbier

Brauerei Heller-Trum
Schlenkerla
6 Dominikaner Strasse
8600 Bamberg
Germany

To avoid any confusion, the actual label reads "Aecht Schlenkerla Rauchbier ges. gesch. Marzen," which in effect means smoky old marzen. Rauchbier is a smoked beer, and it is a wonderful treat. If you like smoked ham and other meats, smoked fish, and smoked cheeses, you will love this stuff. However, if you don't liked smoked things, then this beer isn't for you.

The Heller-Trumm brewery has been making smoked beer since its founding in 1678. The original brewery was in fact a brewpub, but it has since been turned into a brewery. The Trumms bought the business and have run it successfully for five generations.

The barley is smoked on racks on the premises, and then the beer is brewed. It is an ale, and after brewing it is stored for seven weeks. This dark beer smells and tastes of smoke. Great with foods—either smoked or not.

Ireland

Guinness Extra Stout

Arthur Guinness & Son Ltd.
St. James Gate
Dublin 8
Ireland

Guinness is one of the truly great beers of the world. Guinness, an Irish or dry stout, is a rich and creamy stout that is the envy of the stout-brewing world. This beer was one of the few nonpilsner beers favored by Americans in the bleak beer years of the '60s and '70s. Brewed in the Republic of Ireland, Guinness beer is one of the few things both Irishmen and Englishmen can agree on. Dark brown, almost black, Guinness leaves a fine Belgian lace and has a body that won't quit. This is one of those beers that doesn't taste so bad at room temperature. It tastes good at any temperature.

Murphy's Irish Stout

Lady's Well Brewery
Leitrim Street
Cork
Ireland

Much like its more famous countryman, Guinness, Murphy's Irish Stout is one of the world's premier Irish stouts. It gives its older, fellow Irish brewery a good run for its money. A little smoother and creamier, it lacks the bite of Guinness. Some pubs—some towns—in Ireland will serve one or the other. Roasty, with an almost coffee-like after taste, Murphy's is as dark as they come. Taste the two and compare for yourself.

Italy

Moretti Baffo D'Oro
Moretti La Rossa Double Malt Beer

Birra Moretti
Udine, Italy

Baffo D'Oro is a golden pale lager that is full-bodied and somewhat bitter. The manufacturer of this beer, Birra Moretti, was founded in 1859 and manufactures many beers. Baffo D'Oro is its signature beer.

Moretti La Rossa Double Malt Beer is a very flavorful beer. It has a very complex taste with roastiness to it, as well as malt and plenty of hop bitterness. A reddish amber beer, it has great aroma and great taste.

Peroni Beer
Peroni Italia Pilsen Export Beer
Peroni, E.C. S.P.A
V. Delle Forze Armate
310/5
Milan Italy

Peroni is one of the best known and largest beer producers in Italy. They make solely lager beers, and their range is somewhat limited. However, their Peroni Beer and their Italia Pilsen Export are two very high-quality, bitter, golden pilsner-style beers that are dry and refreshing.

Japan

Kirin Beer
Kirin Brewery Company, Ltd.
Tokyo, Japan

Kirin Beer is a light golden lager with a strong hops flavor, clean taste, and dry finish. This lager may not be incredibly memorable like a stout or a lambic, but it is a very tasty beer.

Mexico

Dos Equis Amber Lager
Dos Equis
Mexico

Dos Equis is one of the few remaining true Vienna lagers left in the world. It is one of the most notable beers brewed outside the United States and Europe. Reddish to amber in color, this lager is brewed using a roasted malt. It is dry, clean, clear, and crisp.

Negro Modelo
Corona Extra
La Cerveceria Modelo
Mexico City, Mexico
Negro Modelo, more than Dos Equis, is perhaps more reminiscent of a Vienna lager. It's bolder, darker, and more robust than Dos Equis, yet smooth, clean, and crisp. This is not a heavy beer. This beer has remained true to its roots, and is the same brewer that brews Corona Extra.

Corona Extra is a very light beer, golden and clear in color and mass-produced and mass-marketed all across the western hemisphere. It is often served with a wedge of lime. What it lacks in bountiful flavors it makes up for in its refreshing taste. When the sun is beating down and you want something cool and refreshing, Corona served with a lime wedge squeezed and pressed into the bottle is an exceptional beer.

Scotland

MacAndrew's Scotch Ale
Caledonian Brewing Company
42 Slateford Road
Edinburgh
Lothian EH11 1P4
Scotland
You want to know what a real Scotch ale tastes like? MacAndrew's is a beer that instantly brings you to the northern shores of Scotland. A burly barley flavor and a high alcohol content make this an excellent winter brew to snuggle up with. This is an amber-colored ale with little carbonation and a slight hint of caramel; a little lighter in finish than McEwan's.

McEwan's Scotch Ale
McEwan's Fountain Brewery
Scottish & Newcastle Breweries PLC
Edinburgh
Scotland
McEwan's Scotch Ale dates as far back as 1856. While this brewery has been bought and merged many times, the name and

the taste have been consistently exceptional. Very dark brown in color—but not black like a stout—you will smell the roasty flavors in its aroma. This tastes so good that you'll almost want to try another Scots specialty, haggis.

Newcastle Brown Ale

Scottish Courage Ltd.
Abbey Brewery
111 Holyrood Road
Edinburgh EH8 8YS
Scotland

Possibly the best known brown ale in the world, Newcastle Brown Ale is the classic common brown ale. No fancy spin on this simple and exquisite amber brown beer with a reddish tinge. This particular brew dates back only to the 1920s, which for the beer industry, especially in England, makes this a relative newcomer. It is smooth and easy to drink, with a nutty flavor.

BREWING IN AMERICA AND THE MICROBREWING REVOLUTION

While America's modern microbrew revolution did not happen until the 1970s, the first real microbrewing revolution owes its start to the passion of the Founding Fathers. Not only were men like Samuel Adams, John Hancock, George Washington, and Thomas Jefferson busy creating a new world, they were also creating a few new brews and spawning through their enthusiasm a new industry on this continent.

However, the importance of beer in this country goes back even further in our roots to the colonists. The opening chapters of this country's history were almost started by accident, all because of beer. Those heroic souls on the *Mayflower* who came here to carve out a place to live free overshot their original destination and were running out of beer. The ship's log records its passengers' thirst for that frothy beverage. Instead of turning the ship around to look for its original destination, the ship's captains decided it would be smarter to land, carve out a spot, settle in, and make beer (along with other priorities like houses and fences). In fact, a brewery was one of the first few buildings to be built in the New World.

The Pilgrims, and Puritans sometime later, most often brewed their beer from hops imported from England. The best beers in the colonies were long considered to be those brewed from English malted barleys. But the colonists were ingenuous people, forced by deprivation and necessity, who invented new methods of brewing until new rations from England could be had. These new concoctions were brewed mostly with corn as an adjunct or substitute. Some of the popular recipes called for bran, potatoes, molasses, nutmeg, ginger, sassafras, juniper, bark, parsnip, and pumpkin, among other things.

Beer was such an important part of colonial life that many taverns and alehouses doubled as courts of law and were used for town meetings and to ferment (no pun intended!) political upheaval. (Samuel Adams planned the Boston Tea Party at a pub.) This was not uncommon in England either, as the East English Company's original headquarters was a London pub where much trading went on. By the time of Washington and Jefferson, there were hundreds of commercial alehouses in the colonies. And, as it was in ancient Egypt, Ben Franklin reported that men were paid their day's wages in beer. Harvard was one of the first universities to establish its own pub.

The first brewery established in what is now the United States was founded in 1633, in what was then New Amsterdam (now New York). Another brewery was established in Boston four years later. Philadelphia, the city that spawned more brewers than any other, including Milwaukee, established its first brewery in 1685.

It was at this time that many of Canada's most famous breweries were founded as well. Molson's, a modest-sized brewery, was established by John Molson in Montreal in 1786. In the mid-1800s the Carling and O'Keefe breweries, now one of the world's largest breweries, and Labatt's were founded.

The most popular drinking vessel of pre-Revolutionary War America was called a blackjack. A blackjack was a bottle-like container with four square or rectangular sides and a flat bottom. Some had a spout and a cork, and others were open like a mug.

Blackjacks were made of thick leather and highly waxed to make them watertight. The leather was also highly oiled and colored black, hence the name. Later, no self-respecting colonist would be seen drinking from anything other than a pewter tankard, and by the time of the Revolution, wealthy Americans were drinking from glasses. However, commercially made glass was not available to the middle and lower classes until the mid-1800s.

The beers that the early settlers drank were classic English ales, including porters. Because of the Dutch and English settlers, the beers of the new continent were very much like the beers you would find in the British or Belgian pubs of that time.

The beers in the colonies were classified into four distinct groupings, divided by strength. The four classifications were small beer, ship's beer, table beer, and strong beer. Homemade beer, the weakest, was called small beer. Ship's beer was the next strongest and was so called because it was conditioned, just as India Pale Ale, to withstand long voyages. Table beer was next in strength, followed by strong beer. These two were most likely brewed by brewers or other experts, and were most often commercially made.

George Washington was a well-known beer enthusiast who brewed his own beers at Mount Vernon. One of his beer recipes, preserved in his diaries that date back to 1757, included a large amount of molasses. Washington's favorite beer concoction was called a flip. This beer drink was made with beer, cream, rum, and eggs. As the final touch, a red-hot poker pulled from the fireplace was used to stir this sweet brew, causing a rather moderate explosion of beer head to spew forth. Jefferson also brewed at his home, Monticello. He had one of the most extensive beer and wine libraries in the world at the time. Benjamin Franklin went so far as to propose a national brewery. William Penn, who not only brewed beer in his house, sold it from his Bucks County home as well.

Early beer laws were very interesting. For example, you could not serve beer if it was not in half-pint, pint, or quart containers. And as early as 1637 the Massachusetts Bay Colony set the price of beer at one penny a quart. Other laws precluded anyone from making beer who was not already an expert and exempted beer and all related products from taxation, prohibiting the collection of beer debts through the courts. In early America, only landowners and church members were allowed to brew beer for public consumption.

However, it is important to note that many of the beers that colonists were drinking were still brewed in England. The beer was held in casks that were conditioned just before they were loaded from the docks into the ships' holds and transported across the Atlantic. After the English Crown levied a high tax on beer, patriots advocated the homemaking of beer to avoid paying the Crown's tax and to help create and foster an American beer industry.

After the First Revolution

After the Revolution, beer was a major topic of conversation. British beer was no longer being imported, and there was even some talk of establishing a national brewery. Breweries and brew-pubs were establishing themselves all over the fledgling nation.

The first wealthy brewer in America was Matthew Vassar. His beer was named Poughkeepsie Do and Ale, and his brewery was founded in 1798. Between father and son, the Vassars created one of the first beer empires. In 1860, Matthew Vassar, Jr. founded Vassar University. Vassar, however, was neither the only nor the last of the beer barons. Soon local breweries were competing regionally with others, and competition began to intensify. Into this fray came the driving force of the modern beer industry, lager.

Golden lager, first introduced in Plzen, Bohemia (now the Czech Republic) in 1842, took America and Europe by storm. This style of beer became so popular that by 1860 it was already the beer of choice in the United States. At this time, the United States was going through its golden age of beer. No other country in the world offered the countless varieties of beer that were available in the United States. Nowhere else did lagers and ales coexist like they did here. The United States went from 1.31 million barrels of beer produced in 1860 to 6 million barrels in 1867, and there were more than 1,200 breweries.

By 1880 there were more than 2,400 breweries and brewpubs. Before the close of the 1800s, each of America's major cities could boast many local brands. Philadelphia supported 94 breweries all on its own, and there were 115 breweries in New York and Brooklyn, 41 in Chicago, 33 in Detroit, 29 in St. Louis, and 23 in San Francisco. Names like Anheuser-Busch, Miller, and Schlitz, still known today, were the largest brewers and sold their beer nationwide by rail and refrigerated box cars.

The Volstead Act: Prohibition and the Dark Ages of American Brewing

By the time the Volstead Act was passed in America in January 1919, the beer industry was already in decline. While competition forced smaller brewers to abandon the business, teetotalers were also wreaking havoc on an embattled industry. Prohibition laws passed in small conservative states like Maine and Vermont were soon adopted by larger states like New York. The Women's Christian Temperance Union was founded to combat the consumption and manufacture of alcoholic beverages. The scourge of all barrooms was Carrie Nation, a six-foot-tall, axe-wielding prophet of sobriety who, along with her minions, busted up barrooms and terrorized patrons for decades.

Despite the fact that Prohibition was aimed more at rum, gin, and other hard liquors, the wine and beer industries were very hard hit. America's consumption of alcoholic beverages did not decrease with Prohibition as much as some might have thought. Bathtub gin, moonshine, and homemade beers were incredibly popular. In many general stores, it was very easy to find the ingredients to make some of these concoctions—especially beer. With the consumption of these home-brewed and distilled products, the federal government lost out on quite a bit of tax revenues. It has been estimated that the government lost more than $35 billion in tax revenues because of Prohibition.

These were tough times for brewery owners. This sad chapter produced some interesting products like Blatz' Industrial Alcohol, Coors Malted Milk, and Schlitz Chocolate. Other brewers revamped their plants to make ice cream, soda, and near beer. Finally, on April 7, 1933, President Roosevelt called for an end to Prohibition. Seven hundred breweries reopened but nine hundred breweries either stayed in their new lines of work or shut their doors to business forever.

PROHIBITION BEER

Many breweries stayed in business during the Depression and Prohibition by manufacturing and selling malt extract. Brewers sold malt as an excellent additive to foods to increase vim and vigor, but it was actually used to make beer. Many manufacturers included the recipe to make beer on the label. Manufacturers selling malt extract included Anheuser-Busch, Coors, and Pabst.

The Beer Wars

Prohibition was a bust because it had not stemmed the tide of the manufacture and consumption of alcoholic beverages, especially wine and beer. Crime went up, tax revenues went down, and so did a huge number of jobs. President Roosevelt wanted to end Prohibition and put people into honest jobs in what was obviously a booming business.

Many brewers reopened with mixed results after the repeal of Prohibition. After Prohibition, brewing beer and owning a pub were not allowed. This was designed to help small brewers expand in the newly reopened market; however, it actually became a death knell for many of them. While some brewers had relied on their small breweries and maybe a string of small pubs, these businesses, with little capital in the Depression era, did not have the capital to begin large-scale bottling and distribution operations.

Because of these new regulations, many of the smaller breweries were either sold to larger breweries or went out of business altogether. As these smaller brewers went out of business, their distinctive beer styles went with them. Coupled with this sad trend was the fact that people who were thirty years old and under had never tasted a legal beer. Manufacturers were trying to brew light, golden-color, pilsner-style lagers to market their beers to the widest possible audience. These young drinkers were not the discerning ale and lager purists that their fathers were. For an audience that had not previously been able to choose from a large variety of styles, the new watery, weak, fizzy beers that larger brewers were creating were actually quite appealing.

The beer wars heated up after the Second World War. During the war, servicemen and women became used to drinking beer from cans, and the beer being canned was mostly pilsner-style lagers because they traveled better and appealed to the widest range of tastes. With the return of many war veterans, canned beer made it back to the home front. Tin cans (and later aluminum) were cheaper and easier to manufacture and transport. The larger breweries latched onto this new technology right away. However, many of the smaller, local breweries could not afford the capital-intensive machinery necessary to make the switch and got left behind.

Canned beer was as much a sign of where you were as it was a sign of where you weren't. It was also a sign of where you were stationed during the war. Beers served on the home front were the second weakest of all. If you were unlucky enough to be serving in the Pacific, you were drinking some of the worst government-issue beer that was ever brewed. However, those "lucky" enough to be serving in Europe (horrible as the situation was) were drinking good beers brewed by experts. Those who served in Europe tasted beers long extinct in America and brought home cravings for the good stuff, much as their fathers and grandfathers had from the First World War. While brewing supplies were hard to come by in Europe, many beers were still being brewed that were not available in the States.

Once home, GIs and their wives settled into a new lifestyle full of gas-guzzling cars, canned meats, and canned beer. Canned beer now enabled brewers to sell their beers farther and farther away from their breweries. Brewers were going national. Not that there hadn't been national brewers before, but with the newest canning processes and the creation of the highways in the 1950s, beer distribution could expand at a much bigger and faster rate than ever before.

But the very biggest thing that ever happened to the beer industry was television. The bigger breweries that had canning and good distribution found the medium that would transform their businesses into the largest the brewing industry had ever seen. The biggest brewers were getting exposure everywhere—and they were delivering. The biggest winners were Anheuser-Busch, Miller, Schlitz, Coors, and Stroh's.

By the 1960s and 1970s, the brutal realities of the beer industry were such that only the biggest of the big could survive. Eventually, even Schlitz was taken over leaving just Anheuser-Busch, Miller, Coors, and Stroh's. These four breweries behind approximately two dozen different labels supplied nearly eighty percent of all the beer consumed in the United States. With the advent of light beers to accommodate the health and fitness era of the 1970s, the American beer industry hit an all-time low. This was our nation's bleakest beer hour.

This is probably a good time in the story to salute those smaller brewers who were able to survive the beer wars. Among them were

RECIPE FOR PROHIBITION KITCHEN BEER

1 can malt extract (hopped)
5 lbs. white or brown sugar
2 packets baking yeast

1. In 2 gallons of water, boil extract and sugar for 15 minutes.
2. Add 4 gallons of water. Boil for 60 minutes. If you have hops, steep them for the full boil.
3. Add yeast.
4. Place in basement for 10 days.
5. Bottle and drink.

many Pennsylvania brewers. More than any other state, Pennsylvania preserved a great brewing heritage for the rest of the country. It has been supposed that because Pennsylvania's liquor stores are state controlled, the industry there was in part responsible for keeping alive many of the smaller breweries. One must also suppose that consumer demand for these brews helped their cause. In Pennsylvania there was LaTrobe Breweries (Rolling Rock), D.G. Yuengling (the country's oldest surviving brewer), Jones, Straub, and The Lion, Inc.

Other smaller brewers to survive the wars were Dixie Brewery in New Orleans, Louisiana; National Brewery in Baltimore, Maryland; Gennessee and F.X. Matt in New York State; and August Schell and Cold Spring in Minnesota.

While the megabrewers had reached their pinnacle of success, many Americans were growing discontented with the pallid beers being offered. Coupled with this was the advance of the strong dollar that saw many Americans traveling to Europe. These Americans, like the veterans of World War II, discovered a whole new world of beers and brought back a desire to drink these beers here in the States. The seeds of discontent had been sown in the victory of the megabrewers, and now their lack of real vision was about to be exposed.

Fermenting Revolution

Because of their losses incurred during World War II, breweries in Europe were going through their own beer wars. While Europe still had a much more varied selection of styles than we did (that is to say, a couple dozen styles as compared with one), many of the beers famous before the outbreak of the war were no longer available. Also, many of the beers now being brewed were not of the same quality as they once had been. Modernization and competition both helped deteriorate the European brewing product.

By early 1971, there was a growing backlash in Britain against what many thought of as the Americanization of their beer. It was at this time that CAMRA was formed, or the Campaign for Real Ale. This self-appointed watchdog group's mission was to save real ale in England. What started as a small group of disenchanted pub draft drinkers soon grew into a very well-respected and recognized

consumer watchdog and savior of the English brewing tradition. The movement started by CAMRA forced many British brewers to give up their cheap processes and bring back more traditionally finished products. The success of CAMRA was noticed in other European countries and led to the revitalization of quality brewing in Belgium, the Netherlands, and Scandinavia.

By the late 1970s and early 1980s, Americans began demanding European beers, and names like Heineken began to pop up on American menus. When Mexican food became popular, beers like Tecate, Corona, and Dos Equis also grew in popularity. These were all shots fired across the bow of the megabrewers, but still little was done to counteract these hints of growing consumer dissatisfaction.

Of Wineries and Breweries

In the 1970s, the wine industry was going through the same growing pains as the beer industry. Dozens of small wineries were opening in California's Napa and Sonoma Valleys, and thousands of Americans were tracking up into the northern California hills and vineyards to drink new and different wines. Chief among this movement of vintners was Robert Mondavi.

Fritz Maytag was to microbrewing what Robert Mondavi was to California winemaking—a trailblazer and lightning rod. As a young Stanford college student, Fritz became aware of a small brewery called Anchor Steam. Anchor Steam had been in business for more than a century as both a brewer and a brewpub. While in his sophomore year, Fritz heard that Anchor was closing. Fritz Maytag, born Francis Louis Maytag III, told them not to close and came back the next day with a check and bought the place for $5,000 in 1965. The heir to the famous Maytag dishwasher and washing machine fortune, Fritz was determined to save the last of the approximately 150 steam brewers that had once populated California.

It took Fritz ten years to finally turn a profit, and now Anchor Steam is one of the most successful and well-known brewers in America. Fritz is also responsible not only for saving steam beer from extinction, but for reintroducing porters to the United States. Anchor Brewing was the first American brewer to reintroduce porter in 1973. Anchor was also one of the first to reintroduce barley wine

HOW FAR WOULD YOU GO FOR A BEER?

During the late '60s and '70s, Coors was a regional brewer available only west of the Mississippi. Stories about people living in the Midwest and East Coast driving 1,000 or 1,500 miles across the country just to purchase Coors were not that uncommon. Coors finally went national in the late '80s, ending another excuse for a road-trip party.

to the American market. By 1977, Anchor Brewing was expanding and turning out 82,000 barrels per year.

Another pioneer in the cause of good beer was Jack McAuliffe. McAuliffe had been a naval technician stationed in Scotland. Upon his return home, McAuliffe realized what a dirth of quality beers there was here and decided to change those fortunes. He bought a small brewing system, rented an old fruit warehouse, and set up shop as New Albion brewery in 1973, in Sonoma, California. Unfortunately, McAuliffe was not as successful as Maytag. New Albion was run on a shoestring budget and monetary constraints proved to be too much for McAuliffe to handle. Between the mounting costs of producing, bottling, and marketing, New Albion went out of business in 1982. While McAuliffe did not prosper, he helped blaze a new trail and was the first of the new microbrewers.

McAuliffe was eventually succeeded by a new breed of microbrewers, two of which were much more successful. Sierra Brewing Company was founded in Chico, California, in 1981, and in 1984 the Boston Beer Company was founded and started selling Samuel Adams beers.

One of the first brewpubs of note was the Mendocino Brewing Company, founded in 1983 by Bill Owens, aka Buffalo Bill Owens. Owens is best known for two beers: Alimony Ale, The Bitterest Beer in America, and Buffalo Bill's Pumpkin Ale. Owens had to twist a lot of arms to establish a brewpub since the law prohibited a brewer to own a bar or drinking establishment, but his was the first brewpub in the land in at least sixty years. Bert Grant also pioneered this territory in Yakima, Washington, eventually opening a brewpub and then a brewery.

These few brewers helped lead a brewing revolution and create a new world of beer. No longer were the citizens of the United States required to pay high prices for European beers just because they wanted to drink a different style. Today there are more than one thousand brewpubs and microbreweries—and the numbers are still growing.

AMERICAN BEERS YOU SHOULD KNOW

The beers listed here are as good as their European counterparts. America has benefited from having the younger brother's intense focus on outdoing his elder sibling's accomplishments. These beers are accomplished and well-crafted beers, not straight knock-offs of their European cousins. While many beers here may duplicate a particular European style, others are unique, including pumpkin ale, ginger beer, apricot beer, and some porters and stouts of unrivaled quality.

Not all of the American microbrews that make tasty beer could be included. If a particular microbrewery is not listed, it does not mean that it produces a lesser quality beer. This list is a starting point for the beer enthusiast to journey forward with and explore.

Abita Turbodog Beer
Abita Brewing Company
P.O. Box 762
Abita Springs, Louisiana 70420
(504) 893-3143

The Abita Brewing Company was established in 1986 by a former anthropology professor at Southeastern Louisiana University. Abita Springs is located on Lake Pontchartrain across from the city of New Orleans. Abita Brewery specializes in German-style beers that other breweries of that region might think were too heavy for their customers, considering the climate. Turbodog is an excellent brown ale with caramely flavors and a nice roast quality. Its color is a light brownish red. It's a good drinking beer that is well suited to go with food.

Alimony Ale, The Bitterest Beer in America
Buffalo Bill's Pumpkin Ale
Buffalo Bill's Brewery
P.O. Box 510
Hayward, California 94543-0510
(510) 538-9500

Bill Owens founded his brewpub in 1983, and one of his most famous beers by far is Alimony Ale, the Bitterest Beer in America. This is more bitter than any ESB you're likely to have. If you like hops and bitter beers, you're going to love this beer. Owens got the idea for Alimony Ale when his brewery's CPA was going through a bitter divorce.

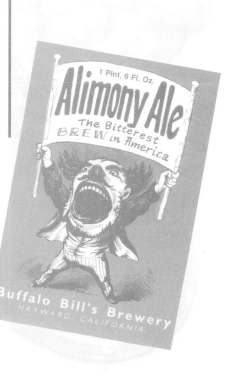

Buffalo Bill's Pumpkin Ale was one of the first beers to bring back this colonial taste treat. Pumpkin Ale tastes of pumpkin and nutmeg, but it's not too sweet and has a pleasant aftertaste. This ale is based on the recipe of George Washington's Pumpkin Ale. Buffalo Bill serves this with some allspice at the time of drinking.

Anchor Porter, Anchor Steam Beer, Old Foghorn Barleywine Style Ale

Anchor Brewing Company
1705 Mariposa Street
San Francisco, California 94107
(415) 863-8350

Anchor Porter is a perfectly solid porter that is respectable in every way. It is thick, creamy, and sweet with a dry finish and some strange tastes, including licorice, caramel, and a somewhat smoky flavor. It stands tall as a unique porter in the world.

Anchor Steam Beer is an odd duck because it is neither a lager nor an ale. It is clean, clear, and crisp with a smooth taste and a dry and somewhat light finish. A deep amber in color, Anchor Steam is slightly fruity. It is an excellent beer to drink alone or with food, as good with hot dogs or pizzas as with steamed mussels or steak.

Old Foghorn Barleystyle Wine is an old-fashioned, hardboiled barley wine. Fruity, rich, and powerful, it is a taste-filled treat with an aroma that goes on and on. If you want to taste what barley wine is all about, this is the model for all American barley wines.

Baderbrau Pilsner Beer

Pavichevich Brewing Company
383 Romans Road
Elmhurst, Illinois 60126
(630) 617-5252

This tastes so much like a European pilsner that it even looks like an import on the shelves. If you are looking for an American beer that tastes just like Pilsner Urquell, this is the beer. This is a light-colored beer with a wonderful nose and a crisp, clear body and dry, hoppy finish. This is what pilsner beer should taste like.

Blue Ridge Steeple Stout, Hempen Ale, Birch Beer

Frederick Brewing Company
4607 Wedgewood Boulevard
Frederick, Maryland 21703
(301) 694-7899

Steeple Stout is something to look forward to. Brewed in honor of St. Patrick, this stout is as full-bodied as they come. An excellent mouthfeel with sweet overtones and a relatively dry finish make this an excellent stout. All of Frederick's entries into the beer market are solid beers made from only the freshest ingredients. They also make a nice ESB Red Ale. A solid group of people making a very high-quality product, you can't go wrong with any Blue Ridge beer.

Hempen Ale is the only beer in the world made with hemp (they've taken all the hallucinogens out of it). Clean, with a hop bite and a dry finish, this is an excellent beer to drink on its own, and it has enough body to stand up to any cuisine. Refreshing, fun, and different, don't be afraid of the name; it really is a solid ale.

If Blue Ridge Birch Beer is available, you really ought to try it. It's clear and sweet, but with bite and a nice aftertaste; a truly wonderful experience.

Brooklyn Black Chocolate Stout

Brooklyn Brewery
79 North 11th Street
Brooklyn, New York 11211
(718) 486-7422

Brooklyn Black Chocolate Stout is one of the best beers in the world. It is also brewed by contract with the F.X. Matt Brewing Company, who also makes Harpoon and Saranac beers. The recipe and the beer belong to Brooklyn Brewing Company, and they use the facilities of F.X. Matt.

Brooklyn Brewing Company's Black Chocolate Stout rates with anything from Samuel Smith's. This is as good as it gets. Make sure this is not the first stout you try, or you will not like it. It's heavy, almost like someone took a chocolate malted milkshake and poured a dark beer into it. It is an exceptional experience like nothing else on this Earth. The Europeans can't touch this!

Give me a woman who loves beer and I will conquer the world.

—KAISER WELHELM

Catamount Bock, Catamount American Wheat, Catamount Oktoberfest Beer, Catamount Christmas Ale
Catamount Brewing Company
58 South Main Street
White River Junction, Vermont 05001
(802) 296-2248

Catamount is one of the best American brewers. While many brewers have one or two good beers, and several mediocre beers, Catamount is as consistent as they come. Established in 1986, Catamount is named for the cougars of the mountains of the Northeast, the "cat of the mount." Catamount makes some strong beers. Their offerings are not for the faint of heart in either taste or alcohol.

Catamount Bock is an ale that looks very much like a lager. This seasonal beer is very clean and clear. Its upfront taste is full of caramel and slight butterscotch flavors. It finishes hoppy and dry; a unique taste treat.

Catamount American Wheat is not as tart as some European wheat beers. Cloudy and lightly colored with a frothy white head, this is an excellent drink for the long, hot summers. The Europeans would like this one.

Catamount Christmas Ale is a classic deep-colored pale ale, reddish in color with malt and hop to spare. It's a strong beer and an excellent example of a winter warmer. Try this during the winter months and you may not want to drink anything else.

Catamount Oktoberfest Beer is a deep gold, almost orange, or amber colored beer with malt and hops in perfect balance in the true sense of the Vienna style. A lager of a special caliber, it goes well with all foods and is flavorful enough to be imbibed alone.

Cave Creek Chili Beer
Black Mountain Brewing Company
6245 East Cave Creek Road
Cave Creek, Arizona 85331
(602) 488-6597

This has the wildest thing you'll ever see in a beer—an edible chili pepper. The beer is a very well-crafted, authentic, pilsner-styled beer with a strong malt and a dry, bitter bite at the end that tastes of pepper. Made of imported barley and hops, with no adjuncts, this is a great treat that everyone ought to try once.

Celis White Beer

Celis Brewery
2431 Forbes Drive
Austin, Texas 78754
(512) 835-0884

Celis White Beer easily stands head and shoulders above its European counterparts. In truth, Celis has an unfair advantage: Pierre Celis, the brewer of Celis White, single-handedly saved the Belgian white wheat beer style. In 1965, Celis sold his dairy and began brewing Belgian wheat beers with his brewery, De Kluis, in Belgium. His were and are the beers that all Belgian wheat beers are judged against. After his brewery burned down, Celis sold his interest in De Kluis and established the Celis Brewery in Austin, Texas.

It is odd to say that this beer stands up to the European beers because it is made by the man who set the standard for all wheat beers. Run, don't walk, to drink this beer. Europe's loss was America's gain.

Dock Street Bohemian Pilsner, Dock Street Illuminator Double Bock

Dock Street Brewing Company
225 City Line Avenue
Suite 110
Bala Cynwyd, Pennsylvania 19004
(610) 668-1480

Dock Street was first brewed by contract with F.X. Matt Brewers in 1986. In 1990, the first Dock Street Brewery and Brewpub was founded in Bala Cynwyd. This beer is brewed in more than one place and is not unique to Dock Street but typical of what goes on in the beer industry.

Dock Street's Bohemian Pilsner is a very real attempt to capture the original flavor of Pilsner Urquell. It is a lighter version of the Pilsner Urquell—but only slightly. This is beer with a big nose: it has lots of fruity and floral essence. Golden with an almost amber color, it is flavorful right from the start. Drink this next to a Budweiser or a Miller and you'll finally understand what's been missing in the United States for the last sixty years.

The Illuminator Double Bock is a solid version of a double bock. Featuring a strong, hoppy flavor and a malty taste, it has both gravity and a big nose; a beer definitely worth tasting.

Door County Raspberry Bier

Cherryland Brewery Ltd.
341 North 3rd Avenue
Sturgeon Bay, Wisconsin 54235
(414) 743-1945

Founded in 1987, Cherryland Brewing Company brews some very nice beers, and nothing stands out as strong as their Door County Raspberry Bier. The Raspberry Bier is a light and true pilsner-style lager that has the taste and aroma of raspberries. Not as big-bodied as a framboise, this has only the hint of raspberry. However, you're still not going to be drinking this with a hot dog or pizza. This is to be nursed with friends when you're not munching on goodies at the bar.

Geary's London Style Porter

D.L. Geary Brewing Company
38 Evergreen Drive
Portland, Maine 04103
(207) 878-BEER

A dark brownish black with reddish tints to it, Geary's London Style Porter is truly an excellent traditional-style porter. It has no overpowering special effects taste treats to it (no chocolate or coffee as do the Brooklyn or Red Hook porters); however, it is a solid porter with a thick roastiness and caramel, coffee, and slight chocolate overtones, like a Taddy Porter. An excellent beer worth tasting again and again.

Grant's Imperial Stout, Grant's Perfect Porter, Grant's Scottish Ale, Grant's India Pale Ale

Yakima Brewing and Malting Company
1803 Presson Place
Yakima, Washington 98903
(509) 575-1900

Bert Grant has been in the beer industry since the 1950s. After thirty years of brewing experience behind him, including stints at Carling's, Molson, Stroh's, and others, Grant decided he could no longer stand the beers he originally liked because they'd been watered down and had become unrecognizable over the years. Grant established the Yakima Brewing Company in 1981. This was Washington's first brewpub since the repeal of Prohibition. There is nothing unrecognizable about any of Bert's beers.

Grant's Scottish Ale is an old-fashioned kick-in-the-pants Scottish ale that's supposed to keep the north wind from shaking you to your bones. It's strong and flavorful with a distinctive flavor that leaves a clean, dry aftertaste. This honey- or amber-colored beer has a nice, thick head but not too much carbonation.

Grant's Perfect Porter is a no-nonsense porter with strong, thick, caramel and chocolate overtones and a malty roastiness; an excellent version of a porter. Bert likes to talk up the oak process he puts this beer through.

Grant's Imperial Stout is one of those few beers that stands up to its European counterparts. It's reminiscent of Samuel Smith's. It's a strong, chocolate, malty brew that is dark and tasty with a kick.

If you want to know what an India Pale Ale tastes like, then you've found one worth drinking. Grant's India Pale Ale is a good old-fashioned India Pale Ale. Grant's is strong with plenty of hops to spare. This beer has some bite to it.

Harpoon Alt

Massachusetts Bay Brewing Company
306 Northern Avenue
Boston, Massachusetts 02210
(617) 574-9551

Harpoon Alt has got a full, round flavor with excellent mouthfeel and a wonderful finish. Sometimes a beer like this can't be consumed with food because it is so different, but Harpoon's alt is very accessible. This beer is a tremendous complement to any dish. This is an extremely good beer and a lot easier to come by than other alt brands. If you see this stuff, buy it and enjoy!

Highland Celtic Ale, Highland Oatmeal Porter

Highland Brewing Company
42 Biltmore Avenue
P.O. Box 2351
Asheville, North Carolina 28802
(704) 255-8240

Highland Celtic Ale is a cross between a classic Scottish Ale and the less robust English/Irish pub ales. Amber in color and strong in taste, it's got a strong, malty flavor and a very powerful hoppiness. A strange brew by definition, but a tremendous mouthfeel and aroma.

Highland's Oatmeal Porter is a distinctive beer. A dark, thick beer, it has enough malt to stand up, and is long on caramel and coffee flavors.

Holiday Russian Imperial Stout

Pacific Coast Brewing Company
906 Washington Street
Oakland, California 94607
(510) 836-BREW

You want a Russian Imperial Stout to rival Samuel Smith? Brewed by the Pacific Coast Brewing Company since 1988, this black, full-bodied brew is the most flavorful, powerful Imperial Stout you will ever taste. This beer is not for the weak-kneed, and it shouldn't be the first stout you try. Let your taste buds mature a little before you raise a glass of this to your lips.

Hubsch Lager, Hubsch Marzen

Sudwerk Privatbrauerei Hubsch
2001 Second Street
Davis, California 95616
(916) 756-2739

The Hubsch family has created a truly unique brewery that makes beergarden-style beers within walking distance from the University of California at Davis' prestigious wine and brewing schools. Hubsch, with a brewery name stolen right out of the German Beer Purity Law, makes some of the best German-style beers available.

Hubsch Lager is an excellent representation of the Munchener helles style. This is as good as any beer from Germany. It's brewed with the finest Bavarian hops, like many of the best European beers of this style, and is of exceptionally high style and quality. Dry, crisp, clear, and clean, it opens almost sweet with malty overtones and finishes dry and bitter with good hops flavor. It will stand up in any taste test.

You want to know what real Marzen beer tastes like? The Hubsch Marzen is another excellent representation of a European style. Almost floral in its bouquet, it finishes dry and clean. Another exceptional beer from this wonderful brewery.

Jet City Rocket Red Ale

Jet City Brewing Company
P.O. Box 3554
Seattle, Washington 98124
(206) 392-5991

This is a real red ale! The American version of a red, Killian's, tastes like water next to this. A deep amber red, this brew has some hops to it! There are even some hints of chocolate and caramel, but it's bitter and clean. Brewed from roasted malted barley, you'll smack your lips after drinking this beer.

Juju Ginger

Left Hand Brewing Company
1265 Boston Avenue
Longmont, Colorado 80501
(303) 772-0258

The first thing which must be said is that the Left Hand Brewing Company makes some wonderful beers and, unfortunately, there is only so much space that can be devoted to singling out all the quality beers in any book that's supposed to be an overview. Both Black Jack Porter and the Sawtooth Ale are excellent beers and should be enthusiastically sought out and tasted.

EVERYTHING BEER BOOK

Left Hand is to be glorified for still making a ginger beer, an almost forgotten style. There are only two American brewers making this type of beer, and you should definitely taste one. A pale ale, this beer is brewed with ginger. It opens with a distinct ginger smell and has a somewhat sweet-peppery taste that finishes dry with hops. It's as if someone turned ginger ale into real beer. This is a taste sensation, and one of the few remaining examples of this type of beer. It is a fairly close representation of what a true ginger beer brewed by the English more than a century ago must have been like.

Lompoc's Ginger Wheat
The Atlantic Brewing Company
30 Rodick Street
Bar Harbor, Maine 04609-1868
(207) 288-9513

This is the other ginger beer still brewed in America. While Juju is made using pale ale as a base, Lompoc's Ginger Wheat uses wheat beer as a base. The Atlantic Brewing Company spices their wheat beer with ginger root, which offsets the sourness and adds a whole new dimension to what is already a strange taste sensation. Juju is closer to the original ginger beers of nineteenth century England, but this is an excellent beer worth tracking down and trying once. Both ginger beers go extremely well with raw fish and seafood and are often found in sushi bars.

Old Brown Dog Ale
Smuttynose Brewing Company
225 Heritage Avenue
Portsmouth, New Hampshire 03801
(603) 436-4026

The beers from Smuttynose are hand-crafted from a small micro-brewery named after a group of islands just off the Portsmouth, New Hampshire, coast. Old Brown Dog Ale is a classic English-style brown ale. Soft with just the right caramely malt flavors and a little hops to finish it out, this is a wonderful brown ale. It only became available in bottles in 1995 and is not as well distributed as we hope it will become.

MAN'S BEST FRIENDS

Man's two best friends are dogs and beer. What better way to a man's heart than to put a dog on the label. The beers listed below, while they may sometimes look like mutts, are really pedigrees. These are certainly some of the best microbrews available on the market, and would garner attention even if not for their funky marketing angle.

Bubba Dog Beer
A product of the Yellow Rose Brewing Company of San Antonio, Texas, this is a wonderful wheat beer. They also make some other wonderful beers, including Vigilante Porter.

Stoudt's Fat Dog Stout
This is thick, chewy, and delicious. Almost like eating a slice of really good brown bread, but with more bite. Many wonderful flavors. An exquisite beer.

Spanish Peak
This Bozeman, Montana, brewery is at the forefront of the beer and cider industries. They consistently make top-notch products. One of their more famous brews is their Black Dog Ale. Try it; it'll have you barking for more.

Old Brown Dog Ale
Brewed by Smuttynose Brewing Company, in Portsmouth, New Hampshire, this is one dog that will definitely hunt. Full-bodied and flavorful, this is an excellent version of a brown ale.

Sea Dog Windjammer Blonde Ale
Brewed in Bangor, Maine, this is an excellent beer and well worth picking up at any time. Great with food or by itself.

Flying Dog (Doggie Style) Classic Pale Ale
This is one bitter dog—when was the last time that was a good thing? Based in Denver, Colorado, Broadway Brewing's version of a pale ale is as classic as it is drinkable.

Bully! Porter
Boulevard Brewing of Kansas City, Missouri, makes one of the most classic porters ever brewed in America, and is well worth your searching it out. Big, flavorful, roasty, chocolaty overtones. This beer is only for Big Dogs. Little pups aren't wanted here.

Adam Hearty Old World Ale
The Hair of the Dog Brewing Company makes some of the most complex and wonderfully hand-crafted beers in the western hemisphere. You'll want this dog to bit you again, and again, and again.

Penn Dark Lager, St. Nikolaus Bock Bier

Pennsylvania Brewing Company
800 Vinial Street
Pittsburgh, Pennsylvania 15212
(412) 237-9400

Penn Brewery is one of the best known breweries of the Mid Atlantic states and is growing in reputation. Established in 1986, Penn was founded by Thomas V. Pastorius as Pennsylvania's first new microbrewery. Pennsylvania has a rich history of small, quality brewers, so his task was daunting. Located in Pittsburgh, Penn Brewery also sports its own brewpub. Penn also offers a very nice Oktoberfest.

Penn Dark Lager is an American version of a Munich-style beer. This is a wonderful beer to drink. It has a wonderful aroma, a vibrant body, and a great aftertaste and an excellent mouthfeel. You cannot go wrong with this beer. The Germans would be happy drinking this brew.

St. Nikolaus Bock Beer is an excellent bock beer. Dark, with a big nose and super mouthfeel, this beer is a great representation of what bock is supposed to taste like. It has a nice roastiness to it with caramely overtones. This is a seasonal beer, but make a point of looking for it.

Pete's Wicked Lager

Pete's Brewing Company
514 High Street
Palo Alto, California 94301
(800) 644-7383

Pete Slosberg is one of the high-profile brewers in America. His beers are well known and have been so since he started brewing in 1986. Chief among his accomplishments is Pete's Wicked Lager. A classic imitation of a pilsner lager, this is a clear, clean beer with a full shock of hops. This is a flavorful, easy-to-drink beer that certainly would fare well in some European countries.

Pike Pale Ale

Pike Brewery
1415 First Avenue
Seattle, Washington 98101
(206) 622-6044

Charlie Finkle is the premier beer importer in America. A visionary, he is responsible for more of the world's best beers coming to America than any other individual. As the founder of Marchant du Vin, Charlie was responsible for telling Samuel Smith's to brew Imperial Stout!

Pike Pale Ale is one of the best pale ales you could ever hope to drink. A big nose, strong first taste, and a well-rounded finish make this an exceptional beer of immense quality. Hoppy, with fruity overtones, it finishes with tremendous mouthfeel and aftertaste.

Pineapple Ale
Star Brewing Company
5231 NE Martin Luther King, Jr. Boulevard
Portland, Oregon 97211
(503) 282-6003
This is a traditional light-bodied pale ale brewed with fresh pineapple. It is indeed a taste treat. This malty brew has strong pineapple overtones and is a good beer for after dinner or on a hot day.

Pyramid Apricot Ale, Pyramid Espresso Stout, Pyramid Kalsch Beer, Thomas Kemper Bohemian Dunkel
Pyramid Ales & Thomas Kemper Brewery
91 South Royal Brougham Way
Seattle, Washington 98134
(206) 682-8322

Hart Brewing Company
110 West Marine Drive
Kalama, Washington 98625
(360) 673-2121
Hart Brewing Company is one of the most diversified craft brewers in America. Hart is comprised of three separate entities: Pyramid Ale, the Thomas Kemper Brewery, and the Hart Brewery & Pub. All three brand names are highly focused to create brand and style recognition. Pyramid makes only ales, Thomas Kemper focuses on lagers; and the Hart Brewery is a brewpub. The folks at Hart have been peren-

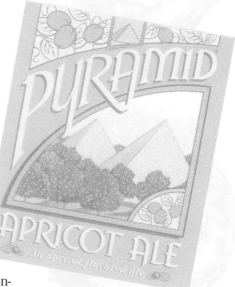

nial winners at the Great American Beer Festival, and after drinking any of their beers you'll understand why.

Pyramid Apricot Ale uses a pale ale for a base and is flavored with apricots. This is a dessert beer. It is hazy and yellow/amber in color. The aroma of this beer is powerful and immediate. There's no guesswork as to the flavors you're going to taste. It's a little sweet in the beginning, but it finishes dry and the apricot taste lingers; a truly different experience.

The Pyramid Espresso Stout is not as rich as you might think or wish. It's black with a heavy dose of espresso and chocolate and smells like coffee when you pour it. It's highly hopped and has a strong malt character that is the result of only being flavored rather than brewed with coffee beans.

Pyramid Kalsch Beer is a kölsch beer, but because it is brewed in Kalama, Washington, they call it Kalsch. This is a wonderful attempt to bring kölsch beer to the United States. This seasonal beer, sold during the summer months, is a light, golden ale that is very drinkable. The nose is somewhat floral, and it has a solid hoppy pop with a nice, dry finish.

Thomas Kemper Bohemian Dunkel is a brownish/reddish dark lager of wonderful proportions. Spicy, aromatic, and flavorful, the sweet malt finishes with a pop. Slight flavors of caramel and chocolate can be found.

Red Hook Doubleblack Stout, Red Hook ESB, Red Hook Rye, Red Hook Hefeweizen

Red Hook Brewery
3400 Phinney Avenue, North
Seattle, Washington 98103
(206) 548-8000

Red Hook Doubleblack Stout is an exciting beer and one of the very best beers brewed in the world. It smells like coffee beans because it is brewed with Starbucks coffee. A lot of body and only a little head, it has the kick of real espresso. This is really an imperial stout–styled beer.

The genesis of this beer lies in the friendship between the founder of this brewery, Paul Shipman, and Starbucks' founder Gordon Bowker, both coffee and beer enthusiasts. An incredible beer with exceptional body and taste. Don't drink this stuff late at night because you will be up until the next morning.

Red Hook ESB is a golden/amber/orange ale of excellent quality. Crafted to taste like the ESBs of English pub fame, this is an excellent example of the style and is for drinking and eating. It has a big nose and a sweet malt and hoppiness that is difficult to achieve. Just as good as anything you'll get from England—you'll think you're in a pub with the first taste.

Red Hook Rye is something special. This beer brewed from flaked rye is a wonderful unfiltered beer in the greatest sense of the English tradition. This hazy, light beer has a powerful aroma and a strong taste with a somewhat floral nose. It's got some wonderful citrusy flavors—almost like a wheat beer, but not quite that tangy— and is a wonderful, refreshing beer. You can really taste the grain and the hops.

Red Hook Hefeweizen is an exceptional hefeweizen. It has some kick to it with a lot of hops, as a beer from Oregon should. This is one of the best entries in the hefeweizen category and is easily drinkable alone or with food. Light, refreshing, and yeasty with a hint of sourness and a great aroma of wheat.

Rogue Shakespeare Stout, Rogue Hazelnut Brown Nectar
Rogue Ales
Oregon Brewing Company
2320 OSU Drive
Newport, Oregon 97365
(503) 867-3660

Rogue Ales market some of the most highly recognizable bottles anyone has ever seen. They feature painted glass bottles and unique paper labels. Rogue Shakespeare Stout is black, with an equally dark, thick head. It has a nice roasty quality and finishes dry with a wonderful aftertaste.

Rogue Hazelnut Brown Nectar is one of the best brown ales brewed in America. The flavor of hazelnut is not overpowering. The malt is sweet and caramely, and there is just enough hops to keep it all honest. Truly a beer to marvel over.

St. Stan's Amber Alt, St. Stan's Dark Alt, St. Stan's Graffiti Wheat

St. Stan's Brewery
821 L Street
Modesto, California 95354
(298) 524-2337

Garith Helm and his wife Romy, beer enthusiasts from their first trip to Germany, decided to start homebrewing because they could not find their favorite beers here at home. St. Stan's was founded in 1981 when they bought a small microbrewing setup. St. Stan's is now one of the truly acknowledged quality microbrewers and the biggest brewpub in all of California.

Alt is a German-style old ale from Dusseldorf. St. Stan's Amber Alt is smooth and very malty. It also has low carbonation. Amber in color, this alt beer has a light hopping that balances out with the malt. This is a creamy beer that is not as powerful in taste as it is smooth. This is a very subtle beer that doesn't hit you over the head. This is a difficult beer to get right, and St. Stan's is an excellent version of this style, on par with the best European versions of this style.

St. Stan's Dark Alt is well known by the experts. This is a beer brewed in the same style as the amber but is darker because it is roasted. There are chocolate and coffee-like flavors. This can stand up to anything the Germans can produce and is an outstanding version of a dark alt.

Do you remember the movie *American Graffiti*? That film was based on George Lucas' high school days in Modesto, California, home of St. Stan's. Each year, the town of Modesto has a Graffiti Festival, and St. Stan's makes a wheat beer that features a different classic car each year on its label. St. Stan's brews its summer wheat in small batches for the summer months. The beer's label has the year right on it so you always know what you're getting. If you like wheat beer, you'll surely like St. Stan's. Tangy and slightly sour with a big nose and clean finish, it is another excellent American version of a classic European style.

Samuel Adams Triple Bock, Samuel Adams Double Bock, Samuel Adams Lager

The Boston Beer Company
30 Germania Street
Boston, Massachusetts 02130
(617) 522-3400

James Koch (pronounced Cook), who founded the Boston Beer Company in 1985, is one of the most important figures in all of the microbrewing revolution. A sixth-generation brewer (his great-great-great-grandfather came over here in 1840 to become a brewer), Koch's father actually tried to talk him out of entering into the brewing business.

Samuel Adams Triple Bock is the world's strongest beer. This is the zenith of the microbrew revolution's brewing achievements. This is not a traditional lager or bock; it is one of the most unique beers in all the world. It almost doesn't taste like beer. It tastes like barley wine or a heavy, brutal sherry. Europeans don't have anything that can touch this stuff. It's thick like a liquor and has a nose that is incredible and practically no carbonation. It comes in small 8.45-ounce blue bottles that are corked. Many liquor stores keep it behind the counter. This is best sipped from a small glass like sherry, brandy, or cognac. And if you think you're going to finish this little bottle, you're either out of your mind or one heck of a drinker.

James Koch has made an exceptional Double Bock full of roasty flavors, a sweetness of malt, and a finish with a wonderful aftertaste. While the Triple Bock leaves the beer world behind and ventures into the liquor world in terms of taste and texture, Double Bock is still a very easily tasted beer. It is much lighter in body than the Triple Bock and not as heavy as a stout or porter. It is an intense beer with tremendous flavor, great aroma, and some carbonation. It's got a roasty quality to the malt with fruity and caramely overtones. Not too sweet, it has enough hops to balance it all out.

Samuel Adams Lager is the beer that started it all for James Koch and for microbrewing in the eastern U.S. Amber in color, Samuel Adams Lager is a flavorful beer with great aroma and excellent barley and hops balance. Clear, crisp, and clean, you can drink it with everything from hot dogs to seafood and foods higher on the culinary scale. This is a wonderful everyday drinking beer.

Scrimshaw Pilsner
North Coast Brewing Company
444 North Main Street
Fort Bragg, California 95437
(707) 964-2739

Founded in 1988, this brewery makes some wonderful beers. Mark Ruedrich, the founder and brewmaster, once lived in England and was unhappy with the selection of beers back in the States—not an uncommon story among microbrewers. This brewery is located in what was once a church and a monastery. Scrimshaw Pilsner is a classic pilsner brewed with the Czech recipes in mind. You can smell the hops in the aroma of the beer, but it is not overpowering. It has an almost floral scent. Crisp and clean, it finishes dry with a good aftertaste. This is a beer that goes with any food and stands up to any other pilsner.

Sierra Nevada Pale Ale, Sierra Nevada Bigfoot Barleywine Style Ale
Sierra Brewing Company
1075 East 20th Street
Chico, California 95928
(916) 893-3520

After a visit to Bill Owens' New Albion microbrewery in 1981, Ken Grossman and Paul Camusi decided to start Sierra Nevada. They built a small brewery in less than eighteen months in their spare time. Sierra Nevada has been synonymous with the microbrewing revolution. Their wide range of beers is consistent and tasty. Sierra Nevada Pale Ale is what an old-time pale ale is supposed to taste like. A golden to amber color, there is plenty of nose and great taste to follow. Caramely with some hops at the end, this is one of the best pale ales being made in the United States.

One of the beers you have to taste before you die is the Bigfoot Barleywine Style Ale. This is an authentic barley wine—thick, fruity, and powerful. Like Samuel Adams' Triple Bock, this is one that can stand up anywhere in the world. And like the Triple Bock, you have to sip it because it's too heavy and too alcoholic to drink like a pilsner. Restraint is sometimes the key to enjoying. This ale is hoppy and malty.

Stoudt's Honey Double Bock, Stoudt's PILS

Stoudt's Real Beer
P.O. Box 880, Route 272
Adamstown, Pennsylvania 19501
(717) 484-4387

Stoudt's is one of the most prestigious breweries on the East Coast, and one of the few microbreweries owned and headed by a woman. Carol Stoudt is also the sole female brewmaster in the United States. A long-time brewing executive, she decided to brew her own beer in 1987 and hasn't looked back. Pennsylvania has found yet another brewer to be proud of.

Stoudt's Honey Double Bock is brewed in the same spirit as the Trappist doppel bock beers. This is a dark-styled lager brewed with a touch of honey. An excellent beer with a wonderful aroma that smells of honey with slightly carmely and floral overtones, it actually smells sweeter than it is.

Like its German and Czech elders, Stoudt's PILS is brewed with plenty of Saaz hops and has a wonderfully floral smell. It is golden, clear, and crisp, and finishes dry. This is what pilsner is really supposed to taste like. Serve this to your friends and you'll be a hero.

Widmer Hefeweizen

Widmer Brothers Brewing
929 N. Russell Street
Portland, Oregon 97227
(503) 281-2437

This excellent hefeweizen is light and flavorful; you can smell the wheat and the yeast. It is an excellent drinking beer, especially in summer. This unfiltered ale must be kept cold. Serve it with a wedge of lemon, and make sure you follow the instructions on the label. Swirl the last third of the contents before you pour to get some extra sediment that lends even more flavor.

Yuengling Black & Tan
Yuengling Brewery
5th and Mahantongo Streets
Pottsville, Pennsylvania 17901
(717) 622-4141

Founded in 1829, Yuengling is hardly what we think of as a microbrewery in the modern sense of the word. Yuengling was brewing beer when many of today's microbrewers' ancestors weren't even in the country yet! Founded by German brewers, Yuengling is still owned by the Yuengling family and still brews an excellent spectrum of beers.

Black and tan was not originally a style but a way of serving a beer by mixing light and dark beers in a glass unstirred. The idea was to drink them while they were still mixing. As time progressed, consumers wanted to take home more and more of their favorite beers. So, brewers hoping to fill the void began brewing a beer that would taste like the best draft-pulled mixtures. Today, brewers use one recipe that duplicates this taste experience. Yuengling Black and Tan is one of the better beers of this new style.

THE U.S. BREWERY BUSINESS

7

CHAPTER

BOTTLED BY
ADAMS MEDIA CORPORATION

There are very distinct groupings of breweries in the United States. First, there are the megabrewers. These are some of the largest brewers in the world, including such well-known giants as Anheuser-Busch, Miller, and Heineken. Then there are the regional breweries, which are newer corporations and older, established breweries that have expanded in the recent brewing boom. Next are the microbreweries and the brewpubs. Some of the larger breweries have beer halls or gardens where food and beer are served, while some brewpubs have beers that are bottled and sold at retail nationally, but what differentiates one from another?

The brewery is the best drugstore.

—PROVERB

THE BIG DAWGS

There are five major brewers in the United States that are considered megabrewers: Anheuser-Busch, Miller, Heineken, Coors, and Stroh's. These breweries are responsible for as much as ninety-five percent of the beer consumed in the United States. Anheuser-Busch, maker of Budweiser, sells 80 million barrels of beer each year. That makes them by far the largest beer brewer in the world. The next closest manufacturers are Miller and Heineken, though these two together do not match what Anheuser-Busch puts out. A microbrewery is classified as being a company that brews no less than 15,000 barrels per year—less than seven percent of what Anheuser-Busch makes in a day. That's definitely micro compared to the big guys.

Many of the megabrewers market and sell beers under many different labels, and not all their beers are consumed in the United States. Budweiser exports a significant amount of its total annual product. Miller Brewing Company is also responsible for a significant number of labels and brand names. More often than not, they all make pretty much the same style of crisp, clear, fizzy, lightly malted, lightly hopped beers lovingly called lawnmower beer.

Anheuser-Busch Brewing Company

Anheuser-Busch is the largest brewing conglomerate in the world and one of the most stable of businesses. Owned and operated by the Busch family since the late 1800s, Anheuser-Busch now controls some 43–45 percent of the domestic beer market.

Soap king Eberhard Anheuser bought a dying brewery in St. Louis in 1857. He shored up the shaky brewery, and some years later his daughter married a brewery supply salesman named Adolphus Busch. After his father-in-law's death, Busch assumed control of the company and changed the name of the corporation to the Anheuser-Busch Brewing Association. A true beer maven, he—like the rest of the world—was impressed by the new lagers from Pilsen and Budweis. Busch established Budweiser. He quickly trademarked the name in the United States, even though there were other Budweiser beers already in existence at the time, and set out to nationally market his brand. By the turn of the century, Budweiser was one of the top three beers in the country.

During Prohibition the brewery was well known for making Bevo, a non-alcoholic near beer. After Prohibition was repealed and World War II was over, Anheuser-Busch was back on the offensive and became the dominant force in U.S. brewing. The original St. Louis, Missouri, brewery is still one of the premier breweries to visit in the world. You can still see them wash their beer through a giant filter of beechwood chips. Aside from the various incarnations of Budweiser, Anheuser-Busch also produces Michelob, Busch, Anheuser, O'Doul's Non-Alcoholic, and Red Wolf beers.

Their recent efforts have been to improve on their market share through Budweiser on the general beer market and with a number of specialty beers under the Michelob label. Michelob was originally a draft-only beer, considered fairly high quality in the 1940s. Now it is substantially watered down, lightly hopped, and a pale imitation of what it once was.

Miller Brewing Company

The original Milwaukee, Wisconsin, brewing company was purchased by Frederick Miller in 1855 from the Best family. It was not officially known as the Frederick Miller Brewing Company until 1888.

The company was a solid one, but it was the marketing power of Philip Morris, who bought out Miller in 1970, that revolutionized the company and inspired a beer craze.

The marketing teams brought in by Phillip Morris created, positioned, and marketed the "Lite" beer campaign that changed the beer industry and gave Miller an opportunity to expand its sagging market share. Trying to cash in on the fitness craze, Miller increased their business ninefold, and they are now producing 45 million barrels per year.

Miller is also the brewer of such well-known brands as Lowenbräu, Meister Bräu, and Milwaukee's Best. Their most recent attempt to regain market share was a new brand called Red Dog. Red Dog is a subsidiary but was promoted as a product of the Plank Road Brewery with no mention or attachment to Miller's name. This, marketers felt, would make the beer stand out as opposed to being just another new beer from Miller. The strategy worked, and the beer is very popular.

Heineken

While the original brewery was founded in Amsterdam in the Netherlands in 1592, it did not acquire the name Heineken until 1864 when it was acquired by Gerard Adriaan Heineken. Heineken immediately set about to improve the company's distribution throughout the Netherlands and Europe. Exports to the United States began after Prohibition when Leo Van Munching, a cruiseship steward, began importing it first for friends, and then for profit. Through a series of complex acquisitions, licensing, and rights deals, the beer is now one of the best distributed in all the world. Eventually, these licensing agreements were bought out, and the U.S. importer's office, now the world headquarters, is known as Heineken USA.

Heineken is now the nation's number-one imported beer and is the fourth largest supplier. While Anheuser-Busch and Miller both have multiple labels, most of their beers are made in just a few large facilities. Heineken has taken a completely different approach. Heineken is sold the world over and is brewed in more than fifty different countries. While they do own and operate Canadian breweries, Heineken refuses to brew its beer in the United States, otherwise it might lose its

BARRELS OF BEER

Brewer	# of barrels per year
Anheuser-Busch	80 million
Miller Brewing Company	45 million
Heineken	40 million
Coors	20 million
Stroh's	19 million

HEINEKEN AND THE BARON

Lest you get any ideas that the beer business is a genteel one, consider the high-pressure sales tactics of Leo Van Munching, Sr., the original importer of Heineken. Dubbed "the Baron" by numerous Manhattan bartenders and bar owners, Van Munching was known for being a little fast and loose with the truth, especially when selling his favorite beer. Van Munching worked for the Holland America cruise line, as a steward. Taking much of his savings, he bought a large quantity of Heineken and brought it with him to America in the 1930s after the repeal of Prohibition. Heineken had not been able to penetrate the American market in the past and was willing to take a risk on Van Munching.

Van Munching was famous for his favorite gambit, known by some salesmen (and con artists) as "day-and-night." Philip Van Munching confesses his sales tactics in his wonderful history of the beer wars, *Beer Blast* (Times Business, 1997). Van Munching

title as the number-one imported beer—a huge marketing angle for the company. Other beers produced and marketed by Heineken include Amstel Light, Buckler Non-Alcoholic Beer, and Murphy's Irish Stout.

Adolph Coors Company

Coors was originally founded in 1873 by Adolph Coors and another partner who dropped out a few years later. Since then, Coors has been a family-run business and only recently a national powerhouse. Coors emerged as a late bloomer in the national game. Long a regional beer, loved by those living in the Rockies and the West Coast, Coors beers gained notoriety in the late 1970s and were largely nationally established by the early 1980s. Stories are plentiful of those consumers, desperate for anything different from the national brands of the time, who braved the drive across the Midwest and the Continental Divide to buy this beer by the vanload.

While the company brews out of three plants, including ones in Tennessee and Virginia, their Golden, Colorado, plant is the world's single largest brewery. While Coors Light is now the nation's fourth bestselling beer, the Coors Brewing Company has also made forays into the specialty market. Their Blue Moon beers are made by contract brewers. Much like Miller's Red Dog beer, the affiliation between beer and brewery is not stressed to the consumer in order to help the brand establish its own unique identity. Coors is also the brewer of Keystone beers, George Killian's Irish Red Lager, and, most notably, the malt beverage that doesn't taste anything like beer, Zima.

Stroh Brewery Company

Bernhard Stroh established the Stroh Brewery Company in Detroit, Michigan, in 1850. Known as the Lion Brewing Company until the early 1900s, Stroh's was a regional brewer for many years and only recently jumped onto the national stage. Long before Prohibition, Stroh's promoted its beer as being fire-brewed, but it was neither the first or the only fire-brewed beer in the world. Beer is brewed in one of two manners: by steam or hot water that runs through pipes around the kettles. Fire-brewing requires that the flame actually come into contact with the kettle. This process causes some caramelization during the brewing process and adds a distinctive flavor.

Like most breweries during Prohibition, Stroh's made near beer, malt extract, and other things until that onerous Amendment was appealed. In the years since, Stroh's has expanded exponentially via the introduction of new labels and brands and by acquiring other brewers. Currently they are responsible for producing a number of well-known beers, including Schlitz, Old Milwaukee, Piels, Augsburger, and Schaefer—all names acquired during the beer wars. Stroh's also contract brews Pete's Wicked beers.

REGIONAL BREWERS

While not as big as some of the megabrewers, there are many regional brewers, large and small, across the United States. In this classification, many of these regional brewers not only service a region with their own name brands but do quite a bit of contract brewing for both microbrewers and megabrewers. Regional breweries generally produce from 15,000 to 1,000,000 barrels per year.

Two of the most well-known regional brewers are G. Heileman Brewing Company and F.X. Matt Brewing Company. These two breweries both brew a wide variety of beers and supply a wide variety of customers. A third brewer that is worth mentioning is Yuengling Brewery, the oldest continually operating brewery in the United States.

G. Heileman

G. Heileman is probably the largest of the regional breweries. They have breweries in LaCrosse, Wisconsin; Seattle, Washington; Baltimore, Maryland; Portland, Oregon; and San Antonio, Texas. With operations spread out all over the country, how does this qualify as a regional brewery? Heileman does not brew and market a national brand. Almost all of the beers it makes are distributed in specific regions, with the exceptions of several of its smaller specialty beers. There is not one beer in its stable that holds a significant market share of the beer industry. Heileman is one of the largest brewers in the country because in terms of total output, they're huge.

(continued)

Sr. would go into a bar early in the morning and approach the bartender, doing everything necessary to sell his beer. Scream, shout, or laugh, he would goad the bartender to carry even the smallest amount of Heineken.

After closing the sale, he would return to the establishment very late in the evening, checking to see if the morning man was still on the job. If he wasn't, Van Munching would approach the bar and, posing as an unknowing customer, ask what kind of beers were available. Of course, he would choose the fancy new import, Heineken. Pounding the bar with his fist and carrying on, he would insist to other customers that this beer was the best ever brewed, and if he could not convince them to buy one themselves, he would buy them one. In short, he would create a run on the beer. The next day he would show up and the bartender would be astonished and happy to see him to order more of this wonderful new brew.

Heileman brews beers that range from the lowest of the lows to the higher quality brands. Heileman is famous for producing low-market entries such as Carling's Black Label, Champale Malt Liquor, Crazy Horse Malt Liquor, and Colt 45. Conversely, they do brew some quality lagers and ales such as Jet City Rocket Red Ale, Oregon Nut Brown Ale, and Rhino Chaser Lager. In their stable, you will also find names that are an echo from a bygone era of beer such as Schmidt's, Blatz, Rheingold, and Tuborg Gold. They are also the producers of McSorely's, Lone Star, Rainier, and Weinhard's.

Recently, this company has come into some financial difficulties due to its growth through acquisition. However, the group of breweries that are included under this umbrella are well known and produce huge quantities of popular beers.

F.X. Matt

If G. Heileman runs the gamut from sublime to slime, then F.X. Matt is a cut above. However, they are not without sin either. F.X. Matt is based in Utica, New York, and their most notable transgression to all of beerdom is D'Agostino Fresh Real Pub Beer. However, they are also the contract brewer of one of the world's best beers—Brooklyn Black Chocolate Stout. F.X. Matt is also the brewer of such notable beers as Dock Street, New Amsterdam, Harpoon, and Saranac. F.X. Matt also brews Rhino Chaser Amber Ale. While many of these beers are contract beers, Saranac is the family's new signature label that caters to the quality beer market at a mid-level price.

F.X. Matt is owned and operated by Francis Xavier Matt, II, whose grandfather founded the brewery in 1888. Back then it was known as the West End Brewery, a local brewery in Utica, New York. To this day, Matt continues to sell its original brands in and around New York state and in several connecting states. Some of their original brand names were Utica Club and Matt's Premium. While F.X. Matt expanded quickly after World War II, it did slow down by the early 1980s. After some family wrangles were worked out in the executive suite, F.X. Matt made a stunning comeback, joining the quality beer market and increasing its total output to more than 800,000 barrels per year. While the total quantity is impressive, it is also important to keep in mind that they do it producing some quality beers.

S&P Company

S&P Company is a conglomerate made up of a group of companies, including the Fallstaff, General, Pabst, and Pearl brewing companies. While there are a number of brewery locations, their executive headquarters are in Madera, California. Stroh's brewery contract brews some of the beers for S&P so that they can be distributed on the East Coast. S&P has a stable of beers that range from swill to better quality beers. Some of the names they make that you might recognize are Ballantine, Pabst, Hamm's, Olympia, Texas and Texas Pride, Olde English 800 Malt Liquor, and Burgemeister. Some of the Ballantine ales are pretty good beers, including the Ballantine's Twisted Red Ale and Ballantine India Pale Ale.

D.G. Yuengling & Son

D.G. Yuengling & Son Brewing Company is the oldest operating brewery in the United States. Yuengling was founded by David Gottlieb Yuengling, a German immigrant brewer, in Pottsville, Pennsylvania, in 1829. Originally named the Eagle Brewery, Yuengling crafted only draft beer, which was transported by draft horse teams in its early days. The beer was transported in wooden casks and hand pulled as it was served at the pub. While Yuengling has grown in popularity, it suffered greatly during Prohibition and during the beer wars of the 1960s and 1970s. While Heileman and Matt have expanded their businesses through contract brewing, D.G. Yuengling improved their business the old-fashioned way: they rebuilt their brand name.

Yuengling's ability to survive the beer wars brings up an interesting point about Pennsylvania and its brewers. Pennsylvania had more regional breweries survive the beer wars than any other state. While Pennsylvania has always had more brewers than any other state through the course of history, Pennsylvanians seem loyal to their brands.

Yuengling was strong in its belief that it could continue to brew quality beers. One of the things the beer world owes Yuengling dearly for is the Pottsville Porter. While even in Great Britain a Londoner could not buy himself a porter at his own pub, Yuengling single-handedly kept the porter tradition alive. D.G. Yuengling's Pottsville Porter was the only porter available in the world for almost fifteen years during the dark years of the '70s. This is still a wonderful, quirky beer full of rich coffee and caramel overtones and a solid malty nose.

While Yuengling is still family owned and operated, they have moved to increase both their image and their sales. They have expanded their line, as well as spent money to repackage their beer. They also make two other notable beers: Yuengling Black and Tan and Chesterfield Ale.

MICROBREWERIES AND CONTRACT BREWING

Traditionally, a microbrewery produces less than 15,000 barrels of beer a year. At this time there are approximately 200 microbreweries in the United States. The difference between a brewpub and a microbrewery is that the bulk of a microbrewery's beer is sold through retail sales, not through an associated bar or restaurant. Another of the things that differentiates microbrewers from brewpubs is bottling equipment. Bottling equipment is too cumbersome and expensive for the average brewpub. Shelf life is also important to a microbrewer, while a brewpub serves its beers for consumption immediately.

One of the best known microbrewers of the Midwest is Boulevard Brewing Company. They are the makers of an exceptional porter named Bully! Porter. Based in Kansas City, Missouri, they are owned by John McDonald and make upward of 20,000 barrels per year. They make all their own beer and see themselves as a strong but regional brewer of high quality. They believe in staying regional and not risking a loss in quality of their product by contracting it out.

The microbrewery world is now a strong and independent group of entrepreneurs who have created a whole new world for beer drinkers. Consumers have responded. While places like the Yakima Brewing Company and the Mendocino Brewing Company have grown from brewpubs to microbrewers, there is another option in getting beer to the retail market: contract brewing. Two of the most famous contract brewers are Pete's Wicked and Samuel Adams. For the beer enthusiast who wants to be a beer entrepreneur, contract brewing is very attractive. Contract brewing is when the beer is brewed at a regional brewery or another microbrewer, but is owned by the person or company that orders the beer.

Pete's Wicked

One of the best known contract brewers in America is Pete Slosberg, president of Pete's Wicked Brewing Company. Pete's Wicked is based out of Palo Alto, California. Pete's owns no breweries and brews no beers, yet their sales are extraordinary. How? Pete's Wicked contract brews their beers with regional breweries that can produce the quality and quantity necessary.

Pete didn't have enough money to start a brewery, but he was a wild beer enthusiast who decided he could promote better than he could brew. The recipes are owned by Pete's Wicked Brewing Company and were originally brewed out of Schell Brewing in New Ulm, Minnesota. But when things got a little bigger, Pete's got a new contract and moved his operations to the bigger Minnesota Brewing Company in St. Paul, Minnesota. But in 1995 Pete's Wicked grew even more popular and they moved their base of brewing to Stroh's Brewery, also in St. Paul.

The great thing about being a contract brewer is that it lets the organization worry about the marketing and selling of the beer, while the day-to-day brewing of the beer is contracted out. There is no outlay in expensive brewing copper or in bottling machinery. One of the negatives cited by some is that the contract brewer gives up his control of the crafting of the product, and when made by bigger, more industrial brewers the quality is sacrificed. With some beers that has indeed been the case. But there are many quality beers made in places like G. Heileman and F.X. Matt, and one should be more than happy that some of these beers are made in large enough quantities that consumers all over the United States can enjoy them.

Boston Beer Company

Unlike Pete's Wicked, the Boston Beer Company does own a brewpub where it serves some of the well-known Samuel Adams beers. They also serve a number of hand-crafted beers not available in stores and test their newest brewing concoctions that don't always make it to your favorite beer distributor's shelves.

Jim Koch (pronounced Cook) is also one of the most well-known contract brewers. Most of his beers are made by the Pittsburgh Brewing Company, F.X. Matt, and G. Heileman.

Dock Street Brewery

Dock Street Brewery is based in Philadelphia and has a brewpub there. They are also a microbrewer and a contract brewer. They have extensive beer works at their brewpub and are capable of producing more than 3,000 barrels a year. Their bottled beer is produced by F.X. Matt, who sells more than 25,000 barrels of their beer, mainly on the East Coast.

BREWPUBS

A brewpub is an establishment that makes and serves most of the beer it produces on its premises. This is usually done through a restaurant or bar. Thus, many of the brewpubs rightfully call themselves breweries. Many of the oldest breweries started out as brewpubs, making small batches of beer fresh for the local customers. As demand grew and grew, these establishments brewed more and more beer—eventually bottling their beers and becoming brewers. This was the case with many of the great brewing houses of Europe.

Brewpubs were quite common in the days before Prohibition. However, after Prohibition, it was illegal to make and serve beer on the same premises. There were originally good intentions behind this law. It was designed to give smaller brewers who were waiting to get back into business after Prohibition a chance to compete. It was thought that many of the largest brewers would eventually buy up all the bars and force smaller brewers out of business by cutting them from the menus of the bars and restaurants they owned.

Many of the beers made by brewpubs are served on tap. It is quite common that the beers served will change frequently and seasonally. Many of these brewpubs serve food, and the staffs of their restaurants are trained to advise you on appropriate beer and food pairings. Some have dishes made from their beers, like breads, meat, vegetable, and seafood dishes. Some of these establishments also feature harder spirits, especially single-malt whiskeys, and cigars. In many cases, these brewpubs have become epicurean adventures. Currently, there are more than one thousand brewpubs in the United States.

Many microbrewed beers that are available on the market were first served in brewpubs across the country. Some of the first brewpubs in America after Prohibition were Buffalo Bill Owens in Hayward, California; Yakima Brewing and Malting in Yakima, Washington; and Mendocino Brewing Company in Hopland, California. One of the best examples is Buffalo Bill's Brewery. Bill Owens was the first to fight city hall to repeal the many laws that were preventing smaller brewpubs from starting. Located in Hayward, California, the brewery is a restaurant that serves the beer it makes on its premises. Bill Owens is famous for two of his ales: Alimony Ale and Pumpkin Ale. Both of these are exceptional beers of great renown, eventually becoming so popular that they are now contract brewed.

There are many fine brewpubs that do not have contract brewing or licensing agreements. One case in point is the Park Slope Brewery, located in Brooklyn, New York. Park Slope is a neighborhood of quiet, tree-lined streets and large, restored Victorian brownstones built during the Gilded Age. The neighborhood surrounds Prospect Park, which was designed by Frederick Law Olmstead. Park Slope Brewery is a neighborhood establishment, serving hand-crafted beers made on the premises. With its pressed-tin ceiling and old-fashioned oak bar, the Park Slope Brewery is always packed, and they make some excellent beers. While Park Slope Brewery does not have a bottled beer available in stores, they will sell you a jug of beer, as will many other brewpubs. It is important to know that when opened, this beer usually needs to be consumed within forty-eight hours. More often than not, these are not pasteurized beers and are not made to sit in your refrigerator for a couple of weeks. Also, once the container is opened, the beer will go flat much more quickly.

IMPORTERS

It would be a sin of omission if this book didn't include a nod to the importers—those tireless individuals and companies that for so long fueled the beer industry with an alternative to the dwindling selections of American offerings. The most famous importer of all time was "the Baron," Leo Van Munching, Sr., a former Holland America steward who went on to found one of the most lucrative businesses the beer industry has ever known—Van Munching Importers, the people who brought you Heineken. Van Munching and his son, Leo Van Munching, Jr., helped to establish the beer import market almost single-handedly.

Another visionary importer, and one of the most visible, is the Marchant du Vin. The U.S. importer of such world-renowned brands as Lindemans, Orval, St. Sextus, Ayinger, Pinkus, and Samuel Smith, the Marchant du Vin is one of the most influential arbiters of import tastes since Leo Van Munching.

Marchant du Vin is just one among many who import some of the best made beers into the world's largest market. Here are some well-known beer importers and their beers.

Acme Food Specialties
P.O. Box 4445
Santa Fe Springs, CA 90670
(310) 946-9494
(310) 944-6809 (fax)
Einbecker Ur-bock, König Pilsener, Ritterbrau, Schultheiss Berliner Weisse

Admiralty Beverages Company
2336 NW 21st Avenue
Portland, OR 97209
(503) 240-5522
Chimay, Dentergems, Duvel, EKU, Hoegaarden, Lucifer, Paulaner, Scottish & Newcastle, Spaten, Young's

All Saints Brands
201 Main Street SE #323
Minneapolis, MN 55414
Christoffel Bier Blond, La Trappe

Amazon
P.O. Box 1466
Brattleboro, VT 05302
(802) 254-3884
Xingu

Anheuser-Busch
1 Busch Place
St. Louis, MO 63118
(314) 577-2000
Carlsberg

Barton Beers
55 E. Monroe Street
Chicago, IL 60603
(312) 346-9200
(312) 346-2213
*Corona Extra, Corona Light, Coronita,
Double Diamond, Modelo Especial,
Negra Modelo, Pacifico, Peroni, San
Miguel, St. Pauli Girl, Tsing Tao*

Belkus Marketing
(609) 589-2414
Young's Beers

Brandevor USA
18211 NE 68th Street #100
Redmond, WA 98052
(206) 881-5095
Simpatico

Bulunda Import-Export Company
Jacksonville, FL
(904) 642-1077
Ngoma

Century Importers
11911 Freedom Drive #100
Reston, VA 22090
(703) 709-6600
(703) 709-6999 (fax)
*Caribe, Courage, Foster's, Kronenbourg,
O'Keefe, Old Vienna*

Cherry Company
4461 Malai Street
P.O. Box 1375
Honolulu, HI 96818
(808) 537-5245
Kirin

Chrissa Imports
50 Cypress Lane
P.O. Box 548
Brisbane, CA 94005
(415) 468-5770
Gösser, König Pilsener, Spaten

Crown Jewel Importers
Fairfield, NJ
(201) 575-8886
Monrovia

DAB Importers
770 East Main Street #1A
Morristown, NJ 08057
(609) 234-9400
(609) 234-9640 (fax)
DAB Beers

Dribeck Importers
57 Old Post Road #2
Greenwich, CT 06830
(203) 622-1124
Beck's Beers

East Coast Importing
P.O. Box 2739
Acton, MA 01720
(508) 692-8466
Bitburger, Maisel

Efco Importers
P.O. Box 741
Jenkintown, PA 19046
(215) 224-9022
(215) 885-4584 (fax)
*Brahama, Broyhan, EKU, St.
Bernard Bräu, Tyrolian*

L. Fatato
318 Second Street
Brooklyn, NY 11215
(718) 965-7200
Canadian Ace, Malta El Sol

Fischer Beverages International
393 Totten Pond Road
Waltham, MA 02154
Fischer

Gambrinus Importing
14800 San Pedro #310
San Antonio, TX 78232
(210) 490-9128
*Cobra,Corona, Modelo, Pacifico,
Red Back*

Joseph Gies Import
3345 Southport Avenue
Chicago, IL 60657
(312) 472-4577
EKU, Kulmbacher

Grolsch Importers
1985 N. Park Place
Atlanta, GA 30339
(404) 955-8885
(404) 955-7571 (fax)
Dinkelacker

Guinness Import Company
Landmark Square
9th floor
Stamford, CT 06901
(203) 323-3311
*Bass, Dos Equis, Guinness, Harp,
Moosehead, Pilsner Urquell*

G. Heileman Brewing Company
100 Harborview Plaza
La Crosse, WI 54601
(608) 785-1000
Castlemaine, Hacker-Pschorr, Swan

Heineken USA
1270 Avenue of the Americas
New York, NY 10020
(212) 332-8500
Amstel, Grizzly, Heineken

Highland Distributing Company
Houston, TX
(713) 862-6364
Mamba

Hilton Commercial Group
P.O. Box 2026
Toluca Lake, CA 90610
(818) 953-4160
Bergbrau, Giovane, Vienna Lager

Holsten Import Corporation
120 White Plains Road
Elmsford, NY 10523
(914) 345-8900
Holsten

Hudepohl Schoenling
1625 Central Parkway
Cincinnati, OH 45214
(513) 241-4344
(513) 241-2190 (fax)
*Cerveza Panama, Mackeson's,
Whitbread Ale*

International Beverages
65 Shawmut Road
Canton, MA 02021
(617) 821-2712
*Aass, August Schell, Burghoff,
Chimay, Eggenberger, Holsten,
Mamba, Schloss, Timmermans,
Upper Canada, Young's*

International Brands
441 North Klibourn Avenue
Chicago, IL 60624
(312) 826-4001
*Bass, Bohemia, Carta Blanca,
Dinkelacker, Guinness, Harp, Kirin,
Kiwi, Mamba, Nordik Woll, OB,
Ringnes, St. Pauli Girl*

Jacquin International
2633 Treton Avenue
Philadelphia, PA 19125
(215) 425-9300
Birell

Kelwill Importers
P.O. Box 1987
Bloomfield, NJ 07003
(201) 748-9010
Silver Dragon, Yin Long, Zhuhai

Kirin USA
600 Third Avenue
New York, NY 10016
(212) 687-1865
Kirin

Labatt Importers
23 Old Kings Way S
Darien, CT 06820
(203) 656-1876
*Dos Equis, Fister's Whitbread,
Labatts, Mackerson, Moretti*

Marchant du Vin Corporation
140 Lakeside Avenue #300
Seattle, WA 98112
(206) 322-5022
(206) 322-5185 (fax)
*Ayinger, Brasseurs, Lindemans,
Orval, Pinkus, Samuel Smith, St.
Sixtus, Watou*

Paterno Imports
2701 S. Western Avenue
Chicago, IL 60608
(312) 247-7070
(312) 247-0072 (fax)
Berliner Kindl

Phoenix Imports
2925 Montclair Drive
Elliott City, MD 21043
(800) 700-4ALE
*Corsendonk, Gouden Carolus,
Hexenbräu, Liefmans, Royal Oak,
Rubens Red & Gold, Samichlaus,
Thomas Hardy's Ale*

Sapporo USA
1290 Avenue of the Americas
New York, NY 10104
(212) 765-4430
Sapporo

Scottish & Newcastle Importers
444 De Haro #125
San Francisco, CA 94107
(415) 255-4555
*McEwan's, Newcastle Brown Ale,
Theakston's Old Peculiar*

Sieb Distributors
418 Seneca Avenue
Ridgewood, NY 11385
(718) 386-1480
(718) 821-8120 (fax)
Spaten

Suntory International
1211 Avenue of the Americas
New York, NY 10036
(212) 921-9595
(212) 398-0268 (fax)
Suntory

Vanberg & DeWulf Importers
52 Pioneer Street
Cooperstown, NY 13326
(800) 656-1212
*Affligem Abbey, Blanche de Bruges,
Boon Lambics, Castelain, Duvel,
Jenlain, Mort Subite, Rodenbach,
Saison Dupont, Scaldis*

Wisdom Import Sales Company
17401 Eastman Avenue
Irvine, CA 92713
(714) 261-5533
*Bohemia, Carta Blanca, Tecate,
Watney's Red Barrel*

WHERE TO GET GOOD BEER

CHAPTER

8

BOTTLED BY
ADAMS MEDIA CORPORATION

Sounds like a pretty simple dilemma, doesn't it? For some, it's as easy as going to the local bar or package store. However, there are other ways to obtain the beers you want that are not available to you through those channels. Some people explore the world of beers through the very popular Beer of the Month Club, and there are other mail-order services as well as catalogs and Websites.

Let's be honest. If you want really good beer, you're going to have to stretch a little to get it. The first thing you must realize is that the good stuff costs more than a six-pack of your favorite lawnmower beer. Very rarely will a case of some of the fancier beers listed in this book cost less than a combo meal at McDonald's.

If you're lucky and have a retailer near you that carries a large array of beers from various countries, then welcome to paradise. Nowadays, stores that sell beer are under increasing demand to stock more out-of-the-way beers. Beer enthusiasts who are not lucky enough to have a more enlightened purveyor of beers locally are usually more resourceful. There are many things you can do.

One solution is to call friends who live somewhere else in the state. They can be a good source of information regarding stores or distributors that you might not know about. If you're looking for a specific beer, call that manufacturer and ask where the distributor closest to you is located. Or, depending on what state you live in, you can order it straight from the manufacturer.

Of course, you can always make a trip to the brewery. There are many breweries throughout the country and many of them schedule tours. These are a lot of fun. You'll learn first-hand how the beer is made and the intricacies that distinguish one beer from another. Plus, you'll get to sample that brewery's products after the tour to see which is your favorite.

Of course, festivals are fun, too, and that's always another way to go. Festivals are especially good because brewers use these giant beer parties to test new brews on enthusiastic crowds. Many brewers are now on-line, and that is another way to reach them. You need to be resourceful to find some good beers. So dig a little—there are many delicious brews waiting to be found.

I feel no pain, dear mother,
  now
But oh, I am so dry!
O take me to a brewery
And leave me there to die.

—ANONYMOUS

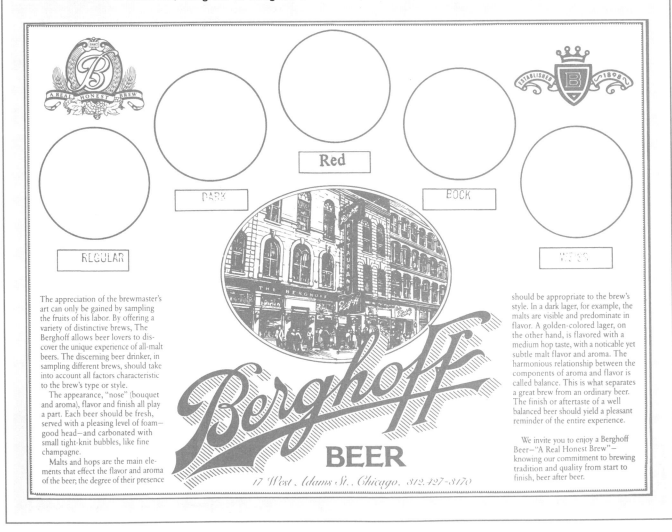

SAMPLING OR SAMPLER MENU

Many microbreweries have what is commonly referred to as a sampler's or a sampling menu. Here, in small quantities, the microbrewery serves each of its brews in order of lightest to darkest. Here is a sampling menu from one of the oldest microbreweries in America, Berghoff's. Berghoff's has been in business since 1989 and is one of those restaurants where Chigagoans go to eat. But the secret is out, because it is also one of the most popular restaurants in the city. Microbrewery? This place was established when McKinley was president! Oh, and the beer? Excellent!

Red

DARK

BOCK

REGULAR

WEISS

The appreciation of the brewmaster's art can only be gained by sampling the fruits of his labor. By offering a variety of distinctive brews, The Berghoff allows beer lovers to discover the unique experience of all-malt beers. The discerning beer drinker, in sampling different brews, should take into account all factors characteristic to the brew's type or style.

The appearance, "nose" (bouquet and aroma), flavor and finish all play a part. Each beer should be fresh, served with a pleasing level of foam—good head—and carbonated with small tight-knit bubbles, like fine champagne.

Malts and hops are the main elements that effect the flavor and aroma of the beer; the degree of their presence should be appropriate to the brew's style. In a dark lager, for example, the malts are visible and predominate in flavor. A golden-colored lager, on the other hand, is flavored with a medium hop taste, with a noticable yet subtle malt flavor and aroma. The harmonious relationship between the components of aroma and flavor is called balance. This is what separates a great brew from an ordinary beer. The finish or aftertaste of a well balanced beer should yield a pleasant reminder of the entire experience.

We invite you to enjoy a Berghoff Beer—"A Real Honest Brew"—knowing our commitment to brewing tradition and quality from start to finish, beer after beer.

Berghoff

BEER

17 West Adams St., Chicago. 312.427-3170

MICROBREWERIES IN THE UNITED STATES AND CANADA

ALABAMA

Birmingham Brewing
3118 Third Avenue, South
Birmingham, AL 35233
(205) 326-6677

ALASKA

Alaskan Brewing & Bottling Company
5429 Shaune Drive
Juneau, AK 99801
(907) 780-5866

Bird Creek Brewery
310 East 76th Street
Anchorage, AK 95540
(907) 344-2473

Ravens Ridge Brewing Company
P.O. Box 81395
Fairbanks, AK 99708
(907) 457-2739

CALIFORNIA

American River Brewing
100 Borland Avenue
Auburn, CA 95603
(916) 889-0841

Anchor Brewery
1705 Mariposa Street
San Francisco, CA 94107
(415) 863-8350

Angeles Brewing
10009 Conoga Avenue
Chatsworth, CA 91311
(818) 407-0340

Blind Pig Brewing
42387 Avenido Alvarito #108
Temecula, CA 92390
(909) 569-4646

Buffalo Bill's Brewery
Box 510
Hayward, CA 94541
(510) 538-9500

Devil Mountain/Bay Brewing
2283 Camel Road
Benicia, CA 94510
(707) 747-6961

El Toro Brewing
17370 Hill Road
Morgan Hill, CA 95037
(408) 778-BREW

Etna Brewery
131 Callahan Street
Etna, CA 96027
(916) 467-5277

Golden Pacific Brewing
5515 Doyal Street
Emeryville, CA 94608
(510) 547-8270

Hangtown Brewery
560 A Placerville Drive
Placerville, CA 95667
(916) 621-3999

Humes Brewing
2775 Cavedale Road
Glen Ellen, CA 95442
(707) 935-0723

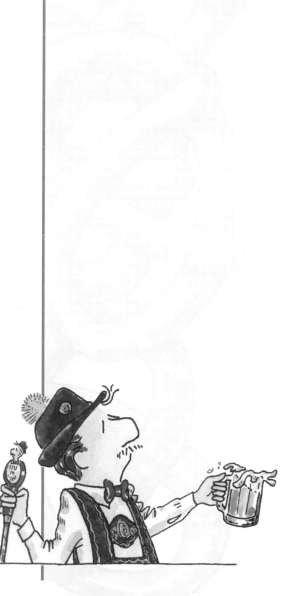

Lind Brewing
1933 Davis
San Leandro, CA 94577
(510) 562-0866

Mad River Brewing
195 Taylor Way
Blue Lake, CA 95525
(707) 668-4151

Moonlight Brewing
P.O. Box 316
Santa Rosa, CA 95401

Murphy's Creek Brewing
Murphy's Grade Road
Murphy's, CA 95247
(209) 736-BREW

Nevada City Brewing
75 Bost Avenue
Nevada City, CA 95959
(916) 265-2446

Pacific Hop Exchange Brewing
158 Hamilton Drive #A1
Novato, CA 94949
(415) 884-2820

Pete's Brewing Company
514 High Street
Palo Alto, CA 94301
(415) 328-7383

Riverside Brewing Company
1229 Columbia Avenue, Suite C4
Riverside, CA 92507
(909) 682-5465

Sudwerk Privatbrauerei Hubsch
1107 Kennedy Place, 1
Davis, CA 95616
(916) 756-2739

Tuscan Brewing
25009 Kauffman Avenue
Red Bluff, CA 96080
(916) 527-7048

COLORADO

Avery Brewing
5763 E. Arapahoe
Boulder, CO 80301
(303) 440-4324

Bristol Brewing
4740 Forge Road
Colorado Springs, CO 80907
(719) 535-2824

Durango Brewing
3000 Main Street
Durango, CO 81301
(970) 247-3396

Golden City Brewery
920 12th Street
Golden, CO 80401
(303) 279-8092

Great Divide Brewing
Denver, CO 80205

H.C. Berger Brewing
1900 E. Lincoln Avenue
Fort Collins, CO 80524
(970) 493-9044

Irons Brewing Company
12354 West Alameda Parkway,
Unit E
Lakewood, CO 80228
(303) 985-2337

Left Hand Brewing
1265 Boston Avenue
Longmont, CO 80501
(303) 772-0258

Lone Wolfe Brewing
898 Highway 133
Carbondale, CO 81623
(970) 963-8777

New Belgium Brewing
350 Linden Street
Fort Collins, CO 80524
(970) 221-0524

Odell Brewing
800 E. Lincoln Avenue
Fort Collins, CO 80524
(970) 498-9070

Pike's Peak Brewery
2547 Weston Road
Colorado Springs, CO 80910
(719) 391-8866

Tabernash Brewing
205 Denargo Market
Denver, CO 80216
(303) 293-2337

Tablerock Brewpub & Grill
705 Fulton
Boise, CO 83702
(208) 342-0944

FLORIDA
Beach Brewing
5905 S. Kirkman Road
Orlando, FL 32819
(407) 345-8802

Florida Beer Brands
645 W. Michigan Street
Orlando, FL 32805

GEORGIA
Atlantic Brewing
1219 Williams Street, N.W.
Atlanta, GA 30309
(404) 892-4436

Marthasville Brewing
3960 Shirley Drive, S.W.
Atlanta, GA 30336
(404) 713-0333

IDAHO
Beier Brewing Company
202 East 37th Street
Boise, ID 83714
(208) 338-5133

ILLINOIS
Chicago Brewing Comany
1830 N. Besly Court
Chicago, IL 60622
(312) 252-8196

Golden Prairie Brewing
1820 W. Webster Avenue
Chicago, IL 60614
(312) 862-0106

Pavichevich Brewing Company
383 Romans Road
Elmhurst, IL 60126
(630) 617-5252

RJ's Ginseng Company
14828 McKinley Avenue
Posen, IL 60469
(708) 389-4274

Star Union Brewing
P.O. Box 282
Hennepin, IL 61327
(815) 925-7400

Woodstock Brewing & Bottling
202 E. Calhoun
Woodstock, IL 60098
(815) 337-1970

INDIANA
Indianapolis Brewing
3250 North Post Road
Indianapolis, IN 46226
(317) 898-1235

Mishawaka Brewing Company
3703 N. Main Street
Mishawaka, IN 46545
(219) 256-9994

IOWA
Dubuque Brewing and Bottling
Company
East Fourth St. Extension
Dubuque, IA 52001
(319) 583-2042

KANSAS

Miracle Brewing
311 S. Emporia
Wichita, KS 67202
(316) 265-7256

KENTUCKY

Oldenberg Brewery
2477 Royal Drive
Ft. Mitchell, KY 41017
(606) 341-2804

LOUISIANA

Abita Brewing Company
P.O. Box 762
Abita Springs, LA
(504) 893-3143

MAINE

Andrew's Brewing
RFD #1
Lincolnville, ME 04849
(207) 763-3305

Bar Harbor Brewing
Route 3 Otter Creek
Bar Harbor, ME 04609
(207) 288-4592

Casco Bay Brewing Company
57 Industrial Way
Portland, ME 04103-1071
(207) 797-2020

D.L. Geary Brewing
38 Evergreen Drive
Portland, ME 04103
(207) 878-2337

Lake St. George Brewing
RR 1, Box 2505
Liberty, ME 04949-9738
(207) 589-4690

Shipyard Brewery
86 Newbury Street
Portland, ME 04101
(207) 761-0807

MARYLAND

Frederick Brewing
103 South Carroll Street
Frederick, MD 21701-7899
(301) 694-7899

Oxford Brewing
611 G
Hammonds Ferry Road
Linthicum, MD 21090
(410) 789-0003

Wild Goose Brewery
20 Washington Street
Cambridge, MD 21613
(410) 221-1121

MASSACHUSETTS

Atlantic Coast Brewing
50 Terminal Street
Boston, MA 02129
(617) 242-6464

Berkshire Brewing Co.
12 Railroad Street
South Deerfield, MA 01373
(413) 665-6600

Boston Beer Company
30 Germania Street
Boston, MA 02930
(617) 728-4182

Brewery on Martha's Vineyard
43 Oak Bluffs Avenue
Oak Bluffs, MA 02557
(508) 696-8400

Ipswich Brewing
25 Hayward Street
Ipswich, MA 02938
(508) 356-3329

Massachusetts Bay Brewing
Company, Inc.
306 Northern Avenue
Boston, MA 02210
(617) 574-9551

Oak Salem Village Brewing
(Private Residence)
Danvers, MA 01923
(508) 777-2260

Ould Newbury Brewing
50 Parker Street
Ould Newbury, MA 01951
(508) 462-1980

MICHIGAN
Detroit & Mackinac Beer
15408 Mack Avenue
Detroit, MI 48224
(313) 881-2337

Frankenmuth Brewery
425 South Main Street
Frankenmuth, MI 48734
(517) 652-6183

Kalamazoo Brewing
315 East Kalamazoo Avenue
Kalamazoo, MI 49007
(616) 382-2338

MINNESOTA
Cold Spring Brewing Company
219 North Red River Avenue
Cold Spring, MN 56320
(612) 685-8686

James Page Brewing
1300 Quincy, N.E.
Minneapolis, MN 55413
(612) 331-2833

Summit Brewing
2264 University Avenue
St. Paul, MN 55114
(612) 645-5029

MISSOURI
Anheuser-Busch, Inc.
1 Busch Place
St. Louis, MO 63134
(314) 577-2626

Boulevard Brewing Company
2501 Southwest Boulevard
Kansas City, MO 64108
(816) 474-7095

MONTANA
Lang Creek Brewery
655 Lang Creek Road
Marion, MT 59925
(406) 858-2200

Montana Beverages
(Kessler Brewery)
1439 Harris Street
Helena, MT 59601
(406) 449-6214

Whitefish Brewing
P.O. Box 1949
Whitefish, MT 59937
(406) 862-2684

NEW HAMPSHIRE
Smuttynose Brewery
225 Heritage Avenue
Portsmouth, NH 03801
(603) 433-2337

NEW MEXICO
Eske's: A Brew Pub/
Sangre de Cristo Brewing
P.O. Box 1572
106 Des Georges Lane
Taos, NM 87571
(505) 758-1517

Rio Grande Brewing
3760 Hawkins, N.E.
Albuquerque, NM 87109
(505) 343-0903

Russell Brewery
1242 Siler Road
Santa Fe, NM 87501
(505) 438-3138

Santa Fe Brewing
Flying M Ranch
Galisteo, NM 87540
(505) 466-3333

NEW YORK
The Brooklyn Brewery
118 North 11th Street
Brooklyn, NY 11211
(718) 486-7422

Buffalo Brewing Company
Abbott Square
1830 Abbott Road
Buffalo, NY 14218
(716) 828-0004

F.X. Matt Brewing Company/Saranac
811 Edward Street
Utica, NY 13502
(315) 732-3181

Woodstock Brewing
20 St. James Street
Kingston, NY 12401
(914) 331-2810

NORTH CAROLINA
Dilworth Micro Brewery
655 R. Pressley Road
Charlotte, NC 28217
(704) 522-0311

Loggerhead Brewing
2006 W. Vandalia Road
Greensboro, NC 27407
(919) 292-7676

OHIO
Columbus Brewing
476 South Front Street
Columbus, OH 43215
(614) 224-3626

Crooked River Brewing
1101 Center Street
Cleveland, OH 44113
(216) 771-BEER

Gambrinus Brewing
1152 South Front Street
Columbus, OH 43207
(614) 444-7769

Lift Bridge Brewing Company
1119 Lake Avenue
Ashtabula, OH 44004
(216) 964-6200

OREGON
Deschutes Brewery & Public House
1044 N.W. Bond Street
Bend, OR 97001
(503) 382-9242

Hair of the Dog Brewing Company, Inc.
4509 S.E. 23rd Street
Portland, OR 97202
(503) 232-6585

Oregon Trader Brewing
140 Hill Street
Albany, OR 97321
(503) 928-1931

Saxer Brewing
5875 Southwest Lakeview SR
Lake Oswego, OR 97035
(503) 699-5924

Star Brewing
5231 N.E. Martin Luther King, Jr. Boulevard
Portland, OR 97211
(503) 282-6003

Widmer Brewing
929 North Russell Street
Portland, OR 97227
(503) 281-2437

PENNSYLVANIA

Arrowhead Brewing Company
1667 Orchard Drive
Chambersburg, PA 17201
(717) 264-0101

Latrobe Brewing Company
119 Jefferson Street
Latrobe, PA 15650
(412) 537-5545

Stoudt Brewing Company
Route 272, Box 880
Adamstown, PA 19501
(717) 484-4386

D.G. Yuengling and Son, Inc.
5th and Mahantongo Streets
Pottsville, PA 17901
(717) 628-4890

SOUTH CAROLINA

Palmetto Brewing
289 Hugar Street
Charleston, SC 29403
(803) 937-0903

TEXAS

Celis Brewery Inc.
2431 Forbes Drive
Austin, TX 78754
(512) 835-0884

Hill Country Brewing & Bottling
730 Shady Lane
Austin, TX 78702
(512) 385-9111

Saint Arnolds Brewing
2522 Fairway Park Drive
Houston, TX 77092
(713) 686-9494

Texas Brewing
703 McKinney Avenue
Dallas, TX 75202
(214) 871-7990

Yellow Rose Brewing
17201 San Pedro Avenue
San Antonio, TX 78232
(210) 496-6669

UTAH

Schirf Brewing Company/Wasatch
Brew Pub
250 Main Street
P.O. Box 459
Park City, UT 84060
(801) 645-9500

Uinta Brewing
389 W. 1700 South
Salt Lake City, UT 84115
(801) 467-0909

VERMONT

Catamount Brewing Company
58 South Main Street
White River Junction, VT 05001
(802) 296-2248

The Jasper Murdock Alehouse at the
Northwich Inn
P.O. Box 908
Main Street
Norwich, VT 05055
(802) 649-1143

Magic Hat Brewing Company
180 Flynn Avenue
Burlington, VT 05401
(802) 658-2739

The Mountain Brewers, Inc.
P.O. Box 140
Bridgewater, VT 05034
(802) 672-5011

Otter Creek Brewing, Inc.
74 Exchange Street
Middlebury, VT 05753
(802) 388-0727

VIRGINIA
Old Dominion Brewing
44633 Guilford Drive
Ashburn, VA 22011
(703) 689-1225

Potomac River Brewing Company
14141-A Parke Long Court
Chantilly, VA 22021
(703) 631-5430

WASHINGTON
Hale's Ales
East 5634 Commerce Street
Spokane, WA 99212-1307
(509) 534-7553

Hart Brewing
110 West Marine Drive
Kalama, WA 98625
(206) 673-2962

Hart Brewing Inc./
Pyramid Breweries, Inc.
91 South Royal Brougham Way
Seattle, WA 98134
(206) 682-8322

Maritime Pacific Company
1514 Northwest Leary Way
Seattle, WA 98107
(206) 782-6181

Northern Light Brewing
1701 South Lawson
Airway Heights, WA 99001
(509) 244-4909

Onalaska Brewing
248 Burchett Road
Onalaska, WA 98570
(206) 978-4253

The Pike Brewing Company
1432 Western Avenue
Seattle, WA 98101
(206) 622-3373

Seattle Brewers
530 South Holden
Seattle, WA 98108
(206) 762-7421

Yakima Brewing and Malting
Company
1803 Presson Place
Yakima, WA 98902
(509) 575-1900

WEST VIRGINIA
Cardinal Brewing
927 Barlow Drive
Charleston, WV 25331
(304) 344-2900

WISCONSIN
Appleton Brewing Company
1004 South Olde Oneida Street
Appleton, WI 54915
(414) 735-0507

Capital Brewery
7734 Terrace Avenue
Middleton, WI 53562
(608) 836-7100

Gray's Brewing
2424 West Court Street
Janesville, WI 53545
(608) 752-3552

Lakefront Brewery
818A East Chamber Street
Milwaukee, WI 53212
(414) 372-8800

New Glarus Brewing
County West & Highway 69
New Glarus, WI 53574
(608) 527-5850

Sprecher Brewing
701 West Glendale Avenue
Glendale, WI 53209
(414) 964-BREW

WYOMING
Otto Brothers' Brewing
1295 West Street
Wilson, WY 83014
(307) 733-9000

Snake River Brewing Company,
Inc./Jackson Hole Pub and Brewery
P.O. Box 3319
Jackson Hole, WY 83001
(307) 739-2337

CANADA
Brick Brewing Company
181 King Street South
Waterloo, Ontario
Canada
(1-519) 576-9100

Columbia Brewing Co.
1220 Erickson
P.O. Box 1950
Creston
BC V0B 1GO
(604) 428-9344

Granite Brewery
1222 Barrington Street
Halifax, Nova Scotia
(902) 423-5660

Granville Island Brewing Co.
1441 Cartwright Street
Granville Island
Vancouver
BC V6H 3R7
Canada
(604) 688-9927

Labatt Alberta
P.O. Box 1818
Edmonton
ALTA T5J 2P2
Canada
(709) 579-0121

Molson Breweries
1892 15th Street S.E.
Calgary
Canada
(403) 233-1786

Moosehead Breweries
49 Main Street
St. John
NB E2M 3H2
(506) 635-7000

Unibroue
80 Des Carriers
Chambly
Quebec J3L 2H6
Canada
(1-514) 658-7658

BREWPUBS IN THE UNITED STATES AND CANADA

ALABAMA
Port City Brewer
25 Dauphin Street
Mobile, AL 36602
(205) 438-BREW

ARKANSAS
Ozark Brewing
4430 Dickson Street
Fayetteville, AR 72701
(501) 521-BREW

Vino's
923 West 7th Street
Little Rock, AR 72201
(501) 375-8466

Weidman's Old Fort Brew Pub
422 North 3rd Street
Fort Smith, AR 72901
(502) 782-9898

ARIZONA
Bandersnatch Brewpub
125 E. 5th Avenue
Tempe, AZ 85281
(602) 966-4438

Whistle Stop Cafe
11 S. Beaver Street
Flagstaff, AZ 86001
(602) 779-0079

Coyote Spring Brewing & Cafe
4883 N. 20th Street
Phoenix, AZ 85016
(602) 468-0403

Crazy Ed's Black Mountain Brewery
6245 E. Cave Creek Road
Cave Creek, AZ 85331
(602) 253-6293

Flagstaff Brewing
16 E. Highway 66
Flagstaff, AZ 86004
(602) 773-1442

Gentle Ben's Brewing
841 N. Tyndall
Tucson, AZ 85719
(602) 624-4177

Hops! Bistro & Brewery
841 N. Tyndall
Tucson, AZ 85016
(602) 468-0500

7000 E. Camelback Road
Scottsdale, AZ 85251
(602) 423-5557 or 945-HOPS

2584 East Camelback Road
Phoenix, AZ 85016
(602) 468-0500

Prescott Brewing
130 W. Gurley Street
Prescott, AZ 96301
(602) 771-2795

CALIFORNIA
Anderson Valley Brewery
The Buckhorn Saloon
14081 Highway 128
Boonville, CA 95415
(707) 895-2337

Belmont Brewing
25 39th Place
Long Beach, CA 90803
(213) 433-3891

Bison Brewing
2598 Telegraph Avenue
Berkeley, CA 94704
(510) 841-7734

Blue Water Brewing
850 North Lake Boulevard
Tahoe City, CA 96145
(916) 581-2583

Bootleggers Brewing
3401 Chester Avenue #H
Bakersfield, CA 93301
(805) 323-2739

Boulder Creek Brewing
(Boulder Creek Grill & Cafe)
13040 Highway 9
Boulder Creek, CA 95006
(408) 338-7882

Brewery at Lake Tahoe
3542 Lake Tahoe Boulevard
South Lake Tahoe, CA 96150
(916) 544-BREW

Brewski's GasLamp Pub
Bistro & Brewery
310 Fifth Avenue
San Diego, CA 92101
(619) 231-7700

Buffalo Bill's Brewpub
1082 B Street
Hayward, CA 94541
(510) 886-9982

Butterfield Brewing, Bar & Grill
777 East Olive Avenue
Fresno, CA 93728
(209) 264-5521

Cafe Pacifica/Sankt Gallen Brewery
333 Bush Street
San Francisco, CA 94104
(415) 296-8203

Callahan's Pub & Brewery
8280-A Mira Mesa Boulevard
San Diego, CA 92126
(619) 578-7892

Covany Brewing
359 Brand Avenue
Grover Beach, CA 93433
(805) 489-4042

Crown City Brewery
300 South Raymond Avenue
Pasadena, CA 91105
(818) 577-5548

Dempsey's Sonoma Brewing
50 East Washington Street
Petaluma, CA 94952
(707) 765-9694

Downtown Joe's Brewery &
Restaurant
902 Main Street
Napa, CA 94559
(707) 258-2337

Fremont Brewing
3350 Stevenson Boulevard
Fremont, CA 94538
(510) 651-5510

Fullerton Hofbrau
323 N. State College Boulevard
Fullerton, CA 92631
(714) 870-7400

Gordon Biersch Brewing
640 Emerson Street
Palo Alto, CA 94301
(415) 323-7723

41 Hugus Alley
Pasadena, CA 91103
(818) 449-0052

2 Harrison Street
San Francisco, CA 94120
(415) 243-8246

33 E. San Fernando Street
San Jose, CA 94301
(408) 294-6785

Heritage Brewing
24921 Dana Point Harbor Drive
Dana Point, CA 92629
(714) 240-2060

Hogshead Brewpub
114 J Street
Sacramento, CA 95814
(916) 443-BREW

Hops Bistro & Brewery
4353 La Jolla Village Drive H-29
San Diego, CA 92122-1212
(619) 587-6677

Humboldt Brewery
856 Tenth Street
Arcata, CA 95521
(707) 826-BREW

Huntington Beach Beer Company
201 Main Street #E
Huntington Beach, CA 92648
(714) 960-5343

Karl Strauss Brewery Gardens
9675 Scranton Road
San Diego, CA 92121
(619) 587-BREW

Karl Strauss' Old Columbia Brewery
& Grill
1157 Columbia Street
San Diego, CA 92101
(619) 234-BREW

LaJolla Brewing
7536 Fay Avenue
San Diego, CA 92037
(619) 456-2739

Live Soup Brewery Cafe
1602 Ocean Street
Santa Cruz, CA 95060
(408) 458-3461

Los Gatos Brewing
130G N. Santa Cruz
Los Gatos, CA 95030
(408) 395-9929

Lost Coast Brewery & Cafe
617 4th Street
Eureka, CA 95501
(707) 445-4480

Manhattan Beach Brewing
124 Manhattan Beach Boulevard
Manhattan Beach, CA 90266
(310) 798-2744

Marin Brewing
1809 Larkspur Landing Circle
Larkspur, CA 94939
(415) 461-HOPS

Mendocino Brewing
(Hopland Brewery Restaurant)
13351 S. Highway 101 S.
Hopland, CA 95449
(707) 744-1361

Monterey Brewing
511 Tyler Street
Monterey, CA 93940
(408) 375-3634

Napa Valley Brewing
(Calistoga Inn)
1250 Lincoln Avenue
Calistoga, CA 94515
(707) 942-4101

North Coast Brewing
444 N. Main
Ft. Bragg, CA 95437
(707) 964-2739

Pacific Beach Brewhouse
4475 Mission Boulevard
San Diego, CA 92109
(619) 274-ALES

Pacific Coast Brewing
906 Washington Street
Oakland, CA 94607
(510) 836-BREW

Pacific Tap & Grill
812 4th Street
San Rafael, CA 94901
(415) 457-9711

Pizza Port Solana Beach Brewery
135 N. Highway 101
Solana Beach, CA 92075
(619) 481-7332

Red, White & Blue
2181 Hill Top Drive
Redding, CA 96002
(916) 222-5891

Redondo Beach Brewing
1814 S. Catalina Avenue
Redondo Beach, CA 90277
(310) 316-8477

River City Brewing
545 Downtown Plaza #1115
Sacramento, CA 95814
(916) 447-BREW

Riverside Brewing
3397 7th Street
Riverside, CA 92501
(909) 784-BREW

Rubicon Brewing
2004 Capitol Avenue
Sacramento, CA 95814
(916) 448-7032

San Andreas Brewing
737 San Benito Street
Hollister, CA 95023
(408) 637-7074

San Diego Brewing
10450 Friars Road
San Diego, CA 92120
(619) 284-BREW

San Francisco Brewing
155 Columbus Avenue
San Francisco, CA 94133
(415) 434-3344

San Marcos Brewery & Grill
1080 San Marcos Boulevard
San Marcos, CA 92069
(619) 471-0050

San Rafael Brewery
(TJ's Bar & Grill)
7110 Redwood Boulevard
Novato, CA 94947
(415) 892-3474

Santa Clarita Brewing
20655 Soledad Canyon Road
Santa Clarita, CA 91351
(805) 298-5676

Santa Cruz Brewing
(Front Street Pub)
516 Front Street
Santa Cruz, CA 95060
(408) 429-8838

Santa Rosa Brewing
458 B Street
Santa Rosa, CA 95401
(707) 544-HOPS

Seabright Brewery
519 Seabright Avenue #107
Santa Cruz, CA 95062
(408) 426-2739

Shields Brewing
24 E. Santa Clara Street
Downtown Ventura, CA 93001
(805) 643-1807

Sierra Nevada Taproom & Restaurant
1075 E. 20th Street
Chico, CA 95928
(916) 345-2739

SLO Brewing
1119 Garden Street
San Juis Obispo, CA 93401
(805) 543-1843

Southern California Brewing
(Alpine Inn)
833 W. Torrance Boulevard
Torrance, CA 90502
(310) 329-8881

Stoddard's Brewhouse & Eatery
(Benchmark Brewery)
111 S. Murphy Avenue
Sunnyvale, CA 94086
(408) 733-7824

St. Stan's Brewery & Restaurant
821 L Street
Modesto, CA 95354
(209) 524-4PUB

Sudwerk Privatbrauerei Hubsch
2001 Second Street
Davis, CA 95616
(916) 756-2739

Tied House Cafe & Brewery
954 Villa Street
Mountain View, CA 94042
(415) 965-BREW

65 N. San Pedro
San Jose, CA 95110
(408) 295-BREW

Tied House Pub & Pool
8 Pacific Marina
Alameda, CA 94501
(510) 521-4321

Triple Rock Brewing
1920 Shattuck Avenue
Berkeley, CA 94704
(510) 843-2739

Truckee Brewing
(Pizza Junction)
11401 Donner Pass Road
Truckee, CA 95734
(916) 587-5406

Twenty Tank Brewing
316 11th Street
San Francisco, CA 94103
(415) 255-9455

COLORADO
Avery Brewing
5763 E. Arapahoe
Boulder, CO 80301
(303) 440-4324

Baked & Brewed in Telluride
127 S. Fir
Telluride, CO 81435
(970) 728-4775

Breckenridge Brewery
2220 Blake Street
Denver, CO 80205
(303) 297-3644

Broadway Brewing
2441 Broadway
Denver, CO 80205
(303) 292-5027

Carver's Bakery Cafe Brewery
1022 Main Avenue
Durango, CO 81301
(970) 259-2545

Casa De Colorado Brewery
320 Link Lane
Fort Collins, CO 80524
(970) 493-2739

Champion Brewing
1442 Larimer Square
Denver, CO 80202
(303) 534-5444

CooperSmith's Pub & Brewing
No. 5 Old Town Square
Fort Collins, CO 80524
(970) 498-0483

Crested Butte Brewery
(The Idlespur)
226 Elk Avenue
Crested Butte, CO 81224
(970) 349-5026

Estes Park Brewery
470 Prospect Village Drive
Estes Park, CO
(970) 586-5421

Flying Dog Brewpub & Grille
424 E. Cooper
Aspen, CO 81611
(970) 925-7464

Great Rocky Mountain Beer Festival
Copper Mountain, CO
(303) 968-2318 (Ext. 6505)

Heavenly Daze Brewery & Grill
1860 Ski Time Square Drive
Steamboat Springs, CO 80479
(970) 879-8080

Hubcap Brewery & Kitchen
143 E. Meadow Drive
Vail, CO 81657
(970) 476-5757

Judge Baldwin's Brewing
4 S. Cascade
Colorado Springs, CO 80903
(719) 473-5600

Mountain Sun Pub & Brewery
1535 Pearl Street
Boulder, CO 80302
(303) 546-0886

Oasis Brewery & Restaurant
1095 Canyon Boulevard
Boulder, CO 80302
(303) 449-0363

Phantom Canyon Brewing
2 E. Pike Peak Avenue
Colorado Springs, CO 90803
(719) 635-2800

Rock Bottom Brewery
1001 16th Street
Denver, CO 80265
(303) 534-7616

Rockies Brewing
(Wilderness Pub)
2880 Wilderness Place
Boulder, CO 80301
(303) 444-8448

San Juan Brewing
300 S. Townsend
Telluride, CO 81435
(970) 728-4587

Steamboat Brewery & Tavern
435 Lincoln Avenue
Steamboat Springs, CO 80477
(970) 879-2233

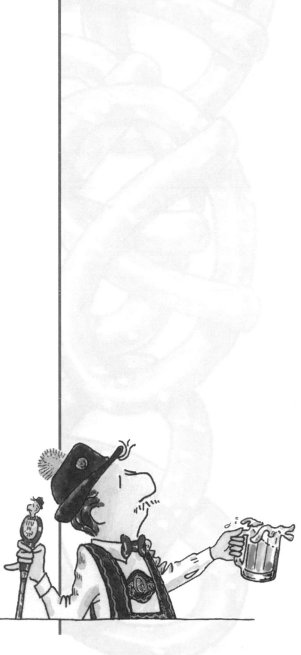

Tablerock Brewpub & Grill
705 Fulton
Boise, CO 83702
(208) 342-0944

Tommyknockers Brewery & Pub
1401 Miner Street
Idaho Springs, CO 80452
(303) 567-2688

Walnut Brewery
1123 Walnut
Boulder, CO 80302
(303) 447-1345

Wild Wild West Gambling Hall &
Brewery
443 E. Bennett Avenue
Cripple Creek, CO 80813
(719) 689-3736

Wynkoop Brewing
1534 18th Street
Denver, CO 80202
(303) 297-2700

FLORIDA
Beach Brewing
5905 S. Kirkman Road
Orlando, FL 32819
(407) 345-8802

Hops Grill & Bar
4502 W. 14th Street
Bradenton, FL 34207
(313) 756-1069

18825 U.S. Highway 19 North
Clearwater, FL 34624
(813) 531-5300

9826 San Jose Boulevard
Jacksonville, FL 32257
(904) 645-9355

4820 S. Florida Avenue
Lakeland, FL 34744
(813) 471-6200

33086 U.S. Highway 19 North
Palm Harbor, FL 34684
(813) 789-5678

14303 N. Dale Mabry Highway
Tampa, FL 33618
(813) 264-0522

326 N. Dale Mabry Highway
Tampa, FL 33609
(813) 871-3600

Irish Times Pub & Brewery
9920 Alt. A1A
Palm Beach Gardens, FL 33410
(407) 624-1504

Kelly's Caribbean Bar, Grill &
Brewery
301 Whitehead Street
Key West, FL 33040
(305) 293-8484

Market Street Pub
120 S.W. First Avenue
Gainesville, FL 32601
(904) 377-2927

McGuire's Irish Pub & Brewery
600 E. Gregory Street
Pensacola, FL 32501
(904) 433-6789

Mill Bakery, Eatery & Brewery
11491 Cleveland Avenue
Fort Meyers, FL 33907
(813) 939-2739

330 Fairbanks
Winter Park, FL 32789

Ragtime Tavern & Grill
207 Atlantic Boulevard
Jacksonville, FL 32233
(904) 241-7877

River City Brewing
835 Museum Circle
Jacksonville, FL 32207
(904) 398-2299

Riverwalk Brewery
111 S.W. 2nd Avenue
Fort Lauderdale, FL 33301
(305) 764-8448

Santa Rosa Bay Brewery
54 Miracle Strip Parkway
Fort Walton Beach, FL 32548
(904) 664-BREW

Sarasota Brewing
6607 Gateway Avenue
Sarasota, FL 34231
(813) 925-2337

Thai Orchid Restaurant & Brewery
317 Miracle Mile
Coral Gables, FL 33134
(305) 443-6364

HAWAII
Gordon Biersch Brewing
101 Ala Moana Boulevard #1123
(at Aloha Tower Marketplace)
Honolulu, HI 96813
(808) 599-4877

IDAHO
Coeur D'Alene Brewing
(T.W. Fisher's Brewpub)
204 N. 2nd Street
Coeur D'Alene, ID 83814
(208) 664-BREW

Harrison Hollow Brewhouse
2455 Harrison Hollow Boulevard
Boise, ID 83702
(208) 343-6820

McCall Brewing
807 N. 3rd Street
McCall, ID 83638
(208) 726-1832

Sun Valley Brewing
202 N. Main Street
Hailey, ID 83333
(208) 788-6319

Thunder Mountain Brewing
591 4th Street East
Ketchum, ID 83340
(208) 726-1832

Treaty Grounds Brewing
W. 2124 3rd Street
Moscow, ID 83843
(208) 883-4253

ILLINOIS
Blue Cat Brewpub
113 18th Street
Rock Island, IL 61201
(309) 788-8274

Box Office Brewery & Restaurant
145 N. 3rd Street
DeKalb, IL 60115
(815) 748-2739

Berghoff's
17 West Adams Street
Chicago, IL 60610
(312) 427-3170

Brewbakers Ale House & Deli
425 15th Street
Moline, IL 61265
(309) 762-3464

Capitol City Brewing and Bar & Grill
107 W. Cook Street
Springfield, IL 62704
(217) 753-5725

Galena Main Street Brewpub
300 N. Main Street
Galena, IL 61036
(815) 777-0451

Goose Island Brewing Company
1800 N. Clybourn
Chicago, IL 60614
(312) 915-0071

J.D. Nick's
1711 W. Highway 50
O'Fallon, IL 62269
(618) 632-BREW

Joe's Brewery
706 South 5th Street
Champaign, IL 61820
(217) 384-1790

Mickey Finn's Brewery
412 N. Milwaukee Avenue
Libertyville, IL 60048
(708) 362-6688

Mill Rose Brewing
45 S. Barrington Road
South Barrington, IL 60010
(708) 382-7673

River West Brewing Company
925 W. Chicago Avenue
Chicago, IL
(312) 226-3200

Rock Bottom Brewing Company
One West Grand Street
Chicago, IL 60610

Taylor Brewing
200 5th Avenue, E.
Naperville, IL 60563
(708) 717-8000

Weinkeller Brewery
6417 W. Roosevelt Road
Berwyn, IL 60402
(708) 749-2276

651 Westmont Drive
Westmont, IL 60559
(708) 789-2236

INDIANA
Bloomington Brewing Company
(Lennie's)
1795 East 10th Street
Bloomington, IN 47407
(812) 339-2256

Broad Ripple Brewpub
840 E. 65th Street
Indianapolis, IN
(317) 253-2739

Lafayette Brewing
622 Main Street
Lafayette, IN 47901
(317) 742-2591

Mishawaka Brewing
3703 N. Main Street
Mishawaka, IN 46545
(219) 256-9993

Oaken Barrel Brewing
50 N. Airport Parkway
Greenwood, IN 46143
(317) 887-2287

IOWA
Babe's: The Brewery
417 6th Street
Des Moines, IA 50309
(515) 244-9319

Dallas County Brewing
301 S. 10th Street
Adel, IA 50003
(515) 993-5064

Fitzpatrick's Alehouse
525 S. Gilbert
Iowa City, IA 52240
(319) 356-6900

Front Street Brewing
208 E. River Drive
Davenport, IA 52801
(319) 322-5280

Millstream Brewing
Lower Brewery Road
Amana, IA 52203
(319) 622-3672

KANSAS
Free State Brewing
636 Massachusetts
Lawrence, KS 66044
(913) 843-4555

Little Apple Brewing
110 W. Loop Center
Manhattan, KS 66502
(913) 539-5500

River City Brewing
150 N. Mosley
Wichita, KS 76202
(316) 263-BREW

KENTUCKY
Bluegrass Brewing Company
3929 Shelbyville Road
Louisville, KY
(502) 899-7070

Oldenberg Brewery & Entertainment
Complex
I-75 & Buttermilk Pike
Fort Mitchell, KY 41017
(606) 341-2802

Silo Microbrewery
630 Barret Avenue
Louisville, KY 40204
(502) 589-BREW

LOUISIANA
Crescent City Brewhouse
527 Decatur Street
New Orleans, LA 70130
(504) 522-0571

MAINE
Gritty McDuff's Brew Pub
396 Fore Street
Portland, ME 04101
(207) 772-BREW

Kennebunkport Brewing
(Federal Jack's Brew Pub)
8 Western Avenue
Kennebunk, ME 04043
(800) BREW-ALE

Lompoc Cafe & Brewpub
(Atlantic Brewing)
34-36 Rodick Street
Bar Harbor, ME 04609
(207) 288-9513

No Tomatoes Restaurant
(Great Falls Brewing)
36 Court Street
Auburn, ME 04210
(207) 784-3919

Sea Dog Brewing
43 Mechanic Street
Camden, ME 04843
(207) 236-6863

Sugarloaf Brewing
(Theo's Pub)
RR #1, Box 2268
Carrabasset Valley, ME 04947
(207) 237-2211

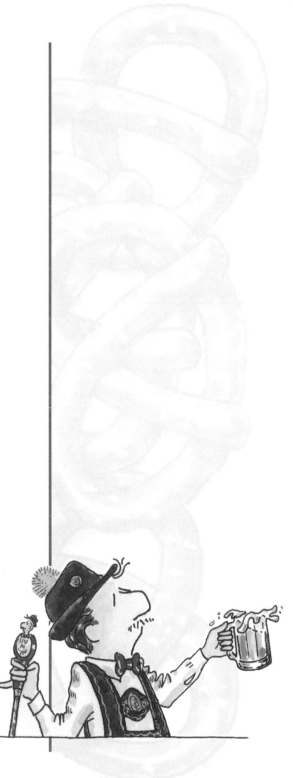

Sunday River Brewing
(The Moose's Tale)
1 Sunday River Road
Bethel, ME 04217
(207) 824-3541

MARYLAND
Baltimore Brewing
104 Albemarle Street
Baltimore, MD 21202
(410) 837-5000

Brewer's Alley
124 North Market Street
Frederick, MD 21701
(301) 631-0089

Olde Town Tavern & Brewery
227 E. Diamond Avenue
Gaithersburg, MD 20877
(301) 948-4200

Sisson's
(South Baltimore Brewing)
36 East Cross Street
Baltimore, MD 21230
(410) 539-2093

Wharf Rat Camden Yards
(Oliver Breweries)
206 W. Pratt Street
Baltimore, MD 21201
(410) 244-8900

MASSACHUSETTS
Atlantic Coast Brewing
50 Terminal Street
Boston, MA 02129
(617) 242-6464

Boston Beer Works
61 Brookline Avenue
Boston, MA 02215
(617) 536-2337

The Brewery at 34 Depot Street
34 Depot Street
Pittsfield, MA 01201
(413) 422-2072

Cambridge Brewing
1 Kendall Square, Bldg. 100
Cambridge, MA 02139
(617) 494-1994

Cape Cod Brew House
720 Main Street
Hyannis, MA 02601
(508) 775-4110

Commonwealth Brewing
138 Portland Street
Boston, MA 02114
(617) 523-8383

John Harvard's Brewhouse
33 Dunster Street
Cambridge, MA 02138
(617) 868-3585

Lowell Brewing
(Brewhouse Cafe & Grill)
199 Massachusetts 01854
(508) 937-1200

Northampton Brewery
Brewster Court Bar & Grill
11 Brewster Court
Northampton, MA 01060
(413) 584-9903

MINNESOTA
Rock Bottom Brewery
825 Hennepin Avenue
Minneapolis, MN 55402
(612) 332-BREW

Sherlock's Home
11000 Red Circle Drive
Minnetonka, MN
(612) 931-0203

MISSOURI
Flat Branch Pub & Brewing
115 S. 5th Street
Columbia, MO 65201
(314) 499-0400

St. Louis Brewery
2100 Locust Street
St. Louis, MO 63103
(314) 241-2337

75th Street Brewery
520 W. 75th Street
Kansas City, MO 64114
(816) 523-4677

Weathervane
1027 E. Walnut
Springfield, MO 65806
(417) 831-6676

MONTANA
Bayern Brewing
(Iron Horse Brewpub)
North Higgens Avenue
Missoula, MT 59807-8043
(406) 721-8705

Miles Town Brewing
(Golden Spur)
1014 S. Haynes
Miles City, MT 59301
(406) 232-3898

Spanish Peaks Brewing & Italian Cafe
120 N. 19th Avenue
Bozeman, MT 59715
(406) 585-2296

NEBRASKA
Crane River Brewpub & Cafe
200 N. 11th Street
Lincoln, NE 68508
(402) 476-7766

Jaipur Brewing
10922 Elm Street
Omaha, NE 68144
(402) 392-7331

Johnny's Brewing
4150 144th Street
Omaha, NE 68137
(402) 895-1122

Jones Street Brewery
1316 Jones Street
Omaha, NE 68102
(402) 344-3858

Lazlo's Brewery & Grill
710 P Street
Lincoln, NE 68508
(402) 474-2337

Sharkey's Brewery
777 Cass
Omaha, NE 68114
(402) 390-0777

NEVADA
Carson Depot Brewing
111 E. Telegraph
Carson City, NV 89701
(702) 884-4546

Great Basin Brewing
846 Victorian Avenue
Sparks, NV 89431
(702) 355-7711

HOLY COW!
Casino Cafe Brewery
2423 Las Vegas Blvd.
Las Vegas, NV 89104
(702) 732-2697

Union Brewery
28 North C Street
Virginia City, NV 89440

NEW HAMPSHIRE
Martha's Exchange
185 Main Street
Nashua, NH 03060
(603) 883-8781

Portsmouth Brewery
56 Market Street
Portsmouth, NH 03801
(603) 431-1115

Seven Barrel Brewing
Plainfield Road
West Lebanon, NH 03784
(603) 298-5566

NEW JERSEY
Long Valley Pub & Brewery
P.O. Box 368
Long Valley, NJ 07853

The Ship Inn
61 Bridge Street
Millford, NJ 08848
(908) 995-0188

Triumph Brewing Company
138 Nassau Street
Princeton, NJ 08540
(609) 924-7855

NEW MEXICO
Assetts Grille & Brewing
6910 Montgomery, N.E.
Albuquerque, NM 87109
(505) 889-6400

Organ Mountain Brewing
(O'Ryan's Tavern)
700 S. Telshor Boulevard
Las Cruces, NM 88001
(505) 522-8191

Preston Brewery
(Embudo Station Restaurant)
P.O. Box 154
Embudo, NM 87531
(505) 852-4707

Rio Bravo Restaurant & Brewery
515 Central Ave., N.W.
Albuquerque, NM 87102
(505) 242-6800

Sangre de Cristo Brewery
(Eske's Embudo Station)
106 Des Georges Lane
Taos, NM 87571
(505) 758-1517

Il Vincino Wood Oven Pizza
3403 Central Ave., East
Albuquerque, NM 87106
(505) 266-7855

NEW YORK
Abbott Square Brewpub
(Buffalo Brewing)
1830 Abbott Road
Buffalo, NY 14218
(716) 828-0004

Bighouse Brewing Co.
90 North Pearl Street
Albany, NY 12207
(518) 445-2739

Buffalo Brewpub
6861 Main Street
Williamsville, NY 14221
(716) 632-0552

Chapter House Brewpub
400 Stewart Avenue
Ithaca, NY 14850
(607) 277-9782

James Bay Restaurant & Brewery
154 W. Broadway
Port Jefferson, NY 11777
(516) 928-2525

Long Island Brewing
111 Jericho Turnpike
Jericho, NY 11735
(516) 334-BREW

Manhattan Brewing Company
Restaurant
40-42 Thompson Street
New York, NY 10013
(212) 925-1515

Mountain Valley Brewpub
122 Orange Avenue
Suffern, NY 10901
(914) 357-0101

Park Slope Brewing
3556 Sixth Avenue
Brooklyn, NY 11215
(718) 788-1756

Rochester Brewpub
800 Jefferson Road
Henrietta, NY 14623
(716) 272-1550

Rohrbach Brewing
315 Gregory Street
Rochester, NY 14620
(716) 244-5680

Syracuse Suds Factory
210-216 W. Water Street
Syracuse, NY 13202
(315) 471-2254

Troy Pub and Brewery
417-419 River Street
Troy, NY 12180
(518) 273-BEER

Westside Brewing Company
340 Amsterdam Avenue
New York, NY 10024
(212) 721-2161

NORTH CAROLINA
Dilworth Brewing
1301 East Boulevard
Charlotte, NC 28203
(704) 377-2739

Greenshields Pub & Brewery
214 East Martin Street
Raleigh, NC 27601
(919) 829-0214

Mill Bakery, Eatery & Brewery
122 W. Woodlawn Road
Charlotte, NC 28217
(704) 529-6455

Spring Garden Brewing
714 Francis King Street
Greensboro, NC 27410
(919) 299-3649

Spur Steak House & Saloon
(Toisnot Brewing)
513 N. Ward Boulevard
Wilson, NC 27893
(919) 237-0086

Tumbleweed Grill & Brewery
473 Blowing Rock Road
Boone, NC 28607
(704) 264-7111

Weeping Radish Restaurant &
Brewery
Highway 64 E.
Manteo, NC 27954
(919) 473-1157

OHIO
Barley's Brewpub
467 N. High Street
Columbus, OH 43215
(614) 228-2537

Burkhardt Brewing
3700 Massillon Road
Uniontown, OH 44685
(216) 896-9200

Captain Tony's Pizza & Pasta
Emporium
23200 Chagrin Boulevard
Beachwood, OH 44122
(216) 464-TONY

Great Lakes Brewing
2516 Market Street
Cleveland, OH 44113
(216) 771-4404

Hoster Brewing
550 S. High Street
Columbus, OH 43065
(614) 228-6066

Liberty Brewing Company
1238 Weathervane Lane
Akron, OH 44313
(216) 869-BEER

Melbourne's
(Strongsville Brewing)
12492 Prospect Road
Strongsville, OH 44136
(216) 238-4677

OKLAHOMA
Bricktown Brewery
One N. Oklahoma Avenue
Oklahoma City, OK 73104-2413
(405) 232-2739

Cherry Street Brewing
1516 S. Quaker
Tulsa, OK 74123
(918) 582-2739

Interurban Brewing
105 West Main Street
Norman, OK 73069
(405) 364-7942

Norman Brewing
102 W. Main Street
Norman, OK 73069
(405) 360-5726

Royal Bavaria Brewing
3401 S. Sooner Road
Moore, OK 73160
(405) 799-7666

Tulsa Brewing
7227 S. Memorial Drive
Tulsa, OK 74133
(918) 459-BREW

OREGON
Blue Pine Brewing
422 S.W. 5th Street
Grants Pass, OR 97526
(503) 476-0760

Bridgeport Brewing & Public House
1313 N.W. Marshall
Portland, OR 97209
(503) 241-7179

Cornelius Pass Roadhouse &
Brewery
Route 5, Box 340
Hillsboro, OR 97124
(503) 640-6174

Deschutes Brewery & Public House
1044 Bond Street, N.W.
Bend, OR 97701
(503) 382-9242

Edgefield Brewery
2126 S.W. Halsey Street
Troutdale, OR 97060
(503) 669-8610

Full Sail Brewery at the River Place
(The Pilsner Room)
0307 S.W. Montgomery
Portland, OR 97201
(503) 222-5343

Fulton Pub & Brewery
0618 S.W. Nebraska Street
Portland, OR 97201
(503) 246-9530

Golden Valley Brewery & Pub
980 E. 4th Street
McMinnville, OR 97128
(503) 472-BREW

High Street Pub
1243 High Street
Eugene, OR 97401
(503) 345-4905

Highland Pub & Brewery
4225 S.E. 182nd Avenue
Gresham, OR 97030
(503) 665-3015

Hillsdale Brewery & Public House
1505 S.W. Sunset Boulevard
Portland, OR 97201
(503) 246-3938

Lighthouse Brewpub
4157 N. Highway 101
Lincoln City, OR 97367
(503) 994-7238

Lucky Labrador Brewpub
915 S.E. Hawthorne
Portland, OR 97214
(503) 236-3555

McMenamin's
6179 S.W. Murray Boulevard
Beaverton, OR 97005
(503) 644-4562

2090 S.W. 8th Avenue
West Linn, OR 97005
(503) 656-2970

Mt. Hood Brewpub
87304 Government Camp Loop
Government Camp, OR 97028
(503) 272-3724

Nor' Wester Williamette Valley
Brewing
66 S.E. Morrison Street
Portland, OR 97214
(503) 222-9771

Northwestern Brewpub
711 S.W. Ankeny
Portland, OR 97205
(503) 226-2508

Oak Hills Brewpub
14740 N.W. Cornell Road
Portland, OR 97229
(503) 645-0286

Oregon Trail Brewing
(Old World Deli)
341 S.W. 2nd Street
Corvallis, OR 97333
(503) 758-3527

Portland Brewing
1339 N.W. Flanders Street
Portland, OR 97209
(503) 222-7150

Portland Brewing
(The Brewhouse Taproom & Grill)
2730 N.W. 31st Street
Portland, OR 97210

Rogue Ale Brewery & Tasting Room
(Oregon Brewing)
2320 O.S.U. Drive
Newport, OR 97365
(503) 867-3660

Rogue Brewery & Public House
31-B Water Street
Ashland, OR 97520
(503) 488-5061

Steelhead Brewery & Cafe
199 E. 5th Avenue
Eugene, OR 97401
(503) 686-BREW

Thompson Brewery & Public House
3575 Liberty Road
Salem, OR 97302
(503) 363-7286

Umpqua Brewing
328 S.E. Jackson
Roseburg, OR 97470
(503) 672-0452

West Bros. Bar B-Q
(Eugene City Brewing)
844 Olive Street
Eugene, OR 97401
(503) 345-8489

Whitecap Brewpub
(Full Sail Brewery)
506 Columbia Street
Hood River, OR 97031
(503) 386-2247

Widmer Brewing
(The Heathmen Bakery & Pub)
901 S.W. Salmon
Portland, OR 97205
(503) 227-5700

Wild River Brewery
249 N. Redwood Highway
Cave Junction, OR 97523
(503) 592-3556

Wild River Brewing & Pizza
595 N.E. East Street
Grants Pass, OR 97526
(503) 471-RIVR

Willamette Brew Pub
120 Commercial Street, N.E.
Salem, OR 97301
(503) 363-8779

PENNSYLVANIA
Allegheny Brewery & Restaurant
(Penn Brewing)
800 Vinial Street
Pittsburgh, PA 15212
(412) 237-9402

Dock Street Brewing
Brewery & Restaurant
Two Logan Square
Philadelphia, PA 19103
(215) 496-0413

Samuel Adams Brewhouse
1516 Sansom Street
Philadelphia, PA 19102
(215) 563-ADAM

Stoudt Brewery
(Black Angus Restaurant)
Route 272
Adamstown, PA 19501

RHODE ISLAND
Union Station Brewery
36 Exchange Terrace
Providence, RI 02903
(717) 484-4386

SOUTH DAKOTA
Fire House Brewing
610 Main Street
Rapid City, SD 57701
(605) 348-1915

TENNESSEE
Big River Grille & Brewing Works
222 Broad Street
Chattanooga, TN 37402
(615) 267-BREW

Bohannon Brewing
134 2nd Avenue, N.
Nashville, TN 37201
(615) 242-8223

Boscos Pizza, Kitchen & Brewery
7615 W. Farmington #30
Germantown, TN 38138
(901) 756-7310

Smoky Mountain Brewing
424 S. Gay Street
Knoxville, TN 37902
(615) 673-8400

TEXAS
Armadillo Brewing
419 East 6th Street
Austin, TX 78701
(512) 322-0039

Bitter End Brewing
311 Colorado
Austin, TX 78701
(512) 478-2337

Boardwalk Bistro
4011 Broadway
San Antonio, TX 78209
(210) 824-0100

Coppertank Brewing
504 Trinity Street
Austin, TX 78701
(512) 478-8444

Fredericksburg Brewing
245 W. Main Street
Fredericksburg, TX 78624
(210) 997-1646

Hubcap Brewery & Kitchen
1701 N. Market #130
Dallas, TX 75202
(214) 651-0808

Rock Bottom Brewery
6111 Richmond Avenue
Houston, TX 77057
(713) 974-2739

Village Brewery
2415 Dunstan Road
Houston, TX 77005
(715) 524-4677

Waterloo Brewing
401 Gaudalupe Street
Austin, TX 78701
(512) 477-1836

Yegua Creek Brewing
2920 N. Henderson
Dallas, TX 75206
(214) 824-BREW

UTAH
Ebenezer's Restaurant & Naisbitt's
Brewery
4286 Riverdale Road
Ogden, UT 84405
(801) 394-0302

Eddie McStiff's Brewpub
57 South Main
Moab, UT 84532
(801) 259-BEER

Red Rock Brewery
254 S. 200 Street West
Salt Lake City, UT 84101
(801) 521-7446

Salt Lake Brewing
(Squatter's Pub Brewery)
147 W. Broadway
Salt Lake City, UT 84101
(801) 363-BREW

Wasatch Brew Pub
(Schirf Brewing)
250 Main Street
Park City, UT 84060
(801) 645-9500

VERMONT

Latchis Grille
(Windham Brewery)
6 Flat Street
Brattleboro, Vermont 05301
(802) 254-4747

McNeill's Brewery
90 Elliot Street
Brattleboro, VT 05301
(802) 254-2553

Mountain Brewers
Route 4, The Marketplace
Box 140
Bridgewater, VT 05034
(802) 672-5011

Norwich Inn
(Jasper Murdock's Alehouse)
225 Main Street
Norwich, VT 05055
(802) 649-1143

Vermont Pub & Brewery
144 College Street
Burlington, VT 05401
(802) 865-0500

VIRGINIA

Bardo Rodeo
2000 Wilson Boulevard
Arlington, VA 22201
(703) 527-9399

Blue Ridge Brewing
709 W. Main
Charlottesville, VA 22901
(804) 977-0017

Legend Brewing
321 W. 7th Street
Richmond, VA 23219

Richbrau Brewing Co. and Restaurant
1214 E. Cary Street
Richmond, VA 23229
(804) 644-3018

WASHINGTON

Big Time Brewing
4133 University Way, N.E.
Seattle, WA 98105
(206) 545-4509

California & Alaska Street Brewery
4720 California Avenue, S.W.
Seattle, WA 98116
(206) 938-2476

Fish Brewing
(The Fish Bowl)
515 Jefferson Street, S.E.
Olympia, WA 98501
(206) 943-6480

Fort Spokane Brewery
West 401 Spokane Falls Blvd.
Spokane, WA 99201
(509) 838-3809

Grant's Brewery Pub
32 N. Front Street
Yakima, WA 98901
(509) 575-2922

Hazel Dell Brewpub
8513 NE Highway 99
Vancouver, WA 98665
(206) 576-0996

Kirkland Roaster & Ale House
(Hale's Ale)
109 Central Way
Kirkland, WA 98033
(206) 827-4359

Leavenworth Brewing
636 Front Street
Leavenworth, WA 98826
(509) 548-4545

Pacific Northwest Brewing
322 Occidental Ave., South
Seattle, WA 98104
(206) 621-7002

Red Hook Ale Brewery
(Trolleyman Pub)
3400 Phinney Ave., North
Seattle, WA 98103
(206) 548-8000

Red Hook Ale Brewery
(Forecasters Public House &
Taproom)
14300 NE 145th Street
Woodinville, WA 98072
(206) 483-3232

Roslyn Brewing
208 Pennsylvania Avenue
Roslyn, WA 98941
(509) 649-2232

Thomas Kemper Brewing
22381 Foss Road
Poulsbo, WA 98370
(206) 697-1446

Winthrop Brewing
155 Riverside Drive
Winthrop, WA 98862
(509) 996-3183

WASHINGTON, D.C

Capital City Brewing
1100 New York Avenue
Washington, D.C. 20005
(202) 628-2222

WEST VIRGINIA

West Virginia Brewing
1291 University Avenue
Morgantown, WV 26505-5450
(304) 296-BREW

WISCONSIN

Adler Brau
Appleton Brewing
1004 S. Olde Oneida Street
Appleton, WI 54915
(414) 731-3322

Brewmasters Pub Restaurant &
Brewery
4017 80th Street
Kenosha, WI 53142
(414) 694-9050

Cherryland Brewing
341 N. Third Avenue
Sturgeon, WI 54235
(414) 743-1945

Great Dane Brewing Company
123 East Doty
Madison, WI 53703
(608) 284-0000

Oconto Brewing Company
(Main Event Sports Bar & Grill)
121 Main Street
Oconto, WI 54153
(414) 834-4811

Randy's FunHunters Brewery
841 E. Milwaukee Street
Whitewater, WI 53190
(414) 473-8000

Rowland's Calumet Brewing
(The Roll Inn)
25 N. Madison Street
Chilton, WI 53014
(414) 849-2534

Water Street Brewery
1101 N. Water Street
Milwaukee, WI 53202
(414) 272-1195

WYOMING

Jackson Hole Pub & Brewery
265 S. Milward Street
Jackson, WY 83001
(307) 739-2337

EUROPEAN BREWERIES

BELGIUM
Abbaye de Scourmont
294 Route Du Rond-Point
6464 Forges-Lez-Chimay
Belgium
(32-60) 21-03-11

Abdij
Corsendonk
2360 Oud-Turnhout
Belgium
(32-14) 45-33-11

Brasserie Cantillon
Gheudestraat 56,
Anderlecht
1070 Brussels
Belgium
(32-25) 21-49-28

Brasserie de Kluis
46 Stoopkens Straat
3320 Hoegaarden
Belgium
(32-16) 76-98-11

Brasserie d'Orval S.A.
6823 Villers-Devant-Orval
Belgium
(32-61) 31-10-60

Brasserie DuPont
5 Rue Basse
7904 Tourpes-Leuze
Belgium
(32-69) 67-10-66

Brouwerij Boortgat
Breendonkdorp 58
2870 Breendonk-Puurs
Belgium
(32-3) 886-7121

Brouwerij Rodenbach
Spanjestraat 133-141
8800 Roeselare
Belgium
(32-51) 22-34-00

Brouwerij Slaghmuydler
Denderhoutembaan 2
B-9400 Ninove
Belgium
(32-54) 33-18-31

Lindemans Farm Brewery
257 Lenniksebaan
1712 Vlenzenbeek
Belgium
(32-2) 569-03-90

St. Bernardus Bry
Trappistenweg 23
B-8978 Watou-Poperinge
Belgium
(32-57) 38-80-21

Westmalle Abbey
Antwerpsesteenweg 496
2390 Malle
Belgium
(32-3) 312-05-35

CZECH REPUBLIC
Budweiser Budvar Brewery
Karoliny Svelte
370-21 Ceske Budejofice-Budweis
Czech Republic
(42-38) 7705111

Pilsner-Urquell
Plzensky Prazdroj
30497 Plzen
Czech Republic
(42-19) 7061111

Staropramen Brewery
Nadrazni 84
150 54 Prague 5
Czech Republic
(42-2) 245-91456

ENGLAND
Bass Brewers
137 High Street
Burton-on-Trent
Staffordshire DE14 1JZ
England
(44-1283) 511000

Charles Wells, Ltd.
The Brewery
Havelock Street
Bedford MK40 4LU
England
(44-1234) 272766

Einbecker Brauhaus
Papen Strasse 4-7
3352 Einbeck
Lower Saxony
England
(49-5561) 7970

Fuller, Smith & Turner
Griffin Brewery
Chiswick Lane South
London W4 2QB
England
(44-181) 996-2000

Marston, Thompson & Evershed
The Brewery
Shobnall Road
Burton-on-Trent
Staffordshire DE14 2BW
England
(44-1283) 531131

Samuel Smith
The Old Brewery
Radcaster, N. Yorkshire LS24 9SB
England
(44-1937) 832225

Shepherd Neame
17 South Street
Faversham Kent ME13 7AX
England
(44-1795) 532206

T & R Theakston, Ltd.
Wellgarth, Masham,
Ripon, N. Yorkshire HG4 4DX
England
(44-1765) 689544

FRANCE
Brasserie Castelain
13 rue Pasteur
62410 Bénifontaine
France
(33-21) 40 38 38

Brasserie de Saint Sylvestre
1 rue de la Chapelle
F-59114 St. Sylvestre-Cappel
France
(33) 28 40 15 49

Brasserie de Saverne
60 rue de Dettwiler
F-67700 Saverne
France
(33-88) 71 74 74

Brasserie Jeanne d'Arc
38 rue Anatole
France
F-59790 Ronchin
(33-20) 53 62 85

Brasseries KRONENBOURG
Boulevard de l'Europe
F-67210 Obernai
France
(33-88) 27 44 88

GERMANY
Brauerei Aying
Zornedingerstr 1
D-85653 Aying
Germany
080 95 880

Brauerei Pinkus Mueller
Kreuzstr 4-10
D-4400 Muenster
Germany

Bzrari-St. Pauli Brauerei
Hopfenstr 15
Postfach 30 0210
D-2000 Hamburg 364
Germany
040 311 030

Hacker-Pschorr Brau
Schwanthalerstrasse 113
D-8000 Munchen 2
Germany
(49) 51-06-8-00

Kulmbacher Reichelbrau A.G.
Postfach 1860
8650 Kulmbach
Germany
(49-9221) 7050

Lowenbräu
Nymphenburgerstr 4
D-80013 Munich 2
Germany
089 52 000

Paulaner Salvator Thomas Bräu
Hochstrasse 75
8000 Munchen 95
Germany
(49-89) 480050

Privatbrauerei Diebel
Brauerei Diebels Strasse 1
47661 Issum
Germany
(49-2835) 30146

Spaten-Franziskoner-Braeu
Marsstr 46-48
D-80018 Munich 2
Germany
089 51 22 0

HOLLAND
Heineken
Rietveldenweg 37
NL-5222 AP Den Bosch
Amsterdam, Holland
071 457155

Grolsche Bierbrouwerij
Brouwerijstr 1
Postbus 55
NL-7500 AB Entschede
Holland
053 833 333

IRELAND
Arthur Guinness & Son Co., Ltd.
St. James Gate
Dublin 8
Ireland
(353-1) 453-6700

ITALY
Birra Moretti
Viale Venezia 9
1-33100 Udine
Italy
(39-432) 530253

Birra Peroni Industriale
Zona Industriale la Stada 56
I-35100 Padua
Italy
049 773802

SCOTLAND
Caledonian Brewing Company
42 Slateford Road
Lothian EH11 1P4
Scotland
(44-131) 337-1286

Scottish Courage, Ltd.
Abbey Brewery
111 Holyrood Road
Edinburgh EH8 8YS
Scotland
(44-131) 552 9191

BREWERY TOURS

If you think drinking beer is enjoyable, then you'll have a ball at a brewery tour. Breweries are places of mystery and magic. What goes on there is much more complicated than television commercials would lead you to believe. Seeing the bottling and packaging and the huge lauter and mash tuns, smelling the brewery smells, and watching all the brewers walking around in rubber boots (there's a lot of water involved in making beer in both the brewing and cleaning-up processes) is an experience not to be missed.

Of course, one of the really fun things about going to a brewery is tasting all the beers. Every brewery tour is different, but all are highly interesting. After the tour you can usually taste a wide variety of beers brewed by these skilled craftsmen.

Brewery tours are also a great place to take the kids. Breweries are an excellent place to learn about chemistry. A brewery is like a chemistry set on a grand scale. Much can be learned about how foods and beverages are processed and how sugars convert into alcohol, etc. Most breweries have sarsaparilla or root beer to offer the kids.

While almost all the microbrewers and many of the larger commercial brewers have tours these days, some do not. Always call before you go. While all beer tours are unique because of the company's product or history, or both, some tours certainly stand out above the rest.

Anheuser-Busch, St. Louis, Missouri

This is the granddaddy of all brewery tours. It has history, volume, and pizzazz. Whether or not you like their beer, they have one of the best shows on Earth. The entire place is kept in exceptional condition, and you get the feel that

Anheuser-Busch has been making beer the same way for more than one hundred years.

The copper is shiny, and the wrought iron and other hints of the turn of the century make you feel like you're right in the midst of the first U.S. beer boom. Walking through the Anheuser-Busch brewing plant is like looking at a fully restored and well-oiled 1904 Rolls-Royce. How could something this old and this pretty actually work so well? It does. Budweiser is the world's bestselling beer, and visiting here gives a whole new appreciation for their beer. It's difficult to call Budweiser a lawnmower beer after visiting this shrine of beer making.

Heineken, Amsterdam, Holland

If Anheuser-Busch is the shrine of American beer making, Heineken is Mecca. If you are in Amsterdam you have to go on the Heineken tour. Like Anheuser-Busch, there's plenty of copper and stainless steel to go around, and you'll be escorted through their maze of operations. In the beer hall afterward you can watch a movie about the creation of Heineken while sampling the beer and eating cheese and crackers. It is one of the funnest times you will ever have.

Yuengling, Pottsville, Pennsylvania

While the big brewery tours are fun, you really can't call yourself a true beer fancier if you have not gone to America's oldest continuously operating brewery: Yeungling. Yeungling, originally called the Eagle Brewery, was founded in 1829. Their small brewery is still located in the "new" building, built in 1831, and all their beer is still brewed there.

The building is a national landmark, and a tour of it is a fascinating experience. The workers still clock in on punch clocks in use since the Civil War. There is also a wonderful beer museum chock-full of Yuengling memorabilia. Down the street from the brewery is the original Yuengling mansion, which is also on view to the public.

Other breweries within a day's drive of Yuengling include **Stoudt's** in Adamstown, Pennsylvania and **Frederick Brewing** in Frederick, Maryland. Both are excellent counterpoints to Yuengling, since both have been built in the last ten years. Stoudt's is notable for its founder and brewmaster, Carol Stoudt, whose passion for beer has won her respect and success—including fifteen medals from the Great American Beer Festival. At Fredrick Brewing you'll more than likely be given the tour by one of the company's founders. This group of young entrepreneurs fashions high-quality beers in a high-tech brewery. Don't miss trying their Hempen Ale, the only beer in the United States brewed with hemp seeds. It's deliciously refreshing.

Anchor Brewing Company, San Francisco, California

Anchor Brewing is one of the most famous brewing companies in the United States. On their tour you'll get a chance to learn about the unique beer they brew and the story of the man who revived the last of these unique breweries. Established in 1896, this is the oldest craft brewer on the West Coast. One of the funnest things is to watch them making steam beer—a one-of-a-kind process.

After visiting Anchor, go to one of the most famous brewpubs in America, **Buffalo Bill's** in Hayward, California. Bill Hayward is one of the founding fathers of the recent beer revolution. Another newer microbrewery to visit is **Sudwerk Privatbrauerie Hubsch**, also known as just Hubsch. Hubsch, based in Davis, California, makes traditional German-style beers. Founded in 1989, this is a shiny and gleaming brewery, an enjoyable experience for the whole family.

SURVIVING A FESTIVAL

There is one major rule at a beer festival: don't get sloppy drunk! A beer festival is a meeting where beer professionals and beer enthusiasts come to taste, talk, and learn about beer and what is going on in the beer industry. There will be anywhere from a dozen to more than one hundred breweries, each showing any number of beers. Try to take the time to actually comprehend what is going on around you.

1. You're there to taste—not chug. There are many beers at even the smallest of festivals. Don't try to pound down every beer. Taste the beer and try to learn what you're tasting.
2. Eat something before you go or while you're there. Make sure that you're not drinking on an empty stomach. What goes better with food than beer?

BEER FESTIVALS IN THE UNITED STATES AND CANADA

There are many festivals that take place across the United States and Canada, with more being added every year. They are usually well promoted in beer magazines and at beer retailers. To find out if there are any near you, call some of the breweries located nearest to you and ask them if they know of any scheduled in the coming months. Below are some of the better known festivals.

CALIFORNIA
California Festival of Beers
San Luis Obispo, California
(800) 549-1538

California Small Brewer's Festival
Mountain View, California
(408) 243-5861

KQED Beer and Food Fest
San Francisco, California
(415) 553-2200

COLORADO
Colorado Brewers Festival
Ft. Collins, Colorado
(303) 498-9070

Great American Beer Festival
Denver, Colorado
(303) 447-0816

Great Rocky Mountain Beer Festival
Copper Mountain, Colorado
(303) 968-2318, ext. 6505

FLORIDA
WMFE Beer Festival
Orlando, Florida
(407) 273-2300

Walt Disney World Beer Festival
Orlando, Florida
(September)

ILLINOIS
Beer Across America
Midwest Brewers Oktoberfest
Chicago, Illinois
(800) 854-BEER

Blues & Brews Cruise
Chicago, Illinois
(312) 692-2337

Midwest International Beer Exposition
Chicago, Illinois
(708) 678-0071

MASSACHUSETTS
Boston Brewers Festival
Boston, Massachusetts
(617) 547-2233

Great New England Brewers Festival
Northampton, Massachusetts
(413) 584-9903

MICHIGAN
Taste of the Great Lakes
Frankenmuth, Michigan
(517) 652-3445

NEW YORK
New York Beerfest (International
Beer & Food Tasting
Under the Brooklyn Bridge)
New York, New York
(718) 855-7882, ext. 21

NORTH CAROLINA
Craft Brewer's Festival
Manteo, North Carolina
(800) 896-5403

Southeastern Microbrewers
Invitational
Raleigh, North Carolina
(April)

OREGON
Northwest Microbrew Expo
Eugene, Oregon
(800) 284-6529

Oregon Brewer's Festival
Portland, Oregon
(503) 222-7150

PENNSYLVANIA
Great Eastern Invitational
Microbrewers Festival
Adamstown, Pennsylvania
(717) 484-4386

Ironworks Festival of Beers
Pittsburgh, Pennsylvania
(412) 276-0122
Stoudt Oktoberfest
Adamstown, Pennsylvania
(717) 484-4386

RHODE ISLAND
Rhode Island International Beer Expo
Providence, Rhode Island
(401) 274-3234

SOUTH CAROLINA
Octoberfest
(Myrtle Beach Beer Festival)
Myrtle Beach, South Carolina
(910) 579-8985

VERMONT
Vermont Brewers Festival
Burlington, Vermont
(800) 864-5927

Sugarbush Brewers Festival
Warren, Vermont
(September)

WASHINGTON
Great Northwest Microbrewery
Invitational
Seattle, Washington
(206) 232-2982

Northwest Ale Festival
Seattle, Washington
(206) 527-7331
(206) 634-1433

WISCONSIN
Blessing of the Bock
Milwaukee, Wisconsin
(414) 372-8800

Great Taste of the Midwest
Madison, Wisconsin
(608) 256-1100

Southport Brewers Festival
Kenosha, Wisconsin
(414) 694-9050

Wisconsin Microbrewers Beerfest
Chilton, Wisconsin
(414) 849-2534

CANADA
International Brewmasters' Festival
Vancouver, Canada
(604) 688-9609

Le Mondial de la Bière
Montreal, Canada
(514) 722-9640

(continued)

3. Pace yourself. Many people try to drink everything they can to beat the crowds out of the parking lot. Forget it. Take your time. Take only small tastes, and make sure you don't frontload all of your drinking (drink a lot when you first arrive).

4. Finally, and most importantly, you must have a designated driver or access to public transportation. No matter how good you are at an event like this, make sure you have an alternative way to get home. Don't drive drunk.

BEER MUSEUMS

At long last it's possible to combine one's favorite pastime (drinking beer) with one's pursuit of culture (museum-going). All sorts of surprises await in these out-of-the-ordinary shrines. Call ahead for visiting hours, and if tours are available by all means take them!

Of course, like anything else, there is good, better, and best. And the best museum out there in the United States is the American Museum of Brewing History and Arts. Located in Fort Mitchell, Kentucky, it is one of the largest collections of historical beer artifacts currently on display. With more than fifty thousand individual historical items on view, this museum is certainly the biggest and the best. It is actually several different large collections that were bought by the Oldenberg Brewery and are part of their brewery tour.

The collection also features 15 hundred beer bottles (some old, some new) arranged by state, so that you can look and experience some state pride. All fifty states are represented. The tour of the museum and brewery takes about fifty minutes. The tour guides are all collectors themselves, collecting labels, beer cans, and other breweriana. And all of them have an excellent knowledge, not only of the collection, but of the history of brewing and the value and uniqueness of what is there. These people know beer!

David P. Heidrich, owner and president of the beer museum and the Oldenberg Brewing Company also hopes to open the largest public library yet established on brewing. Oldenberg is one of the better Mid-western microbrewers, whose Bock, Winter Ale, and Premium Verum are some of the best beers of their kind and are highly recommended.

Oldenberg Brewery and the beer museum are open seven days a week, 10 A.M.–5 P.M., 12 to 5 on Sundays. There is a fee of four dollars, but this does include a very generous tasting at the end. While it is slightly unusual to charge for a tour of this kind, it is money well spent.

David Heinrich's company is one of the most proactive micro-breweries when it comes to fanning the flames of beer interest. Oldenberg also sponsors two other events that all beer lovers will want to know about. The most well known of their learning excursions is Beer Camp. Approximately three hundred people fill the course twice a year, and beer aficionados spend three glorious days learning about the intricacies of beer. Whether you are a newcomer or an expert, the instructors at Beer Camp are there to help you further your knowledge of one of the world's oldest beverages—including vertical tastings of the brewery's and other beers. As many as three hundred fifty beers have been tasted in one of the weekends. With hotels right across the street from the brewery and museum, it's easy to get to the many discussions, seminars, and other activities jammed into this festive and knowledge-packed weekend.

The second is something quite different: Oldenberg's Brews Cruise. Done in association with Windjammer cruises, the tour starts in Grenada, then goes on to Bequia, St. Vincent, St. Lucia, Dominica, and finally Antigua—all on a Windjammer tall ship. The first cruise was sold out, and Oldenberg intends to schedule more cruises. The stops all coincide with visits to some of the most famous Caribbean breweries, as well as one distillery where rum is made. The package price also includes airfare.

Other beer museums worth seeing are the collections at the Anheuser-Busch tour in St. Louis, Missouri, where you'll also get a guided tour of the Clydesdales. The D.G. Yuengling Brewery, in Pottsville, Pennsylvania is of particular interest. The Yeungling Mansion, which is now a regional arts center, and the Pabst Mansion in Milwaukee, Wisconsin, are great windows into how the world's beer barons used to live. The Museum of Brewing and Brewery in New Ulm, Minnesota, which is part of the Schell Brewing Company, also has an excellent collection and is certainly one of the better tours available.

Of course, for those of you who want that more historic feeling, you'll have to travel to Newport, Rhode Island, to drink in this country's oldest operating tavern, the White Horse Tavern, established in 1673. It is located on the corner of Marlborough and Farewell Streets, in Newport (401) 849-3600.

If you have a deep interest in seeing how barrels are made, you can go to the Cooperage Museum, also in Fort Mitchell, Kentucky. While they make whiskey barrels instead of beer barrels, construction is essentially the same, and it is quite interesting. The other place to go would be the Museum of American Glass in Millville, New Jersey.

Cooperage Museum
I-65 Exit 112 on KY-245
Clermont, KY 40110
(502) 543-9877

Bradburry Barrel Company
100 Main Steet
Bridgewater, ME 04735
(207) 429-8141

Museum of American Glass
Glasstown Road
Millville, NJ 08332
(609) 825-6800

American Beer Museum
Oldenberg Complex
I-75 Exit 186
Ft. Mitchell, KY 41017
(606) 341-2802

City Brewery Museum
Galena, Illinois
(815) 777-0354

One Hundred Center
Mishawaka, Indiana
(219) 259-7861

August Schell Brewing
Company
New Ulm, Minnesota
(507) 354-5528

Wolf Brewery Caves
Stillwater, Minnesota
(612) 439-3588

F.X. Matt Brewery, (formerly the
West End Brewery)
Utica, New York
(315) 732-3181

Seattle Microbrewery Museum
Seattle, Washington
(206) 622-1880

The Pabst Mansion
Milwaukee, Wisconsin
(206) 622-1880

Yuengling Brewery & Mansion
Pottsville, Pennsylvania
(717) 628-4890

BEER BY MAIL

One of the most popular gifts you can give a beer enthusiast is the gift of brew through the mail. Wonderful packages, ranging from four- to twelve-packs, can be sent to the lucky recipient's home once a month. Most of the beers featured are special recipes from American microbrews, some of which are not available on the retail market. These are excellent gifts and will bring at least a year's worth of enjoyment and appreciation.

Ale in the Mail
(800) SEND ALE

Beer Across America, Inc.
55 Albrecht Drive
Lake Bluff, IL 60044
(800) 845-BEER

Beers to You
(800) 619-BEER

The Brew Tour
P.O. Box 471
Oregon City, OR 97045
(800) 660-TOUR

Brewmasters International
(800) 571-7133

Great American Beer Club
480 Scotland Road
Lakemoor, IL 60050
(800) 879-2747

Hog's Head Beer Cellars
620 S. Elm Street #112
Greensboro, NC 27406
(800) 992-CLUB

MicroBrew Express
222 Calle del Luna, Suite 4
Santa Clara, CA 95054
(800) 962-3377

Rare Brews, a division of Sommelier du Courrier
(800) 824-5562

Worldwide Beer Club
(888) 2 BUY BEER

BEER CLUBS DELIVER

There is an alternative way to quench a thirst for crafted beers when a home brew, U-brew, or microbrew is not available—the beer club. These are a more spirited version of the fruit-of-the-month clubs, a beer a month. Tap (pardon the pun) into their 800 numbers and, like the pizza man, they deliver. Call to discuss their microbrew labels and terms. It's easy, and so is drinking up one month's supply before the next arrives.

The following is a sampling of Beer of the Month Clubs at the time of publication:

- The Brewer's Gourmet
  1-800-591-BREW
  42 Pope Road, Box 6611
  Holliston, MA 01746

- BrewTap
  1-800-940-BREW
  336 6th Street
  San Francisco, CA 94103

- Brew to You, Ltd.
  1-800-800-BREW
  Woodstock, IL 60098

- Red, White & Brew
  1-800-670-BREW
  Herndon, VA 22070

COOKING WITH BEER

9

CHAPTER

BOTTLED BY
ADAMS MEDIA CORPORATION

EATING AND COOKING WITH BEER

When you think of beer and food, you might think of the kind of food you'd get at the local bar. However, the great chefs of the world have been cooking with beer longer than they have been cooking with wine. There are wonderful beer and food combinations worth reading about and experimenting with, but there are certain things that you need to familiarize yourself with before you start mixing and matching.

Beer is a lot like wine. White wine is more popular in the summer because it tends to go with lighter fare. Red wine is better to drink in winter because it stands up to hardier foods and is a heavier wine. There are also beers that are better experienced in the fall than in the summer, and there are beers that are better with particular foods. Does that mean you can't have a glass of red in summer? No.

For example, Pete's Wicked Summer Brew, a light ale with a hint of lemon, is perfect for summer with a salad, a large sandwich with cold cuts, or seafood. Summer is a time of year that brings out thirst. You don't want to be drinking double bock or chocolate stout after mowing the lawn. That's why lite beers are popular. And with dessert, which could be a fresh fruit pie or fruit with ice cream or sorbet, are you going to have a porter? Probably not; instead, try a framboise or a cherry wheat.

What if it's wintertime and you've just ordered a nice, thick, hardy stew, a big bowl of chili, or a steak smothered in mushrooms? You don't want a light beer now. You want something with guts to it: a dark ale or maybe a bock. Maybe for dessert you're going to have a hot cobbler or a hot chocolate bread pudding with ice cream. Now would be a perfect time for a thick, creamy stout or a chocolate porter.

Keep in mind that no one will laugh at you if you have a porter when it's 98° out in the shade. It's also okay to order a wheat beer to go with your steak in the deep, cold heart of winter. But in the event that you want to drink these beers as they were originally intended to be drunk, you should seriously take into account the time of year and meal provided.

Wine gentrifies, beer unifies.

—W. Scott Griffiths,
Chefs Cook With Beer

BEER MATCHES BY FOOD AND SEASON

BEER	FOOD	SEASON
American pale lager	Burgers, dogs, pizza	All seasons
American dark lager	Chili, potato skins, roasted meats	Fall, Winter, Early Spring
Bock beers	Roasted meats, especially game	Fall, Winter
Eisbock (ice beer)		
Doppelbock		
Hellesbock		
Maibock		
Tripelbock		
Weizenbock		
Diat pils (pils)	Burgers, dogs, pizza	All seasons
Dunkel	Roasted meats	Fall, Winter
Export lager	Seafood	All seasons
German pale lagers	Spicy foods and seafood	All seasons
German dark lagers	Stews and meat dishes	Fall, Winter
Ice beer	Roasted meats	Fall, Winter, Early Spring
Malt liquor	Does not go well with food	All seasons
Marzen	German sausages	Fall, Winter
Munchener	German sausages and veal dishes	All seasons
Pilsners (imports)	All foods	All seasons
Rauchbier (smoked beer)	Especially good with smoked foods	Fall, Winter, Early Spring
Red beer (rojo, rouge, or rot)	Spicy foods; meat dishes	Fall, Winter, Spring
Vienna lager		
Belgian Flanders beer		
Brown ale	Stews and foods with heavy sauces	Fall, Winter, Spring
Pale ale	All foods	All seasons
Porter	Thick steaks, chops	Fall, Winter, Early Spring
Scottish ales	Meat dishes	Fall, Winter, Early Spring
Stout	Thick steaks, chops	Fall, Winter, Early Spring
Trappist	All foods	All seasons
Wassail	Desserts	Winter
Wheat beers	Burgers, sausages, seafood	Spring, Summer
Witbier (biere blanche)	Burgers, sausages, seafood	Spring, Summer

BEER IN FOOD: THE RECIPES

Now that we've looked at which beers go best with which
types of foods at what times of year, let's explore beer's versa-
tility in the foods we love. The following recipes are divided into
these categories:

1. Soups, Sauces, and Dressings
2. Meats
3. Fish
4. Breads
5. Vegetables
6. Desserts

Each category and recipe has suggestions for beers
that complement the other ingredients. However, you as
the chef make the final decision, and the best thing to do
is experiment with the recipes until you find the beer that
tastes best.

Many beer enthusiasts simply substitute beer for wine
in a well-loved recipe. This is a good way to experiment—
don't by shy! If you're a beer lover, you probably already
know that the variety and quality of beer now available is
inspiring chefs across the country. The result is that more
and more recipes are being published in fine cooking
magazines and books, so keep an eye out in your local
kiosk or bookstore for new recipes. Never forget that
beer has been a culinary pleasure for as long as
humankind has been cooking, so congratulate yourself on
being part of history by adding an ale, lager, or stout to
your next meal.

SOUPS, SAUCES, AND DRESSINGS

HEARTY BEER AND VEGETABLE SOUP

1/2 cup olive oil
1 large onion, chopped
2 large carrots, chopped
3 large celery stalks, chopped
8 small new potatoes with skin, quartered
1 cup water
2 bottles beer (preferably an amber or red beer)
5 beef- or chicken-flavored bouillon cubes
2 small zucchinis, chopped
1 medium butternut squash, peeled and chopped
1 large can whole tomatoes
1/2 cup corn
1/2 cup red kidney beans
1/2 cup lima beans
1 1/2 teaspoons salt
1/2 cup Romano or Parmesan cheese, grated

In a large pot, sauté onion, carrots, celery, and potatoes until all are generously coated with olive oil. Cook at low heat for 5–10 minutes. Add water, beer, bouillon cubes, zucchinis, butternut squash, tomatoes, and corn. Cook for 20 minutes. Then add beans, salt, and grated cheese. Cook another 40 minutes at low heat. Serve hot.

COLD RASPBERRY FRAMBOISE SOUP

2 quarts fresh raspberries or 4 small packages frozen
*   raspberries*
2 1/2 cups Lindemans Framboise Lambic beer
1 tablespoon cinnamon
2 tablespoons cornstarch
fresh whipped cream
fresh mint

In a large saucepan, add raspberries, beer, and cinnamon. Bring to a boil and simmer for 15 minutes. Add cornstarch and mix until thickened. Remove from heat and refrigerate. Serve cold with dollop of fresh whipped cream and garnish with a sprig of mint. Serves 4–6.

OLD-FASHIONED FRENCH ONION SOUP GRATINEE WITH BOCK

¼ cup olive oil
4 cups onion, sliced
1 teaspoon honey
1 tablespoon flour
1 cup bock beer
2 cups condensed beef broth
1 loaf French bread
1 pound sliced Swiss cheese

In a stock pot over medium heat, add oil, onions, and honey. Cook for 10 minutes, making sure not to burn the onions. Stir in the flour and mix well. Add bock beer and the beef broth. Bring to a boil and then lower heat and simmer for about 15 minutes.

Preheat oven to 425°F. While the soup is boiling, slice the French bread into thick, generous slices, one for each person to be served. Toast the slices of bread in the oven until golden brown, turning so both sides are toasted. It should take no longer than 5 minutes. When soup is ready, pour into individual bowls. Into each bowl float a toasted piece of French bread. Place the bowls on a cookie sheet, and place the Swiss cheese slices on top of the bread. Place cookie sheet in oven for 10–12 minutes. Serve with the rest of the fresh French bread on the side.

CHEESE AND BEER FONDUE

2 tablespoons salted butter
1 clove garlic, crushed
2 cups Gruyere cheese, grated
⅓ cup smoked beer, or bock, ESB, or Scotch ale
1 tablespoon flour
salt and pepper
French bread chunks (or other gourmet hardcrust bread)
fresh fruit chunks (firm fruits like apples, pears, or strawberries)
chunks of cooked ham, beef, turkey, or chicken

What beer you choose for the fondue is up to you. A strong, flavorful beer is recommended, but not a porter or a stout. If you don't want or can't find a smoked beer, a bock, an extra special bitter, or a Scotch ale would be an excellent substitution.

In a large pan melt the butter and add crushed garlic. Make sure the pan is thoroughly coated on the sides to prevent the cheese from sticking to the pan. Add cheese, beer, and flour, and cook over a low flame while stirring with a whisk. Continue to stir as the cheese melts. Add salt and pepper to taste. When the mixture is smooth and creamy, it's ready to serve. Make sure during serving that the fondue is kept warm. Dip in assorted breads, fruits, and meats.

BEER BARBECUE SAUCE

2 tablespoons cooking oil
1 small onion, minced
$1/2$ cup beer
1 small can tomato sauce (approx. 8 ounces)
1 small jar duck sauce (or other sweet-and-sour fruit mixture)
$1/2$ cup brown sugar
1 tablespoon Worcestershire sauce
3 teaspoons chili powder
2 teaspoons salt
2 teaspoons black pepper
$1/2$ teaspoon cayenne pepper

The beer you use can be to your own taste, but try a bock or some kind of beer brewed with honey.

In a saucepan, brown onions in cooking oil until translucent. Stirring constantly, add beer, tomato sauce, and remaining ingredients. Bring to slight boil and remove from heat. Baste chicken, ribs, or any other kind of meat with sauce and serve extra sauce on the side with the grilled meat.

FRAMBOISE VINAIGRETTE

$1/4$ cup Lindemans Framboise
$1/4$ cup olive oil
1 teaspoon raspberry jam
1 tablespoon lemon oil

1 clove garlic, crushed
1 teaspoon Dijon mustard
$\frac{1}{3}$ teaspoon salt
$\frac{1}{2}$ teaspoon pepper

In a cruet or jar with a tight-fitting lid, add the entire contents and mix thoroughly. It is important to make sure the jam is thoroughly incorporated.

MEATS

PORTER CHILI

6 slices bacon, chopped
1 pound ground meat
    (beef or a mixture of pork and beef)
1 large onion, chopped
3 cloves garlic, crushed
1 cup porter of your choice
$\frac{1}{2}$ teaspoon salt
1 teaspoon pepper
1 16-ounce can whole tomatoes
3 tablespoons chili powder
1 teaspoon cumin
2 ears corn-on-the-cob
1 12-ounce can black beans
1 12-ounce can chick peas/garbanzo beans
1 teaspoon Tabasco

Heat large pot and cook bacon slightly. Do not cook fully. Add ground beef, onion, and garlic, and stir until meat is browned and onions somewhat cooked. Add porter, salt, and pepper. Mix in well. Add tomatoes and make sure to break the tomatoes up as you stir and thoroughly mix them in. Add chili powder and cumin, and cook for 10–15 minutes. Slice ears of corn and add the corn (slices), beans, and Tabasco. Cook for 45–60 minutes at medium to low heat. Serve hot.

STOUT BEEF STEW

1 teaspoon salt
2 teaspoons pepper
4 tablespoons all-purpose flour
2¹/₂ pounds beef chunks, cut into 1-inch cubes
4 teaspoons cooking oil
1 large clove garlic, crushed
1 small bag pearl onions
12 ounces stout beer
2 cups beef broth
1 small bag whole baby carrots
1 small bag frozen peas
2 cups mushrooms, chopped
7 new potatoes, chopped
2 bay leaves

Combine salt, pepper, and flour and mix well. Coat each piece of meat in the flour mixture. In a pot, over medium heat, pour in oil. Add meat chunks a few at a time, making sure to brown all the sides. Remove browned meat. Into the drippings, add garlic and onions and sauté for 3–4 minutes. Return the meat and remaining ingredients to the pot. Bring to a slight boil, then cover the stock pot and let simmer on low to medium heat for 2 hours. Stir occasionally, but do not over-stir. Some chefs would prefer to add the vegetables later to ensure their crispness, but this is up to the cook. Remember that the longer you simmer the vegetables in the beer, the more complex and flavorful your dish will be.

PORTER PORTERHOUSE OR LONDON BROIL

1 large steak, either London broil or porterhouse
1 bottle porter
6 tablespoons olive oil
1 tablespoon Worcestershire sauce
2 tablespoons fresh ground pepper

Marinate meat in porter in a deep dish. Generally, this should be done either the night before or as early as possible on the day of cooking, depending on how intense you want the beer taste to be. Just before cooking, separate the meat and the beer. Add ¹/₂ cup beer to olive oil and Worcestershire sauce. Put meat on a hot grill and baste with beer-oil-Worcestershire mixture, then pepper each side. Grill to preferred doneness.

BIG BEER-GLAZED HAM (OR CHICKEN)

1 ham or chicken (whole or pieces)
1 cup chocolate porter
¹/₄ cup dark brown sugar
3 tablespoons cornstarch
2 tablespoons butter
1 tablespoon honey

Preheat oven to 325°F. Place ham in oven when preheated. In a saucepan, mix beer, brown sugar, and cornstarch. Cook over low heat until smooth and thick. Stir in butter and honey. Remove from heat. Spoon the sauce over the meat every 15–30 minutes until done, usually 1–2 hours. For chicken: Use during cooking, basting as you broil or grill.

BEER & SAGE GRILLED CHICKEN

4 whole chicken breasts
8 fresh sage leaves
1 bottle beer (any kind)
salt and pepper to taste

Put 2 sage leaves under the skin of each chicken breast. Marinate the breasts in beer for at least 1 hour. Before grilling, season with salt and pepper to taste. Grill over a hot flame.

PORK CHOPS WITH SPICY BEER SAUCE

2 tablespoons cumin seeds
2 teaspoons red pepper flakes
4 thick-cut pork chops
salt and pepper to taste
1 tablespoon olive oil
1 cup beer (any kind)

Preheat oven to 350°F. Spread cumin seeds on a cookie sheet and toast in oven for several minutes. When cooled, grind the toasted seeds and add the red pepper flakes. Rub the chops generously with this seasoning and salt and pepper. In a cast iron or heavy skillet, add the olive oil. Cook the chops in the olive oil over high heat until crispy on both sides (approximately 4–8 minutes per side).

Remove chops from pan and place on a platter. Pour the beer into the pan and stir the cooked bits of seasoning. Bring the beer to a boil and cook for about 2 minutes. Pour over chops and serve.

MIDWESTERN-STYLE BRATWURST

bratwurst, for as many folks as you want to feed
beer, enough to immerse the bratwurst

Boil the bratwurst in your beer of choice, then grill until crispy on the outside. Serve with other picnic fare.

FISH

TEXAS BEER-BATTERED FRIED SHRIMP

peanut oil (enough to fry within skillet)
1 cup flour
2 teaspoons paprika
1/4 teaspoon cayenne pepper
1 teaspoon salt
1 1/2 cups beer of your choice
extra flour (enough to coat shrimp; approx. 1 cup)
1 1/2 lbs. raw shrimp, peeled and deveined

Preheat peanut oil in a large, deep pot or deep-fryer to 400°F. Combine flour, paprika, cayenne pepper, and salt. Gradually beat in beer until batter is quite thin. Place extra flour in a bowl. Dip each shrimp into extra flour first, and then into the batter. Deep fry in peanut oil for 2 minutes. Place shrimp on paper towels to drain. Serve hot. Serves 4–6.

BEER-STEAMED CRABS

2 bottles beer
1 cup vinegar
2 dozen crabs
1 cup Old Bay seafood seasoning
½ cup salt

In a large seafood steamer, pour in beer and vinegar. We recommend a porter or stout; however, for a lighter flavor, you might want to try some other very flavorful beer. Some people like wheat beer because it imparts a uniquely sour taste. Preheat the steamer for 5 minutes. Layer the crabs in the steamer, covering each layer generously with Old Bay and salt. Continue this process until all the crabs and seasonings are used. Steam for 20 minutes or until all the crabs on top are red.

BREADS

LIA'S MOM'S BEER BREAD

3 cups self-rising flour (or 3 cups regular flour and 2 teaspoons
*   baking soda)*
2 tablespoons sugar
1 cup cheddar cheese, grated
1 bottle beer of choice

Preheat oven to 350°F. In a greased breadloaf pan, mix all the ingredients. Bake for approximately 30 minutes. For a variation, add 2 tablespoons dill or 1 cup diced onions.

ROBIN'S BUCKWHEAT CREPES

¾ cup all-purpose flour
¼ cup buckwheat flour
3 eggs
½ cup water

¹/₃ cup beer (bitter Belgian lambic beer is best)
Savory filling of your choice: shredded barbequed duck or pork,
creamed chicken, roasted vegetables, or stir fry

Combine both flours in a large bowl. In a separate smaller bowl whisk together the milk and eggs. Add the liquid to the flour, whisking until smooth. Add the beer and whisk until smooth. In a crepe pan or a skillet coated with non-stick cooking spray, spread approximately ¹/₄ cup of the crepe mixture in the pan until the entire surface of the pan is coated. Cook 1 minute or so per side. Stack cooked crepes on a plate kept warm over a pan of simmering water until all the batter is used. Fill crepes with savory filling of your choice and, if desired, top with sprinkled cheese.

VEGETABLES
PRENDERGAST BEER CARROTS

1 small bag baby carrots
1 bottle Bass Ale or favorite dark beer
    (such as chocolate porter)
1 teaspoon sugar
1 tablespoon butter
1 tablespoon dried dill

Melt butter in pan. Add carrots and cook well until well coated and cook a few minutes at low heat. Add sugar and cover pan and simmer on very low heat for 10 minutes. Add dill and simmer another 10 minutes without cover. Serve hot.

GREEN BEANS ALMONDINE DOUBLE BOCK

3 cups fresh green beans, snapped
¹/₂ cup double bock beer
3 tablespoons butter
¹/₂ cup sliced almonds

Steam green beans 5–7 minutes. In a separate, large pan pour in double bock and butter. Bring to a boil and reduce for 5–7 minutes, stirring occasionally. Blend in sliced almonds. When string beans have been cooked, place into mixture and toss until coated. Serve hot.

Spicy Sauerkraut

> 1 packet precooked sauerkraut
> 1–2 teaspoons red pepper flakes
> pinch of caraway seeds
> 1/4 cup beer

Strain the sauerkraut and place it in a saucepan over a low flame. Add the red pepper flakes, caraway seeds, and beer. Bring to a boil, then remove from heat and serve.

Randall Elley's Borracho Beans (Drunk Beans)

> 2 cups dried pinto beans
> 1 clove garlic, crushed
> 3–4 strips cooked bacon, crumbled
> 2 teaspoons salt
> 2 tablespoons bacon drippings
> 1 onion, chopped
> 2 jalapeno peppers
> 2 whole tomatoes, or a 16-ounce can, drained
> 1 6-pack of beer (1 beer for the beans and 5 for you)

Soak beans in water overnight. Drain and cover with fresh water. Add garlic, bacon, and salt. Simmer for 2 1/2 hours or until beans are soft. Drink beer while the mixture simmers. Drain the beans, reserving the liquid. Heat bacon drippings and sauté the onion, peppers, and tomatoes until soft. Stir the vegetables into the beans and simmer 5 minutes. Just before serving, add beer and as much reserved liquid as desired into beans. Serve hot. Have the last of the beer with the beans. Any leftover beans can be mashed and used as refried beans in your favorite Mexican recipe.

DESSERT

STRAWBERRIES FRAMBOISE

1 package fresh strawberries
1 heaping tablespoon sugar
1 bottle Lindemans Framboise Lambic Beer
1 quart vanilla ice cream

About one-half hour before dinner is ready to be served, clean and slice strawberries. In a bowl, combine the strawberries, sugar, and beer. Stir thoroughly until completely mixed. Cover bowl and set in refrigerator. When ready to serve, place ice cream in separate bowls and top with strawberry mixture. Top with whipped cream or chocolate shavings, if desired.

MARTI'S SUPER-MOIST DEVIL'S FOOD CAKE

1 package devil's food cake mix
3 eggs
1¼ cup beer
½ cup oil

Combine cake mix, eggs, beer, and oil in a large bowl. With an electric mixer, beat at low speed until moistened. Turn beater to high and beat for 2 minutes. Divide batter into two 8- or 9-inch cake pans and bake according to manufacturer's specifications.

The beer makes the cake supermoist. Try a porter or stout to complement the cake. Blue Hen Chocolate Porter is excellent!

MIXED BEER DRINKS

While real aficionados would never think to mix their beers, there are those who like to experiment and enjoy the surprises. Before you decide which side of the argument you're on, you should know that mixed beer drinks are numerous and ancient. In fact our country's founding father, George Washington, enjoyed such a drink called a Flip. This was an extremely popular drink of the day, and there are many regional variations.

The Victorian English were very much into mixing their beers. They loved to use ales and lagers to make punches and other mixed drinks. The Germans also invented many mixed beer drinks. Bismark liked his dark beer cut with champagne. Some Germans used different sodas to sweeten their beers and cut the alcoholic content. Here, then, are a few concoctions for your anxious taste buds.

ALEHOUSE SPECIAL

1 pint amber ale
1 oz. rye rum

Pour rum into beer. Do not stir. Drink.

ALT SHOT

1 bottle altbier
1 bottle cola

Mix chilled ingredients and stir gently. Serve cold.

BAYOU BEER BUSTER

¹/₂ pint beer
2 oz. vodka, chilled
2 shakes Tabasco

Pour beer into a chilled mug and add vodka. Add Tabasco. Stir slightly.

BEER BUSTER

¹/₂ pint beer
2 oz. vodka, chilled

Pour beer into a chilled mug and add vodka. Stir slightly.

BIKER'S MUG

1 bottle dark lager
6 oz. 7-Up

Mix and stir lightly.

BISMARK

6 oz. dark lager
6 oz. champagne

Mix and serve cold.

BLACK VELVET

6 oz. stout or dark porter
6 oz. champagne or
sparkling wine

Ingredients should be chilled. Pour both into a highball glass at the same time. Do not stir.

BOILERMAKER

1½ oz. whiskey
½ pint beer

Pour the whiskey into a mug or pint of beer. Do not stir. A popular variation is to carefully drop a shot glass full of whiskey into a mug of beer, then drink without stirring.

BROWN VELVET

6 oz. stout or dark porter
6 oz. port

Mix and serve chilled.

COLORADO BULLDOG

1 pint lager
½ oz. Irish creme
½ oz. Kahlua

Into a beer pour Irish creme and Kahlua. Do not mix. Drink.

DEPTH CHARGE

2 oz. peppermint (or any
flavor) schnapps
1 pint beer

Pour schnapps into frosted glass or mug, then pour in beer. Stir slightly.

DRAGOON'S PUNCH

3 bottles porter or stout
3 bottles ale
½ pint brandy
4 tbsp. confectioner's sugar
3 sliced oranges
2 bottles champagne

Mix all ingredients, except champagne, in a large bowl. Stir slightly. Just before serving add large chunks of ice and chilled champagne.

FLIP

2 egg whites
4 egg yolks
3 tsp. honey
1 quart ale

Whip the egg whites to a frothy consistency. Beat the egg yolks. Add the yolks and the honey to the whites. Into a separate saucepan pour ale and bring to boil. Slowly add egg to boiling ale. Remove from heat. Pour into a second saucepan. Pour back and forth between pans until frothy. Pour into mugs and serve hot with cinnamon and nutmeg sprinkled on top.

Foam

1 pint beer
1 oz. dark or light rum

Pour rum into beer. Don't stir. Drink.

Jailhouse Ale

1 pint ale
1 oz. Jagermeister
½ oz. rum

Pour Jagermeister and rum into the beer and stir gently. Drink.

Moscow Mule

1½ oz. vodka
1½ tsp. lime juice
1 bottle ginger beer

Combine in shaker with ice and shake gently. Strain into glass.

Ogge

2 bottles amber ale
4 egg yolks
2 tbsp. sugar

Pour beer into a saucepan, and heat to boiling. Separately, mix yolks and sugar and beat. Add the yolk mixture to the beer while constantly stirring. Serve hot, sprinkled with nutmeg or cinnamon.

Panachee

12 oz. lime soda
1 tsp. lime juice
2 tsp. confectioner's sugar
1 bottle beer

Mix ingredients and stir. Pour in a tall glass over lots of ice.

Punch with Beer

1 bottle ginger ale
1 bottle orange juice
1 bottle beer
4 oz. sugar
2 tbsp. lime juice

Mix and stir slightly. Serve over ice.

Sangaree Ale

1 tsp. confectioner's sugar
10 oz. cold ale

Add sugar to ale and stir slightly. Lightly sprinkle cinnamon and nutmeg on top.

Shandy Gaff

6 oz. ginger ale
6 oz. ginger beer

Ingredients should be chilled. Pour both into a highball glass at the same time. Do not stir.

Skip and Go Naked

1 oz. gin
1 oz. lime juice or juice of half a lime
beer to fill

Pour gin and juice into a chilled beer mug over ice. Fill with beer. Stir slightly.

HOMEBREWING

10

CHAPTER

BOTTLED BY
ADAMS MEDIA CORPORATION

I f homebrewing weren't so fun and the end result so enjoyable, it would not be one of the fastest growing hobbies in the United States. But is it really worth the time and effort with the variety of beer now available at stores and through the mail? Yes. Beer tastes better when you've made it yourself. Homebrewing also provides the opportunity to learn more about beer—its splendid nuances and variations.

The amazing thing about beer is that there are only a small, finite number of core ingredients: barley, water, hops, and yeast. There are many different types of barleys, hops, and yeasts and variations in water can make a huge difference, too. By varying each one or all of these four basic ingredients, you can produce a great number of different beers. When you make beer yourself, you begin to understand how different taste effects are achieved with just these simple ingredients, and you become a better beer consumer—or at least more savvy. Buying and tasting beer will never be the same for you.

You may want to learn how to homebrew Budweiser or Miller, but the real fun comes in making extraordinary beers. From choosing what style of beer to make to putting together the ingredients, waiting for the day when you pop the top on another new batch, and tasting the efforts of your hard work, making beer with friends is truly a great experience. Isn't that what beer is all about? Beer is about friends and enjoying other people's company. And you will be the envy of your crowd when you start microbrewing the best beer in the world.

THE MAIN INGREDIENTS

As you already well know, there are four main ingredients that go into making beer. These four simple ingredients, in varying degrees, can change the entire complexion of beer—how it smells, how it feels in the mouth, how it tastes, and what lingering tastes it leaves on the tongue.

Water

Water sounds like such a simple thing, but as a homebrewer you will find out differently. The quality and type of water you use will determine

Not all chemicals are bad. Without chemicals such as hydrogen and oxygen, for example, there would be no way to make water, a vital ingredient in beer.

—Dave Barry

what kind of and how good a beer you produce. Bass Ale gets its distinctive taste from hard water, while the delicate taste of Pilsner Urquell shines through because it is made with soft water. Good water is worth its weight in gold because there are a thousand things that your tap water may have in it that can harm your brewing process.

Chlorine

Most municipal water filtration plants use chlorine in differing amounts to help purify water for consumption. They traditionally use more in the summer than they do in the winter because algae grows quickly in the summer and can contaminate water. Chlorine forms very nasty smelling and tasting compounds when it is present in the brewing process.

If chlorine is your only problem, then you're in luck. Sometimes, especially in the fall and winter, boiling the water you're going to use before beginning the brewing process will rid the water of some chlorine. However, activated (carbon) charcoal water filters will do an even better job. You can use the single-container jug kinds, or a system that is fitted into your everyday water supply. The latter range in price from $50 to $400, but this is a good value over the life of the unit and will improve the overall drinkability of the water in your home.

Nitrates and Nitrites

Whether you want to talk about nitrates or nitrites, the important thing to remember is that nitrates are not bad, necessarily, but nitrites are. The amount of nitrates in the water varies from area to area. Depending on which kinds of yeasts you are using during fermentation, nitrites may result. Nitrites may negatively affect the fermentation process, either slowing it considerably or eventually ruining the taste of the final product.

Minerals

Minerals can wreak havoc in your fermenter. Heavy, dark beers are not as badly affected as some of the more delicate beers. The darker the beer you're making, the less you have to worry. Here's what to keep in mind:

Bicarbonate is just as bad as carbonate, but the good news is it can be simply removed from the water by boiling the water before beginning the brewing process.

Calcium is good for yeast and color. Too little is not good and will result in a darker, hazier beer. Calcium is good in any style beer.

Carbonates inhibit the brewing process and are bad. They can be overcome when making a stronger, darker beer, but on the whole contribute nothing to the brewing process.

Chloride has no direct impact on the actual brewing like calcium, sulfates, and magnesium; however, it does contribute to a beer's overall flavor.

Iron is a very bad influence. It will ruin the taste of any beer and must be minimized.

Magnesium can usually be found in the malt. In small amounts it acts like calcium; too much will result in a nasty, sour-tasting beer.

Sodium is good in a small amount. Too much and your beer will be undrinkable.

Sulfates are good for increasing the character of the hops. If you're making bitter beer, sulfates are your friends.

Zinc, in small amounts, is fine for the brewing process, but in abundance, it will impart a flavor not unlike iron.

Hard/Soft—What's the Difference?

There are two kinds of water: hard water and soft water. Hard water is high in minerals and has a higher pH or alkalinity. Soft water is relatively devoid of minerals and is more acidic. If the water is alkaline, then it is hard. If it is not alkaline, then it is soft. Alkaline is determined by the amount of calcium and calcium sulfate. For any of you who have had a tropical fish tank or a pool, you already understand this problem. If you don't understand it, don't worry. Water treatment kits are available from your homebrewing supplier. Follow the kit's instructions, and you will have a better brewing experience. While this sounds like a lot of mumbo-jumbo, or worse, like chemistry class, you're right. But it's not as difficult as it sounds. The kits are easy to use and will correct any problems you might have.

TYPES OF BEERS AND THEIR MALTS

Pales, Ales and Lagers
- American Klages
- American 6-row (pilsner) and 2-row (ale)
- Belgian 6-row (pilsner) and 2-row (ale)
- English 6-row (pilsner) and 2-row (ale)

Amber Beers and Brown Ales
- American caramels (5 to 7 different varieties)
- Belgian Caravienne
- Belgian Munich
- English Crystal or Caramels
- German Dark Crystals

Darker Beers
- American Black Roast
- American Chocolate
- American Victory/Biscuit Malt
- Belgian Biscuit
- Belgian Black Roast
- Belgian Chocolate
- English Brown/Amber
- English Black Roast
- English Chocolate

If your water is less than 7.0 pH, and if the hardness is less than 225–250 ppm, you are ready to brew! If not, you need to either ask your local brewing supply outfit or local homebrewers what they recommend.

The good news for those of you who have hopelessly hard water is that you get to brew all the stouts, porters, or other strong amber and dark ales you want. If you have soft water, you will have to treat it if you want to make those beers, as they require more minerals to create their flavors.

Barley

While barley is the worst cereal grain to make bread with because it has too many natural starches that turn into sugar, it is, however, the best possible cereal grain from which to brew beer. Barley looks like a wheat stalk, and various barleys produce a wide range of flavors. Most of the barley used in the United States is grown in the Pacific Northwest and Canada.

There are essentially two kinds of barley: two-row and six-row. Two-row barley is called this because of the number of kernels visible on the cone-shaped flowers as viewed from above. The same goes for six-row barley, except that there are six kernels that can be viewed from above. Generally speaking, lagers are brewed with six-row barley and ales are brewed with two-row barley. There is no real difference in the quality of beers brewed with two- or six-row barley. Two-row barley is more expensive. Six-row barley is most often used for brewing lager—the predominant style in the United States—and is more plentiful and cheaper.

Barley eventually becomes malt. Malting is the process of turning the barley from starch into sugar. Large breweries use barley that has already been malted. To make malt, barley is sprayed down with water and left for a few days to stimulate growth. After a few days, the barley will develop a little green shoot that would normally become a root. Before these shoots get too big, they are quick-dried with hot air and then sold to the breweries.

To create different styles of beer, some malt is roasted, which gives beer a specific flavor and color. After roasting, these malts are baked in giant ovens. This is called kilning. Malts are kilned to specific finishes. When the malt becomes crystallized, or better caramelized, it is called crystal malt or caramel malt. When the malt is charred, it is known as black malt.

Another popular kind of malt is called roasted barley. Roasted barley should not be confused with kilned malt. Roasted barley is barley that is kilned without first germinating. It is roasted until almost burnt. This results in a different finish and a different flavor. Another kind of malt is smoked. Rauchbier is made with malt that has been smoked after kilning to give it an extra smoked flavor. Many red beers are made with Victory or Biscuit malt.

After the malt achieves its particular finish, it is milled, or ground, until it is coarse so that the barley is just broken up. The resulting milled product is called grist. The grist is thrown in the mash tun and mixed with hot water. The mixture is referred to as the mash. This thick concoction is then heated, but not boiled, for one to four hours. It is at this time that the starches finally turn into sugar. The liquid that is drained off is called the wort. The wort is then boiled in the brew kettle to kill off bacteria.

Malt Extracts

There is nothing wrong with homebrewing using kits, and kits mean malt extracts. Some beginners may groan at the idea of using malt extracts. They may want to make their own malt. Using a kit reduces your chances of a giant, expensive, and time-intensive mess. It is a good thing that most kits come with malt extract syrup, because making your own is too difficult for the novice homebrewer. It's like making a pie from scratch without ever having baked before.

That said, there *is* something wrong with a brewery that uses malt extracts. Beer that is mass-produced with malt extracts is usually an inferior beer. These brewers are called extract brewers. Many lawnmower beers are made that way.

Another product available to homebrewers is dry malt extract. This is nothing more than dehydrated malt extract, and many popular kits are sold using this type of malt extract. There is nothing inherently wrong with using this. Dry extracts are usually easier to get because dry malt is sold separately, while malt extract is usually sold in 1.5 liter containers. Some homebrewers use kits and augment them with extra dry malt to make sure the flavor is pronounced.

(continued)

Light Specialty Beers
- American Vienna
- Belgian Wheat
- English Vienna
- German Light Crystal
- German Vienna
- Midwest Wheat
- Pacific Northwest Wheat
- Rye Malt

Dark Specialty Beers
- Black Roasted Barley
- German Smoked
- Roasted Barley

The great thing about malt extracts is that they save home-brewers time and expense and give them the opportunity to home-brew beers they might not otherwise be able to.

Hops

Hops is a type of plant, and it is the hops flowers that are used to make the beer. The flowers look like little acorns. Hops add stability to beer during the brewing phase. Hops is a clarifying agent that makes beer easier to store and last longer. Hops adds aroma, often a floral nose, but that is not always true. And finally, hops adds bitterness, which is good, because some beers brewed without hops might be too sweet. Hops counteracts that sweetness and brings the flavor back down to a more palatable taste.

As with barleys, certain hops are used to produce certain beers. Saaz is one of the most popular hops used in producing pilsners and other lagers. Many English beers are made with Kent hops, and many American beers are made with Cascade hops.

Hops are added to the brewing process when the wort is ready to be boiled. Sometimes hops are added later in the brewing process, during the aging. This is called "dry hopping." Some brewers feel this adds a more floral nose and other flavoring agents to the beer. Do this only when making recipes that call for this technique.

Freshness is always an issue. Stale hops do not improve the flavor of your beer, but go a long way toward ruining it. This doesn't mean you have to buy your hops from the farm. If your hops have been prepared and stored properly, then they will keep for a long time.

But how do hops do it? What is it in hops that imparts the funky flavors we have grown to value in the brewing industry? First, it's important to know that the hops flower has many important parts that make it so valuable. The flower, which grows on vines, is shaped like a pine cone and is made up of leaves. Each leaf has a gland, which is known as a lupin gland. These lupin glands contain oils, resins, and waxes, all of which add to the flavor of the beer. Some hops flowers may have seeds, while others on the same vine do not. All hops flowers are female.

The resins are very important. There are hard resins and soft resins. While the hard resins don't contribute much, the soft resins do. Resins are broken up into alpha acids, beta acids, and others. Hops high in alpha acids are better for adding bitterness to beer. While beta acids do contribute some bitterness, they are more renowned for what they add to the aroma of a beer. A bittering hop is generally added in the last fifteen minutes of the boil, while a hop intended to add aroma is added in the last five minutes.

Oils in hops also lend different flavors. Some of these flavors are desirable and some are not. Hops high in oils like humelene are more highly regarded, as that oil tends to give beer a more pleasant aroma. Saaz, a popular hops, is high in humelene. Cascade hops is unique because it contains oils not found in other hops. Cascade is an American hops grown in the Pacific Northwest. The oils in it contribute a wonderful floral bouquet as well as what some might call a citrusy flavor. The only problem with Cascade hops is that they don't keep as well as other hops and tend to oxidize faster. Oxidation is a no-no in brewing. Make sure your Cascade hops are as fresh as possible, or use something else.

Hops come in many different forms and can be bought whole, in pellets, or in plugs. There are advantages and disadvantages to each of these forms.

Whole hops look like a pine cone, and storing them in your refrigerator can take up a lot of space. Whole hops are also shipped in a bag in which there is air. This leads to oxidation in the hops, which is bad. "Real" homebrewers would use nothing but fresh hops, but if you're a beginner and you don't want stale hops, try pellets or plugs.

Pellets are hops that have been milled or pulverized and look like rabbit food. They are easy to store and because they are so concentrated, you need less pellets than whole hops to brew a batch of beer. The bad thing about pellets is that the lupin glands have been crushed, and while the oils, resins, and waxes will dissolve more quickly, they also stand a better chance of oxidation. Some aficionados claim that pellets don't add the full

TYPES OF HOPS

Bittering Hops—Higher in Alpha Acids
- Brewers Gold
- Buillion
- Chinnok
- Cluster
- Eroica
- Galena
- Northern Brewer
- Nugget
- Perle
- Spalt

Aroma Hops—Lower in Alpha Acids (also known as Noble Hops)
- Brambling Cross
- Cascade
- Centennial
- Fuggles
- Golding (also known as Kent)
- Hallertaurer (American)
- Hallertaurer (German)
- Herbrucker
- Mt. Hood
- Saaz
- Styrian
- Tettanger (American)
- Tettanger (German)
- Willamette

flavors that whole hops do. But if you're a weekend brewer, they're quite satisfactory.

Plugs offer something for everybody. They are whole hops flowers compressed into little circle-shaped plugs, like drain stoppers. They almost look like a crushed beer can. Plugs are great because they contain whole flowers, which gives you the optimum opportunity to brew tasty beer, and they're easy to store. Just make sure that there is as little air in the package as possible.

Yeast

Yeast is the engine that makes the whole brewing process happen, just like with bread. The same properties in yeast that cause bread to rise give beer alcoholic content and fizz. Yeast is also used to make wine and champagne.

Yeast is a bacteria. Why do we want living bacteria in our brew? Yeast is a hungry little critter that loves sugar, and wort is the best meal it ever had. As the yeast eats up the sugars in the wort, it produces alcohol and carbon dioxide (carbonation). Originally, brewers made casks of beer, then waited for airborne yeasts to float in and, hopefully, corrupt their sterilized sugar water. As these yeasts settled on top of the open barrels of beer, a kind of sludge developed. These were the first top-fermenting yeasts. Single strains of yeasts were not isolated until the 1800s. Now there are over five hundred different strains.

Besides top-fermenting yeasts that are used to brew ales, there are also bottom-fermenting yeasts that are used to brew lagers. Ales are generally fermented at warmer temperatures than lagers. Ale yeasts (top-fermenting) react faster, causing fermentation to happen faster. Sometimes yeast can add fruit flavors such as apple or pear. If the yeast is not carefully regulated, however, it will ruin the finished beer.

Just like hops, yeast comes in different forms and types. For the beginner, dried yeast is the best. It's easier to buy, use, and store. While some homebrewers swear by liquid yeasts, these are much more susceptible to contamination and are not easy to store without going bad once opened.

As with every other part of the brewing process, contamination will ruin your final product. Try to ensure that your yeast is pure.

Two byproducts of yeast are esters and phenolic. In small amounts esters are okay. They give beer a fruit finish that, depending on the beer you're making, is either good or bad. But the very faint apple and pear flavors can quickly become banana flavors—and you don't want that! You also don't want your beer to taste of plastic, which is what happens when the yeast releases phenolic.

Dried yeast is nothing more than freeze-dried yeast. To rehydrate it, first boil water (to kill any bacteria in the water); then when it is cooled but still slightly warm, add the dried yeast. Let the yeast dissolve for fifteen to twenty minutes, making sure it is well mixed and then add it to the cooled wort. Dried yeast that has been rehydrated this way will ferment more quickly, and since rehydrated dried yeast has had time to soak up a lot of oxygen while rehydrating, it goes to work faster.

Liquid yeasts are difficult and messy, and have to be timed just right. If you insist on making your own yeast cultures, it can only be stressed that the containers in which you cultivate your yeast be as clean as possible. Timing is everything in brewing and if either your yeasts or wort are ready too soon, something is going to go wrong.

Advanced brewers eventually need to understand the nature of yeasts. When you've gotten to this plateau in the homebrew world, you will be able to expand the number of beers you can make. The drawback of dried yeasts is that they often are only available in lager or ale types and tend to be generic. Liquid yeasts, on the other hand, allow you to be more creative.

Adjuncts

In the mid-1970s, there were few beers on the American market that were not brewed with adjuncts. Most were brewed with corn, rice, or a mixture of both. This doesn't mean they were bad beers; in fact, except for Heineken and the occasional import, they were the only beers available. There is a snobbishness in the brewing world about corn and rice: "Those beers are fine if you don't have to drink them exclusively." What is happening now is even more astonishing.

Homebrewers first started using only malt barleys. Then, after some time, they discovered the joys of adjuncts. First Buffalo Bill Owens made Pumpkin Beer and then American homebrewers were

TYPES OF YEASTS

Ale Yeasts
- Australian
- Bavarian Wheat
- Belgian
- British
- Canadian
- Chico
- Irish
- London
- Sierra Nevada

Lager Yeasts
- American
- Bavarian
- Bohemian or Czech
- Danish
- Munich

off to the races, putting everything in their beers from chocolate to maple syrup to a thousand other things.

Adjuncts are like any other kind of window dressing: they are good when they are not overdone. This is true especially with sugars: a little goes a long way. Too many adjuncts or too much of one adjunct will ruin the beer. This is where the KISS Brewing Method is very important: Keep It Simple, Stupid!

Popular Grain Adjuncts

Corn, wheat, oats, and rice are all used by larger breweries to cut some of the bitterness in beer because they provide more sugar. These ingredients also help lengthen out the barley. Adjuncts are usually cheaper than barley. They add sugar, but not necessarily flavor. Brewers want barley's flavor, but the price of barley sometimes leaves a bad taste in their mouth. Adjuncts are a cheap substitute. This is not necessarily a bad thing. They do make for a somewhat blander beer, but certainly one that appeals to a wider audience.

Millet or sorghum and *rye* tend to add different flavors to beers and are best used only in recipes that call for them.

Popular Sugar Adjuncts

Belgian candy sugar. Used to sweeten Faro, a sweet Belgian beer. Other fruit beers also contain some of this.

Brown sugar. Dark brown or raw sugars are good. The darker the sugar the better the taste of the beer (because it has a stronger taste of molasses).

Cane sugar. Some brewers substitute cane sugar for barley, making the wort an all-sugar and water liquid. This is good for very light beers with little body. When used during the finishing stages, cane sugar can increase sweetness or alcohol content in Trappist beers. Only use this in small amounts unless you're using a tested recipe.

Chocolate. Never use milk chocolate; use only powdered baking chocolate or melted solid baking chocolate. And don't use too much. Only a hint will do.

Corn syrup. Great for finishing beers, just before bottling. Use in small amounts; otherwise stay away. Very sweet stuff.

Fruits. Fruit flavorings come in various kinds of packages. Some do include sugar and some do not. Either way, in correct amounts, fruits can enhance the flavor of a certain style of beer.

Ginger. If you've never had ginger beer, then this is a real treat. Don't use powdered ginger in the brewing process; use real ginge-root. Also used in wassail.

Honey. Honey is delicate and adds a nice aroma.

Licorice. This is for strong or flavorful beers. Added unsweet-ened, it imparts a lot of taste. Use sparingly.

Maple sugar or sap. If you're going to try giving your beer a maple flavoring, don't use the syrup you buy for pancakes: it's mostly corn syrup, anyway, and will not add a noticeable flavor to the beer. Use the most natural form of maple sugar you can find.

Molasses. There are three kinds of molasses: light, dark, and blackstrap. Only the last two are worth anything in brewing. The stronger or more flavorful the beer, the better.

Rice extract. Used to lighten the body of some beers.

Smoke. If you can't find smoked barley, use liquid smoke extract. Smoked beer is a treat and fun to make if you're into that kind of taste. Use the extract sparingly.

Spruce. For a long time, spruce was a popular ingredient in beer and root beer. Use the extract, available from homebrewing sup-pliers, for your favorite beer and root beer recipes.

Vanilla. This is an often-avoided spice in the adjunct world; how-ever, it is used in some winter warmer and wassail recipes. It's tricky to work with. Use extra-sparingly.

They who drink beer will think beer.

—WASHINGTON IRVING

How Beer Is Made

1. *Barley* is made into malt. *Malting* is the process of turning the barley from starch into sugar. Malting is when barley is sprayed down with water and left for a few days to stimulate growth. After a few days, the barley develops little green shoots. At that time, air is blown through to quickly dry them. Some malts are then baked in giant ovens. This is called *kilning*. Malts are kilned to specific finishes. Then the malt is *milled*—or ground down coarsely so that the barley is only broken up, not ground to flour. The resulting milled product is called *grist*.

2. The grist is thrown in the *mash tun* and then mixed thoroughly with hot water. the mixture is referred to as *mash*. This thick concoction is then heated, but not boiled, for anywhere from one to four hours. It is at this time that the starches finally turn into sugars.

3. The liquid that is drained off is called the *wort*. The wort is then boiled in the brew kettle to kill off any bacteria. It is here that the hops are added. *Hops* are used to bitter and finish beer.

4. The wort is then chilled as it is passed onto the *primary fermenter*. In the primary fermenter the *yeast* is added. The yeast interacts with the sugars to make alcohol. This is called *fermentation*. A byproduct of this reaction is carbon dioxide, which gives beer its fizz.

5. The secondary fermenter, or aging tank, is the place where beers are finished—the last steps in beer making. Different styles require different steps, but all beers need to be aged. The aging process is different for different beers. Some setups or styles require only an aging tank; others require both the second fermentation and aging.

6. After aging, the beer is then kegged or bottled and brought to market. In the bottling phases, many beers are pasteurized. The bottled beer is heated to anywhere from 175–200°F. This kills off any bacteria that might ruin the beer during storage and shelving. Some beers are not pasteurized, especially in the microbrew industry where flavor is so important. These beers should be kept refrigerated. Other beers have more sugar or yeast solutions added to them at this time to augment their finish, making them either sweeter or more carbonated or to increase the alcohol content.

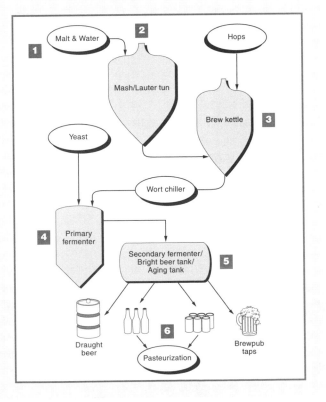

HOW TO BREW BEER: A STEP-BY-STEP GUIDE

Homebrewing is not a cheap hobby, and the initial investment is not insignificant. However, it is cheaper than buying a pair of skis or a motorcycle. The best thing you can possibly do is watch someone else brew first. This is exciting and informative and will let you understand first-hand what is needed in terms of materials and brewing great beer.

While brewing beer is nothing more than cooking, it's also a bit of chemistry. While some of the numbers and terms in more advanced brewing can get intimidating, if you use kits for your first few times, you'll do fine. And from there you'll best be able to judge if this popular hobby is for you.

What Are Beer Kits?

Beer kits are, more than anything, a can of malt extract. Beer is easy to make from a kit and this is recommended for first-time brewers. There are many varieties and manufacturers of kits to brew both ales and lagers. Kits usually come in a 1.5 liter can. Instructions on how to brew beer are included. Follow the instructions carefully. Eventually, when you become an accomplished brewer, you can use beer kits as a starting point, doctoring them up to make your own distinct versions.

Brew an ale first. Lagers are too difficult for a first-timer. Lagers weren't created until the 1800s, 4,000 years after ales were introduced. If it took man as a species 4,000 years to discover lager, you can withstand not brewing it for a few batches, until you get some ales under your belt.

Cleanliness is Next to . . . Nothing!

Cleanliness is your top priority in homebrewing. Everything must be spotless, absolutely cleaned, and thoroughly rinsed. Any germs or bacteria that wiggle their way into the brewing process might completely alter or destroy your beer. And there is nothing worse than spending a Saturday afternoon or night making beer only to find out a week or so later that it was completely for naught.

Some homebrewing experts recommend as many as four different cleansing agents, such as bleach, ammonia, chlorine, and lye. The two best alternatives are cleaning kits from homebrewing supply companies and good old-fashioned household bleach. Two to three ounces of unscented household bleach in five or six gallons of water is the best cleaning solution ever invented for homebrewing purposes. It's cheap and easy to find, and it rinses easily.

A good tip is to leave your equipment in the cleaning solution until you need it, and then rinse what you need just before using it. If you clean something and then lay it down on the counter, it will definitely get contaminated. Take no chances, and be paranoid about germs.

Equipment

There are plenty of beginner kits available from manufacturers and homebrewing suppliers. The cheaper kits are usually a good investment if you don't know much about homebrewing. However, if you know what you're about to get into, then spend a little more to get some equipment that will make your brewing life easier. Some kits can be had for as cheap as $49.50 to $100. There is no lack of good equipment that would cost more. To start off, you'll need the following materials:

Equipment Specific to Brewing (usually comes in a homebrewing equipment kit)

Two plastic buckets with lids

One bucket is the primary fermenter, and the other is the secondary fermenter. These are usually five- or six-gallon buckets with lids. Both should have spigots. The primary fermenter should actually be about seven gallons or more to hold the barm (the foam of fermentation) that will bubble up.

You can buy these new or get them from any local food supplier. Some homebrewers are very picky about where they get their buckets. It is generally recommended that you don't use buckets used to store deli foods such as coleslaw, potato salad, or pickles. Whatever you use, wash it thoroughly. Let it sit with the heavily diluted bleach mixture for half a day. Make sure that the place is well aerated and out of the reach of children and pets.

A bottle brush

This can be found in any housewares store. Some kits come with it and some don't. They're cheap and make life very easy.

A bottle capper with caps

There are two types of cappers: the hand capper and the bench capper. The bench capper is a few dollars more but infinitely easier to use. You will not regret buying it. Make sure you have about fifty to sixty bottle caps per five gallons.

A fermentation lock or air lock

The fermentation or air lock lets oxygen escape but doesn't let it in. This keeps your fermenter from exploding and the beer from oxygenating. Some kits already have the air lock or fermentation lock affixed to the lids of the fermenting vessels. Some do not. If yours doesn't have an air lock, go out and get one.

A filler wand

Also known as a bottling tube or racking cane, this is attached to the tube that leads out of the secondary fermentation bucket during bottling. The end of the nozzle is usually springloaded to let out beer when you want.

A hydrometer

A hydrometer measures the gravity or how much alcohol is in your brew. This is a very intimidating piece of equipment. It looks like a thermometer inside of a test tube or beaker. Get a triple-scale hydrometer. If you have any dreams of being the next Jim Koch, then you better learn how to use this thing. It's actually pretty simple. If you can take your own temperature, then you can do this. The cylinder or flask that holds the hydrometer is sometimes sold separately. Make sure you have this.

WELL-KNOWN BEER KIT MANUFACTURERS

- Alexander
- Black Rock
- Brewferm
- Brewmaker
- Brewmart
- Cooper's
- Edme
- Geordie
- Glen Brew
- Ironmaster Mountmellick
- John Bull
- Laaglander
- Mahogany Coast
- Munton & Fison
- Premiere
- Telford

USING A HYDROMETER

A hydrometer is used to gauge the gravity, or the amount of fermentable material, in your wort. A hydrometer usually comes in two parts. The first looks like a test-tube beaker with a round, flat base, and is narrow and tall. The second piece is the actual hydrometer. It looks like a thermometer, only bulbous at one end.

You will use the hydrometer twice during the brewing process. The first time is after you finish making the wort and add enough water to make it five gallons. Make sure you do this before you pitch the yeast. This is your beer's original gravity. The second reading is done after you've finished brewing your beer. This is the final gravity. The second reading will always register less than the first because there is more alcohol than water and alcohol is lighter than water. If your second reading is higher than your first, it means that the fermentation isn't finished.

1. Take the temperature of your wort.
2. Fill the beaker 1½–2 inches from the top with the wort.
3. Drop in the hydrometer. If it is touching the bottom, add a little more wort until the hydrometer is perceptibly away from the bottom.
4. To take a reading, you want the true water liquid line. You want to take the reading where the wort is at its lowest point, and you want to read right across to get the reading or number indicated on the hydrometer.
5. Now you need to calculate. Water's gravity is 1.000 at 59°F. In order to calculate the correct reading, add .001 for every 10°F above that point. So if your wort is 100°F, add .004 to your reading.
6. Throw out the brew you tested. It may be contaminated. Don't taste it.
7. After the fermentation process is finished, in seven to ten days, take another reading.
8. To gauge the alcohol by volume in your beer, subtract the second number from the first.

A triple hydrometer scale will show you three things: gravity, potential alcohol by volume, and Balling scale. The Balling scale is a way to measure gravity in very precise degrees, known as degrees Plato. Many serious microbrewers prefer this measurement; most homebrewers don't.

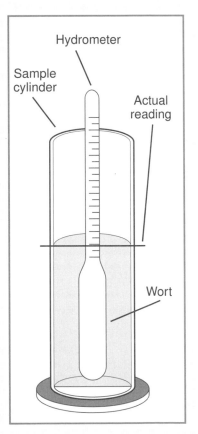

Hydrometer

Sample cylinder

Actual reading

Wort

Plastic tubing

Plastic tubing is important during the bottling and transfer of the wort to the second fermenter. It also connects the secondary fermenter to the bottle filler. The beer should never be exposed to open air after it enters the secondary fermenter until it's time to be consumed (save the few minutes during bottling).

Supplies You Can Find at Home

Fifty to sixty empty beer bottles

The best way to get the bottles ready is to soak them for a few days in a bleach and water mixture. At that point, rinse them out and make sure to get the labels off. Then store them. No matter when you clean them, you will have to wash them again immediately before bottling. But if they've been scrubbed and cleaned off beforehand, it will make bottling go that much more quickly. Twist-off bottles don't cut it. You can't buy the proper capper for those, so they're worthless.

We've had this conversation about bottle colors before, but brown-colored glass is the best. Green is second on the list. It's OK, but it's not the best color. Clear is very bad; unless you intend to drink this stuff pretty quickly, you really don't want clear bottles.

Obviously, you can collect these at home. It will take you longer than you think to collect this many bottles, but you'll have fun doing it. If you're making a lot of beer and you're not going to be able to save up as many bottles as you might need, many homebrewing suppliers will be more than happy to help. All kinds of bottles are for sale.

Homebrewers disagree about certain types of bottles. Most controversial are the self-sealing or Grolsch bottles. They're reusable—so they're good—but the seals will eventually wear out and air will get in—so they're bad. For homebrewers, the original old-fashioned, pry-off caps are the best.

A cooking thermometer

The kind you'd use to test the temperature of candy.

A large pot (to boil the wort)

This pot has to be washed in the exact same way as the rest of your equipment, no matter how clean you think your kitchen is.

A long metal spoon

No wooden spoons. Wooden spoons can't be sanitized, and some brewers contend that if the wood is in contact with the brewing beer for too long it will impart its flavors into the beer.

A strainer

A large one with small holes works best.

Brewing, Step by Step

1. **Clean the two fermenters, the fermentation lock or air lock, the hydrometer, the cooking thermometer, the large pot, the long metal spoon, and the strainer.** Make sure you clean with the bleach and water mixture (three ounces in five gallons) and rinse everything in hot water. Use a new sponge or rag and then toss it. Don't use it again to clean your beer equipment. Also, don't dry anything with a towel! Let everything air dry. Drying with a towel will spread bacteria over where you just cleaned.

2. **Add two gallons of already boiled water to your fermenter and chill in the refrigerator.** You'll need to make room for this. Make sure the lid is tightly fastened.

3. **Put the can of malt extract in hot water for ten to fifteen minutes.** This stuff is thick and difficult to work with. However, if you heat it up, it will be easier to work with. Make sure you take the label off before you start to heat it. Don't put this in the microwave. Even if the can didn't spark, which would be a major scientific breakthrough, it would explode from the gases released from the heated liquid inside.

4. **Bring six quarts of water to a boil in your brewpot.**

5. **In a separate saucepan, bring three quarts of water to a boil.** Once it has begun to boil, lower heat to simmer. This is the water used to rinse the hops, in case you aren't using a hopped malt extract.

6. **Add the malt extract to the brewpot.** Make sure that you empty the can entirely into the brewpot. Boil for approximately fifteen to twenty-five minutes. Total boiling time will be about forty minutes. Remember, too, that you don't want to cover the brewpot. Malt is a very gross commodity, and

you don't want it caking up all over your stove. Also, stir this concoction every five or so minutes. It is important to keep this mixture as homogenous as possible.

Some homebrewers will want you to boil the wort for a whole hour. This is a topic of debate. Follow the instructions included with a recipe or kit unless you have it on good authority from someone else. Once you become an old hand at this, you can experiment in your own kitchen like any good cook or brewmaster.

7. **Add hops and boil for fifteen minutes.** This is where hops makes its big statement, where aroma and bittering come in. Never add the hops at the beginning of the boil, only in the last fifteen minutes or so. If added too soon, the hops will boil off. The resins, waxes, and oils will superheat and rise out of the pot in the whiffs of steam that float away. In the end, your beer will taste like garbage. With hops, bitterness is added in the last fifteen minutes and aroma in the last five minutes of brewing.

8. **After time has elapsed, turn off brewpot and cover.**

9. **Take the fermenter out of the refrigerator. Pour hot wort through the strainer into fermenter containing cold water.** If you couldn't fit your fermenter into the refrigerator, put your covered brewpot in the sink filled part way with cold water. Then drain the sink and repeat the process. The idea is to cool down the wort—the quicker the better. Remember that the wort should be cooled sufficiently before it's poured into a plastic bucket. Never pour boiling wort directly into a plastic fermenter.

10. **Take the hops left in the strainer and pour the boiling water over those that you originally boiled in step 5.** Press the hops in order to get as much out of them as possible. Discard hops.

11. **Add more water until you have five gallons.** Some homebrewers use distilled water or make their own. Boiled water that has been set aside for several days in sealed containers is the best. This water should be cool to continue the cooling process.

12. **In a small bowl, add lukewarm water and the dried yeast packet.** Mix and let stand for fifteen minutes.

13. **Use the cooking thermometer to gauge the temperature of the wort.** You're looking for about 75°F and lower. Anything you can do to cool the wort down is good at this point, but don't add ice.

14. **Take a hydrometer reading of your wort.** To get a sample, use a sanitized wine thief or your metal spoon and fill the flask with wort. Insert your hydrometer into the flask. Record all three numbers on the scale. For your first batch, a hydrometer reading is not necessary; however, if you want to be a really good homebrewer, you eventually have to learn how to use one of these things.

15. **Pitch (add) the yeast.** Stir the mixture thoroughly. Yeast needs air, so make sure you stimulate the wort.

16. **Attach lid to fermenter and lock the lid and the air lock. Store the fermenter in your basement.** Store anywhere it is cool and dark and the temperature is consistent. Avoid direct sunlight!

17. **Wait eight to ten days.** This is definitely the toughest part, whether you're a first-timer or experienced veteran. A foamy head will rise within the first forty-eight hours. This is the yeast at work. It looks sort of funky. The whole process should take ten days.

18. **If the foam that rose up on the second or third day has finally fallen and sunk into the beer, then you're ready for the next stage—bottling. Congratulations!**

Bottling

Bottling uses some of the same equipment you used to brew, but you'll also need some different equipment. You'll also need another pair of hands. If your brewing buddy was helping last time, it's a pretty sure bet he'll want to help out during the bottling. Let him. Bottling isn't hard, but it moves a lot more quickly if you let other people help out.

You'll need the following items: bottles, plastic tubing, bottling bucket with spigot, a bottle filler or filling wand, hydrometer, bottle capper and caps, and bottle washer. You'll also need $^3/_4$ cup corn syrup and two small sauce pans.

Bottling Step by Step

1. **Clean the two fermenters (including bottling bucket with spigot), the bottle brush, the bottles, the filler wand or bottle filler, the hydrometer, and the plastic tubing.** Fill a five-gallon bucket with the usual bleach solution. Fill the bottles with the bleach solution, and then clean and rinse, twice. Do not use soap: it's too difficult to rinse and leaves behind a film that will ruin your beer.

2. **Move the beer through the tubing into the bottling bucket.** What you want to do is siphon off the top liquids if your fermenter does not have a spigot. The bottom of the primary fermenter, which has been stored away for more than a week, is settled with spent yeast. You don't want that in the beer. And you don't want to pour the beer from one vessel to the other, because you'll stir up all the muck at the bottom. Make sure the primary fermenter is in a higher place than the bottling bucket. If you bought a good home-brewing kit, your spigotted fermenter has the spigot positioned $^3/_4$ to 1-inch above the bottom of the fermenter. Then, all you have to do is attach the plastic tubing to the spigot and turn it on, and the beer will flow wonderfully down to the bottling bucket.

3. **Dissolve the corn syrup in one pint of boiling water in one of the saucepans.** Make sure it boils for a few minutes, and then lower the flame and keep warm until needed. You need this sugar to prime the beer. Priming is adding a little sugar to the beer at the bottling stage, which adds carbonation. The sugar is dessert to your yeast; it will eat it up.

4. **In the other saucepan, pour in all of the bottle caps you think you'll need with enough water to cover them, and then boil.** Make sure you boil enough caps because you may mess up a few caps in the beginning. Better to have too many than too few.

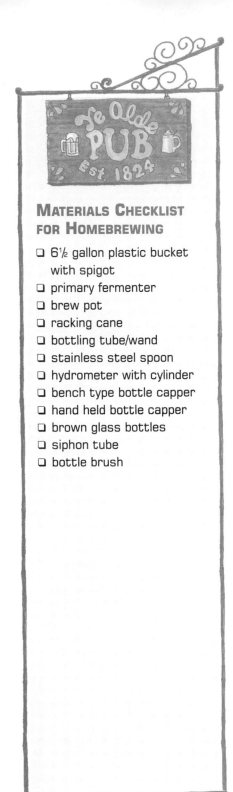

MATERIALS CHECKLIST FOR HOMEBREWING

- ❏ 6½ gallon plastic bucket with spigot
- ❏ primary fermenter
- ❏ brew pot
- ❏ racking cane
- ❏ bottling tube/wand
- ❏ stainless steel spoon
- ❏ hydrometer with cylinder
- ❏ bench type bottle capper
- ❏ hand held bottle capper
- ❏ brown glass bottles
- ❏ siphon tube
- ❏ bottle brush

After the water has boiled for five minutes, turn the flame to low and leave on the stove until needed. Bring to a boil.

5. **Add boiled sugar to the beer and stir until completely dissolved.**

6. **With the hose attached to the filler wand or bottle filler at one end, and the other end attached to the bottling bucket's spigot, begin to fill those beer bottles.** Try to fill as near to the top as possible. A space will result when you withdraw the filler wand. In the wine and beer industry this is referred to as ullage. Don't freak out; your beer won't oxidize. If commercial beers can survive this small amount of air in their mass-produced stuff, then your great work of art won't spoil either—that is, unless you haven't been absolutely immaculate and followed all the instructions to the letter.

7. **Cap your bottles.** Set the unused cap on the top of the bottle so that it rests flat. Then use your capper, regardless of the type you purchased, and voila, bottled beer. The cap should be absolutely secure. If you turn the bottle upside down there should be no spillage. If there is any, take the cap off and try it again. Do not settle for close at this late stage. It is incredibly important that no air or liquid gets in or out.

   Now is a good time to label your beer. The one good thing about labeling is that as you begin to make different beers, you can label them to tell them apart and date them so that you know when different batches were brewed. Labels can be as simple as a blank tag or as complicated as a completely designed and gummed label. Ask your home-brewing supplier for the type you want.

8. **Store your bottles in the basement or somewhere where it's cool and dark. Ales will be ready in two to six weeks.** Ales need a minimum of two weeks before you should even bother to taste them. Lagers need even more time, about four to eight weeks. They are not even worth tasting until four or five weeks have gone by. In either case, do not store the bottles in a refrigerator, as the cold temperatures will interfere with the yeast doing its thing.

9. **Drink and enjoy!** Invite friends over, to prove that you do indeed know what you are doing, and to celebrate your successes.

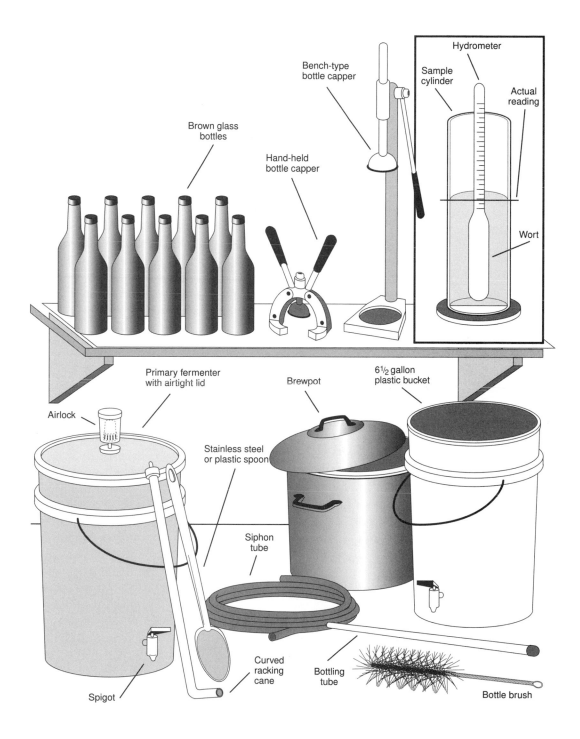

Brown glass
bottles

Bench-type
bottle capper

Hand-held
bottle capper

Hydrometer

Sample
cylinder

Actual
reading

Wort

Primary fermenter
with airtight lid

Brewpot

6½ gallon
plastic bucket

Airlock

Stainless steel
or plastic spoon

Siphon
tube

Spigot

Curved
racking
cane

Bottling
tube

Bottle brush

BREWING RECIPES

For those who are determined to advance beyond basic homebrewing, making exotic and complex beers is the greatest challenge. Don't make these beers until you've done it the simple way at least once, and gotten it right. Many of the following recipes use a combination of malt extracts and complex varieties of hops and other adjuncts. Many are based on old recipes and are quite popular among homebrewers. They require some experience, but in the end, should not pose serious problems for the beginning homebrewer. You will also find in this section recipes for ginger beer and root beer. These require many of the same steps and attention to cleanliness as brewing beer.

Homebrewers are a friendly crowd, always ready to share recipes, tips, and experiences. That is the beauty of homebrewing. The other great thing about it is the wonderful feeling of accomplishment you'll have when drinking beer that took so much time to carefully brew. Watching your friends and family enjoying your beer makes home-brewing even that much more special. So start brewing and enjoy.

Notes on Better Brewing

When you decide to attempt more advanced brews, you will need to know a few more things. Many of the following recipes are brewed based on beer kits—malt extracts—with other grains and hops. The first thing you need to know about is sparging. Sparging is brewing the wort with real grains. You need to strain the wort and grain mixture into the fermenter after the grains have released their flavor. After you have done this, pour water through the spent grains, slowly, until the water runs clear. Use water at 150–175°F when sparging. When the water runs clear, then the grains are truly spent. The water used to rinse the grains also goes in the fermenter. In many cases, the wort is then reboiled.

Steeping is the other thing you need to know about before venturing into the world of more complicated brewing. To steep, you use sparge bags that resemble giant teabags. Fill the bags with fruit or some other adjunct, and then leave them in the brewpot for a specified length of time. Without sparge bags, you'd have to constantly be straining your brew as you went along, especially when making the more complex varieties of beers. Sparge bags make life easy.

Sparge bags come in two different types. Cheesecloth bags are disposable, are very cheap, and work well. Nylon bags are reusable and don't cost much more than $5. Controversy rages about which type is better. In an attempt to avoid accidents and unhappy endings, we recommend the disposable sparge bags.

Another thing that makes life easy is a hops bag. Some homebrewers wrinkle their noses at these, but they reduce the number of steps you need to deal with. Just like a sparge bag, a hops bag is like a giant teabag that holds the hops. We recommend you use them when you are first starting out.

Hale-Bopp Comet Alt Beer

Wyeast 1007 German Ale yeast
3/4 pound 60L Crystal malt
1/3 pound chocolate malt
6.6 pounds Northwestern Amber
1 pound Laaglander DME
3 ounces Hallertaurer hops
3/4 cup corn sugar for priming

1. Add the Crystal malt and the chocolate malt to cold water and bring to boil.
2. Sparge the grains by pouring this mixture through a strainer into the brewpot, adding enough water at this time to make a full 5 gallons. Run the water slowly through the grains in the strainer until it runs clear.
3. Add the extracts and return to boil.
4. Once it has reached boiling, add hops (in a hops bag) and boil for one hour.
5. Cool. Add enough cool bottled water to make 5 gallons. Take out hops bag.
6. Add yeast. Ferment for 7–10 days.
7. Prime and bottle. Let sit for another 2–4 weeks.

Batch size: 5 gallons
Original gravity: 1.047
Final gravity: 1.017

AUSTRIAN LIGHT ALE

Irish Ale (2nd) repitch yeast
3.3 pounds Northwestern Gold malt
3 pounds Muntons Plain Light DME
1½ ounces Northern Brewer hops
¾ cup corn sugar

1. Pour the two cans of malt into 6 quarts of water and bring to boil.
2. At beginning of a rolling boil add hops (in a hops bag). Boil for 1 hour.
3. Cool. Add enough cool bottled water to make 5 gallons. Remove hops bag.
4. Add yeast. Ferment 7–10 days.
5. Prime and bottle. Let sit for another 2–4 weeks.

Batch size:	5 gallons
Original gravity:	1.046
Final gravity:	1.011
Final alcohol:	approx 4%

ED & CAROL'S RYE BEER

Wyeast 1007 German Ale yeast
1 pound flaked rye
½ pound cara pils
¼ pound chocolate malt
3.3 pounds Northwestern Gold malt
1 pound Munton's Light Plain DME
½ ounce Northern Brewer hops
1 ounce Tettanang hops
1 ounce Spalt hops
½ ounce Saaz hops
1 tablespoon crushed caraway seeds
1 teaspoon Irish Moss
¾ cup corn sugar

1. Bring 5 quarts of water to a boil. Add grains and hold at 122°F for 30 minutes.

2. Boil 3 quarts of water and add to mash until temperature reaches 150–152°F. Hold 15 minutes.
3. Add heat and bring temperature up to 158°F. Hold 15 minutes.
4. Sparge the grains by pouring this mixture through a strainer into the brewpot. Pour 1½ gallons of water at 170°F through the grains to sparge.
5. Add extracts, Northern Brewer, and Tettnang hops and boil for 30 minutes.
6. Add Irish Moss and boil for another 30 minutes.
7. Turn off heat and steep Saaz hops and caraway seeds for 5 minutes.
8. Cool. Add enough cool bottled water to make 5 gallons. Remove hops bag.
9. Add yeast. Ferment for 7–10 days.
10. Prime and bottle. Let sit for another 2–4 weeks.

Batch size:	5 gallons
Original gravity:	1.040
Final gravity:	1.015
Final alcohol:	3.25%

CRANBERRY ALE

European Ale yeast
6.6 pounds John Bull Light malt
2 ounces Hallertaurer hops (bittering)
5¼ pounds cranberries, crushed
½ ounce Tettnang hops (aroma)

1. Add extract to 6 quarts of water. Bring to boil.
2. Add Hallertaur hops and boil for 45 minutes.
3. During the boiling process steep the Tettnang hops for 15 minutes.
4. During boil, but after the Tettnang hops, steep cranberries in sparge bags for 15 minutes.
5. Cool. Add enough cool bottled water to make 5 gallons. Remove hops and cranberry bags.
6. Add yeast. Ferment for 7–10 days.
7. Prime and bottle. Let sit for another 2–4 weeks.

Batch size:	5 gallons
Original gravity:	1.038
Final gravity:	1.013

CZECH PILSNER

Wyeast 2278 Czech Pilsner yeast
¹/₂ pound Munich malt
¹/₄ pound Crystal malt 60 L
3 pounds Laaglander Extra Light DME
3.3 pounds Northwestern Gold
2¹/₂ ounces Saaz hops (bittering)
1³/₄ ounces Saaz hops (aroma)
³/₄ cup corn sugar

1. Steep grain for 30 minutes at 155°F in 6 quarts of water.
2. Sparge the grains with 2 quarts of water.
3. Add extracts and boil for 15 minutes.
4. Add bittering hops and boil for 30 minutes.
5. Add aromatic hops and boil for 5 minutes.
6. Cool. Add enough cool bottled water to make 5 gallons.
7. Add yeast. Ferment for 7–10 days.
8. Prime and bottle. Let sit for another 4–6 weeks.

Batch size: 5 gallons
Original gravity: 1.051
Final gravity: 1.031

ED & CAROL'S FRUITCAKE ALE (A HOLIDAY SPICED ALE)

Wyeast Special London yeast
6.6 pounds John Bull Light
¹/₂ pound Muntons Light DME
1 pound alfalfa honey
¹/₂ pound Crystal malt
¹/₈ pound Black Patent malt
2 ounces Cascade hops
¹/₂ ounce Saaz hops
¹/₂ ounce dried ginger
1 6-inch cinnamon stick
2 grated orange rinds
¹/₂ ounce dried bitter orange peel

1. Add extract and honey to 6 quarts of water and bring to boil.
2. When water comes to a rolling boil, add Cascade hops. Boil 33 minutes.

3. Add ginger, cinnamon, and orange and boil for 8 minutes.
4. Add Saaz hops and boil for 2 minutes.
5. Pour entire mash through strainer. Sparge the spent adjuncts with cold water.
6. Cool. Add enough cool bottled water to make 5 gallons.
7. Add yeast. Ferment for 7–10 days.
8. Prime and bottle. Let sit for another 2–4 weeks.

Batch size:	5 gallons
Original gravity:	1.051
Final gravity:	1.013
Final alcohol:	approx. 5%

Honey Oatmeal Stout

Irish Ale yeast
3.3 pounds Northwestern Amber malt extract
3.3 pounds Northwestern Dark malt extract
9 ounces Crystal 120
4.5 ounces Crystal 60
2¼ ounces Black Patent malt
11½ ounces roasted barley
1 pound oats
2 pounds buckwheat honey
1 ounce Cascade hops (for bittering)
½ ounce Tettnang hops (for aroma)
½ ounce Perle hops (for aroma)
¾ cup malt extract (for priming)

1. In 6 quarts of water, add all grains and boil 30 minutes.
2. After 30 minutes, sparge grains with 1½ gallons of water.
3. Add extracts and honey and bring to boil. Add Cascade hops and boil for 1 hour.
4. Steep Tettnang and Perle hops for the last 15 minutes of boil.
5. Cool. Add enough cool bottled water to make 5 gallons.
6. Add yeast. Ferment for 7–10 days.
7. Prime with malt extract and bottle. Let sit for another 2–4 weeks.

Batch size:	5 gallons
Original gravity:	1.051
Final gravity:	1.015
Final alcohol:	approx. 4.75%

He was a wise man who invented beer.

—Plato

SIX-TOED STOUT

Wyeast 1084 Irish Ale yeast
3.3 pounds Muntons Export Stout
3.3 pounds John Bull Dark Unhopped
¾ pound American Crystal malt 120 Lovibond
⅓ pound roasted barley
⅓ pound Black Patent malt
1 ounce Northern Brewer hops
1 ounce Fuggles hops
1 teaspoon Irish Moss
½ bottle Isinglass
¾ cup corn sugar

1. Steep grains in 2 gallons of cold water. Turn on heat and continue steeping grains until water begins to boil. Boil 5 minutes. Turn off heat and remove grains. (Since you're steeping, you should not have to sparge.)
2. Add extracts and begin boiling again. When rolling boil occurs, add 1 ounce Northern Brewer and ½ ounce Fuggles hops. Boil for 30 minutes.
3. Add Irish Moss and boil for 20 minutes.
4. Add the remaining ½ ounce Fuggles hops and boil 10 minutes.
5. Cool. Add enough cool, bottled water to make 5 gallons.
6. Add yeast. Ferment for 7–10 days.
7. Prime with Isinglass and corn sugar and bottle. Let sit for another 2–4 weeks.

Batch size:	5 gallons
Original gravity:	1.051
Final gravity:	1.016
Final alcohol:	approx. 4.4%

BAYOU XXX

This is a non-traditional recipe from the southern United States, typically brewed from the most basic of kitchen elements. This recipe has been dressed up considerably.

Wyeast 1007 German Ale yeast
1 ounce Tettnang hops
1 pound molasses

1. Dissolve molasses in saucepan with 2 quarts of water. Bring to boil and add hops.
2. Boil for 60 minutes.
3. Cool. Add 2 quarts of bottled water to make 1 gallon.
4. Add yeast. Ferment for 4–6 days.
5. Prime and bottle. Let sit for another 2–3 weeks.

Batch size: 1 gallon

GINGER BEER

one packet baking yeast
2 ounces ground ginger
1½ ounces cream of tartar
3 teaspoons lemon juice
3½ cups light brown sugar
1 tablespoon lemon rind, grated

1. Dissolve packet of yeast in 1 cup of lukewarm water.
2. Dissolve ground ginger in 1 gallon of water. Turn on heat.
3. When water is boiling, add cream of tartar, lemon juice, and light brown sugar. Boil for 60 minutes.
4. Steep lemon rind for 20 minutes during boil.
5. Let cool.
6. Add yeast. Ferment for 4–6 hours.
7. Bottle. Let sit for another 2–3 weeks.

Batch size: 1 gallon

ROOT BEER

1 teaspoon baking yeast
4½ pounds light brown sugar
3 ounces root beer extract
4 gallons water

1. Dissolve yeast in 1 cup of lukewarm water. Let sit.
2. In a pot, combine the 4 gallons of water, sugar, and extract. Mix thoroughly and heat slightly until mixture is consistent. Turn off heat.
3. Let cool.
4. Add yeast. Mix well.
5. Bottle. Let sit for approximately 7–10 days.

Batch size: 4 gallons

BEER KIT SUPPLIERS

The best places to look for beer kit suppliers are in homebrewing and beer magazines. However, if you want a quick guide to some of the better known beer kit suppliers, scan these pages and see what strikes your fancy. All of these places are very experienced at shipping if you need to buy by mail or phone. Call for their brochures and catalogs. Many of the stores listed below are full-service providers. Some sell more supplies than equipment.

Alfred's Brewing Supply
P.O. Box 5070
Slidell, LA 70469
(504) 641-2545

Bacchus & Barleycorn, Ltd.
6633 Neinman Road
Shawness, KS 66203
(913) 962-2501

Beer and Wine Hobby
180 New Boston Street
Woburn, MA 01801
(617) 933-8818

Best Brew
5236 Beach Boulevard.
Jacksonville, FL 32207
(904) 396-7666

The Beverage People
840 Piner Road #14
Santa Rosa, CA 95403
(707) 544-2520
(800) 544-1867

Brewcrafters
3629A Webber Street
Sarasota, FL 34232
(800) 468-9678

Brew and Wine Hobby
68 Woodbridge Avenue
East Hartford, CT 06108
(203) 528-0592

Brewer's Connection
1847 E. Baseline Road
Tempe, AZ 85283
(800) 879-BREW

Brewhaus
4955 Ball Camp Pike
Knoxville, TN 37921
(615) 523-4615

Brew Masters, Ltd.
12266 Wilkins Avenue
Rockville, MD 20852
(301) 984-9557

Brew Masters, Ltd.
1017 Light Street
Baltimore, MD 21230
(410) 783-1258

Brewmeisters Supply Company
3522 W. Calavar Road
Phoenix, AZ 85023
(602) 843-4337

Cellar Wine Shop
14411 Greenwood Avenue N
Seattle, WA 98133
(206) 365-7660
(206) 365-7677 (fax)

Crosby and Baker
999 Main Road
Westport, MA 02790
(508) 636-5154

DeFalco's
5611 Morningside Drive
Houston, TX 77005
(800) 216-BREW

The Home Brewery
Old South Highway 65
Ozark, MO 65721
(800) 321-BREW

Home Sweet Brewery
2008 Sansom Street
Philadelphia, PA 19103
(215) 569-9469
(215) 569-4633 (fax)

James Page Brewery
1300-Z Quincy Street NE
Minneapolis, MN 54413-1541
(800) 347-4042

E.C. Kraus
9001 East 24 Highway
Independence, MO 64054
(816) 254-7448

Larry's Brewing Supply
7405 S. 212th Street #103
Kent, WA 98032
(800) 441-2739

Liberty Malt Supply Company
1419 1st Avenue
Seattle, WA 98101
(206) 622-1880
(800) 990-6258

The Malt Shop
N. 3211 Highway S.
Cascade, MI 53011
(800) 235-0026
(414) 528-8167 (fax)

The Market Basket
14835 West Lisbon Road
Brookfield, WI 53005
(414) 783-5233

Mountain Brew
2793 South State Street
South Salt Lake City, UT 84115
(801) 487-BEER

North Denver Cellar
3475 West 32nd Avenue
Denver, CO 80211
(303) 433-5998

Northern Brewer, Ltd.
1106 Grand Avenue
St. Paul, MN 55105
(800) 681-2739

Ryecor Ltd.
7542 Belair Road
Baltimore, MD 21236
(410) 668-0984

Semplex of USA
4159 Thomas Avenue N
Minneapolis, MN 55412
(612) 522-0500

Something's Brewing
196 Battery Street
Burlington, VT 05401
(802) 660-9007

South Bay Homebrew Supply
23808 Crenshaw Boulevard
Torrance, CA 90505
(800) 608-2739

Stout Billy's
61 Market Street
Portsmouth, NH 03801
(603) 436-1792
(800) 392-4792

Things Beer
100 East Grand River
Williamston, MI 48895
(800) 765-9435

Williams Brewing Company
2549 Nicholson Street
San Leandro, CA 94577
(510) 895-2739

WindRiver Brewing Company, Inc.
7212 Washington Avenue South
Eden Prairie, MN 55344
(800) 266-4677

Winemakers
689 W. North Avenue
Elmhurst, IL 60126
(800) 266-BREW

HOMEBREWING EQUIPMENT SUPPLIERS

Here are many suppliers who specialize in homebrewing equipment. Some are full-service suppliers, and some specialize in only specific things—their names are usually good indicators of their specialties. Many will be more than happy to supply you with catalogs and other information. As with beer kits, another good resource for looking up beer equipment suppliers is homebrewing magazines

Advanced Brewers Scientific
2233 Sand Road
Port Clinton, OH 43452
(419) 732-2200

American Brewmaster
3021-5 Stoneybrook Drive
Raleigh, NC 27604
(919) 850-0095

Asheville Brewer's Supplies
Asheville, NC
(704) 285-0515

Beer, Beer, Beer and More Beer
P.O. Box 4538
Walnut Creek, CA 94596
(800) 600-0033

Benjamin Machine Products
338 Spenker Avenue
Modesto, CA 95354
(209) 523-8874

Beverage People
840 Pines Road #14
Santa Rosa, CA 95403
(707) 544-2520

BITOA Brewing Systems &
Brewers Warehouse
4520 Union Bay Place NE
Seattle, WA 98105
(206) 527-5047

Braukunst
55 Lakeview Drive
Carlton, MN 55718
(218) 384-9844
(800) 972-BRAU

Brew City Beer Gear
P.O. Box 27729
Milwaukee, WI 53227
(414) 276-5093

Brew Company
P.O. Box 1063
Boone, NC 28607

Brewer's Connection
3894 West State Street
Boise, ID 83703
(208) 344-5141
(800) 955-BREW

Brewers Resource
409 Calle San Pablo #104
Camarillo, CA 93012
(805) 445-4100
(800) 827-3983

The Brewery
11 Market Street
Potsdam, NY 13676
(800) 762-2560

The Brewlab
1039 Hamilton Street
Allentown, PA
(610) 821-8410
(800) 900-8410

Chateau Distributors
P.O. Box 2683
Sumas, WA 98295
P.O. Box 8000-391
Abottsville, BC V2S 6H1
(604) 882-9692

Cumberland General Store
Route 3
Crossville, TN 38555
(615) 484-8481
(800) 334-4640

Davison Manufacturing
4025 South 65th #14
Greenfield, WI 53220
(414) 545-9246

East Coast Brewing Supply
P.O. Box 060904
Staten Island, NY 10306
(718) 667-4459

Fermentap
P.O. Box 30175
Stockton, CA 95213
(209) 942-2750

Fermenthaus
P.O. Box 4220
Victoria, BC V8X 3X8
(604) 570-2163

The Filter Store Plus
P.O. Box 425
Rush, NY 14543
(800) 828-1494

Foxx Equipment
421 Southwest Boulevard
Kansas City, MO 64108
(816) 421-3600

Freshops
36180 Kings Valley Highway
Philomath, OR 97370
(541) 929-2736
(541) 929-2702 (fax)

Grainger
333 Kingsbridge Parkway
Lincolnshire, IL 60069
(800) 225-5994

The Grape and Granary
1302 E. Tallmadge Avenue
Akron, OH 44310
(800) 695-9870

Heartland Home Brew
888 East Belvidere (Route 120)
Unit 215
Grayslake, IL 60030
(800) 354-4769

Grainger
333 Kingsbridge Parkway
Lincolnshire, IL 60069
(800) 225-5994

The Grape and Granary
1302 E. Tallmadge Avenue
Akron, OH 44310
(800) 695-9870

Heartland Home Brew
888 East Belvidere (Route 120)
Unit 215
Grayslake, IL 60030
(800) 354-4769

Heart's Home Beer & Wine Making
Supply
5824 North Orange Blossom Trail
Orlando, FL 32810
(407) 298-4103

The Home Brewery
P.O. Box 730
Ozark, MO 65721
(800) 321-BREW

Hop Union
P.O. Box 9697
Yakima, WA 98909
(800) 952-4873

Jack Schmidling Productions
18016 Church Road
Marengo, IL 60152
(815) 923-0031

JET Carboy & Bottle Washer
Company
3301 Veterans Drive
Traverse City, MI 49684
(616) 935-4555

Listermann Manufacturing
1621 Dana Avenue
Cincinnati, OH 45212
(513) 731-1130

Morris Hanbury USA, Inc.
Hop Merchants
P.O. Box 1548
402 East Yakima Avenue
Yakima, WA 98907
(509) 457-6699
(509) 452-9468 (fax)

North Harbor Manufacturing
53 North Harbor Road
Colchester, VT 05446
(802) 893-7500

Precision Brewing Systems
P.O. Box 060904
Staten Island, NY 10306
(718) 667-4459
(718) 987-3942 (fax)

Pico-Brewing Systems
8383 Geddes Road
Ypsilanti, MI 48198
(313) 482-8565
(313) 485-2739 (fax)

Rapids Wholesale Equipment
P.O. Box 396
Cedar Rapids, IA 52406
(800) 553-7906

SABCO Industries
4511 South Avenue
Toledo, OH 43615
(419) 531-5347
(419) 531-7765 (fax)

Shadow Mountain Brewing Company
27590-A Commerce Center Drive
Temecula, CA 92590
(909) 694-6570
(909) 694-6573 (fax)

Valley Brewing Equipment
1310 Surrey Avenue
Ottawa, Ontario K1V 6S9
Canada
(613) 733-5241

Vinotheque
2142 Trans Canada Highway
Dorval, Quebec H9P 2N4
Canada
(514) 684-1331

West Creek Home Brewing
118 Washington Avenue
P.O. Box 623
Endicott, NY 13761
(607) 785-4233

Williams Brewing
P.O. Box 2195
San Leandro, CA 94577
(800) 759-6025

Wine Hobby USA
2306 West Newport Pike
Stanton, DE 19804
(302) 998-8303
(800) 847-HOPS

Wine Enthusiast
8 Sawmill River Road
Hawthorne, NY 10532
(800) 356-8466

Yeast Culture Kit Company
1308 West Madison
Ann Arbor, MI 48103
(313) 761-5914

BEER CAREERS

11

CHAPTER

BOTTLED BY
ADAMS MEDIA CORPORATION

The two easiest jobs to get in the beer industry are those of a ballpark vendor and a bartender. That's a little obvious, but it's not far off from how most people in the industry got started. According to Kevin O'Bannon, CEO of the Frederick Brewing Company, the beer-related job he held before his present position "was on the consumer side." But isn't that how everyone started out?

Pete, of Pete's Wicked, didn't want to make beer. He wanted to make wine but balked at the time it took to yield a finished product. He didn't even like beer originally. Bert Grant, CEO of Yakima Brewing Company, and Carol Stoudt, of Stoudt's Brewing, had both previously held jobs with big firms. Bert was a hops salesman once, too.

So how did they get into the business? Love of the product. As in any popular business, such as movies, books, and professional sports, breaking in is sometimes the most difficult part. Aside from competition, the pay is usually low as well. There are plenty of people who would be willing to replace you in your low-paying, entry-level job. Getting and keeping a job in the beer industry comes down to how badly you want it.

Here are some tips on how to get in. First, try the office staff. Many breweries need people with experience in billing, sales, and marketing. Tour guides are usually required in the summer. Many of the larger breweries are always on the lookout for biologists and chemists to keep healthy strains of yeast alive and multiplying. In the end, breweries are like any other manufacturer. They are constantly turning over positions and have staffs that they have to keep up.

OK, so maybe you don't need to be a brewer, but still, you really want to work for a brewery. Practically speaking, if you have any kind of job experience, with persistence, you could get a job with a brewery, large or small. They need people in order fulfillment, billing, reception, and administration. They need experienced people in marketing, public relations, and advertising. The sales side also requires bodies, but here you need a little more experience, and breweries are always looking for experienced and aggressive sales people who have knowledge of sales and promotions within the beer, wine, or liquor industry. They need salesmen, managers, and delivery men.

Malt does more than Milton can
To justify God's ways to man.

—A. E. HOUSMAN,
BRITISH POET

It is also important to know that you don't have to work for a brewery to be involved with the beer industry. You could work for a distributor or beer wholesaler. These jobs are sometimes more rewarding, because you learn about the entire beer business and about all the brewers, instead of the operations of just one. Again, like breweries, they need people in all kinds of positions, especially warehousing, order fulfillment, sales, promotions, and delivery.

Of course, there are also some less obvious places to work, like the magazines and newspapers that cover the beer industry, as well as advertising and public relations agencies that service these companies. Here, of course, you would need experience in writing, editing, copyediting, and production. Like any other company, these businesses need their own administrative assistants and sales, marketing, and publicity personnel.

Another place to look is the Internet. You can access the *Modern Brewery Age Website* http://www.breweryage.com/index.htm). This job bank allows people to view jobs currently available, and it also has a long form for you to fill out and send into the job bank database. This is a new Website, but many industry insiders say it has a lot of potential.

Also of great use through *Modern Brewery Age* is the yearly *Blue Book*, which offers a huge list of brewers, associations, and executives for immediate access into the world of brewing. This is one of the most important books used by people in the brewing industry.

What you might do is use the list of microbreweries and trade associations in this book and call and learn what jobs the nearest brewer might have available. It is important to remember that the larger brewers have huge plants set up regionally so that they can provide beer quickly and in enough quantity for each region. You'll need to do some investigative digging to find these brewers. *The Beer Directory* by Heather Wood is an excellent guide to some of those larger breweries' regional hubs.

Modern Brewery Age Blue Book

U.S. Brewers
- Alphabetical List of U.S. Breweries, Microbreweries, Brew Pubs and Contract Brewers
- Beer Brands in Use
- Directory of U.S. Breweries, Microbreweries, Brew Pubs and Contract Brewers

Foreign Brewers
- Alphabetical List of Worldwide Breweries
- Worldwide Brewery Directory
  - Canada
  - Europe
  - Mexico
  - Middle East
  - West Indies & Caribbean
  - Africa
  - Central America
  - Asia
  - South America
  - Australia/New Zealand

Importers
- Alphabetical List of Import Companies
- Imported Beer Brands by Country and Importer
- Directory of Importers

Non-Beer Beverage Producers and Marketers Trade Associations
- National & State Wholesalers Associations
- Allied Industries Associations
- National Brewers Associations
- State & Regional Brewers Associations
- Foreign Brewers Associations

You can't be a real country unless you have a beer and an airline; it helps if you have some kind of a football team, or some nuclear weapons, but at the very least you need a beer.

—FRANK ZAPPA

Legal Section

- Bureau of Alcohol, Tobacco and Firearms Map
- BATF Listing
- ATF Disaster Relief Regulations Outlined
- State Liquor Control Admin.
- Digest of State Labeling Requirements on Malt Beverages
- Federal Regulations
- Labeling Requirements/Proposed Labeling Requirements
- Brewpub and Microbrewery Legal Section
- Federal Regs on Advertising Displays and Specialties
- State Advertising Regulation
- Credit Regulations
- Container Deposit Requirements
- Container and Connector Restrictions
- Litter Assessments
- Limitations of Container Sizes
- Permissible Alcoholic Content
- State Beer Tax Rates
- Shipping Requirements Affecting Brewers
- Summary of State Laws and Regulations Affecting Brewer Wholesaler Relations

Statistics

- U.S. Beer Sales
- Barrelage of Top 10 Brewers 1995 vs. 1994
- U.S. Sales of Malt Beverages 1968–1995
- U.S. Exports of Malt Beverages 1968–1995
- Leading U.S. Brewers 1972–1995 (28K File size)
- Leading Specialty Brewers 1982–1995 (21K File size)
- Growth of Microbreweries/Brewpubs in the U.S. 1983–1995
- U.S. Microbrewery Production 1983–present
- Top 10 U.S. Brewers—10-Year Comparison
- U.S. Beer Sales, Domestic & Imported
- Year's Market Share—Top Five Brewers
- Domestic Market Share—Top 5
- Top Domestic Brands
- Top Ten Brands

- Top Ten Brands Market Share
- Production, Draft & Package Sales & Total Taxpaid Withdrawals of Malt
- Beverages
- Top 250 U.S. Commercial Brewers
- Withdrawals & Per Capita Consumption of Malt Beverages
- Top 5 Brewers Volume vs. All Others
- Top 10 Regional Breweries
- Import Market Share
- Annual Barrel Shipments 1947–present

BECOMING A PROFESSIONAL BREWER!

Do you feel that unless you're right in the center of the action, the job's not good enough? Are you a control freak who wouldn't be happy as an agent or a move publicist but has to be the director? If that describes you, then the job for you is a brewer or masterbrewer. These positions are the most competitive of professional positions and require schooling.

Brewers and masterbrewers are the coolest and most creative jobs, right? Wrong! They are pressure-filled jobs. You have to keep liquid (beer) pumping out at a rate that keeps the brewery operating at maximum efficiency. And in many cases, you have to brew the same beers over and over again, unless you work for a brewpub. Working in a brewpub might allow you to make staple beers year round and, possibly, two or three seasonal beers. Your beers have to be consistent and good. Mistakes cost thousands of dollars. But whether you want to be a brewmaster for a microbrewery or brewpub, you have to go to school.

The top brewing school in America is the University of California, Davis. They have been turning out some of the best wine and beer makers for the last twenty-five years. This is the Harvard of the wine and beer field. UCal, Davis is known for providing a complete education to their graduates. Not only are you taught how to brew beer, but you also learn biology and agriculture. You learn all about yeast and culturing and what makes for good and bad barley and hops. Graduates are able to run their own show, from first growths to final bottled product. This is a very difficult four-year program that is well worth the time and expense. Top graduates are always highly sought after. UCal, Davis also offers several shorter length programs in brewing and other aspects of the beer/alcohol business.

The newest player in the game is Oregon State University, Corvallis. Their program was established in 1996, in association with the Bureau of Alcohol, Tobacco, and Firearms (BATF) and Nor'Wester Brewing Company, and is also very comprehensive. The fermentation science curriculum is supported by such esteemed brewing bigshots as the Oregon Hops Commission, Great Western Malting, and the Thermaline Company. Oregon State's famed agricultural school is also heavily involved. The school awards a bachelors of science degree in fermentation, which is an offshoot of their foods packaging and processing degree.

Another well-known brewing school that has graduated many fine brewers is the Siebel Institute of Technology. Based in Chicago, Illinois, the Siebel Institute offers eight-week courses in brewing, as well as laboratory work. They also have a degree program, and offer a constantly rotating schedule of courses. Attending the Siebel Institute is a great way for others in the industry to know you mean business.

Also of note are the American Brewers' Guild (ten-week courses), Master Brewers Association of America, the Institute of Brewing in England, and the Technical University at Weihenstephan in Germany. The following is a list of schools that offer brewing degrees and short courses.

BLUERIDGE®

B M N T

American Brewer's Guild
1107 Kennedy Place
Suite 3
Davis, CA 95616
(800) 636-1331
(916)753-0497
http://www.mother.com/abg

University of California, Davis
Brewing Courses, University
Extension
Davis, CA 95616
(916) 757-8899
(916) 757-8558 (fax)

Hands-On Brewing School
23883 Madison Street
Torrance, CA 90505
(310) 375-BREW
(310) 373-6079

Institute of Brewing
33 Clarges Street
London W1Y 8EE
England
011 44 171 499 8144

Master Brewers Association of the
Americas
2421 N. Mayfair Road
Milwaukee, WI 53226
(414) 774-8558

Microbrewers Association of
American Short Courses
4513 Vernon Boulevard #202
Madison, WI 53705
(414) 774-8558
(414) 774-8556 (fax)
(in cooperation with Oregon State)

Microbrewery Planning Course
URI Food Science
530 Liberty Lane
North Kingston, RI 02852
(401) 792-2466

Oregon State University
Dr. Mark A. Daeschel
Brewing and Malting
240 Weingand Hall
Corvallis, OR 97331
(541) 737-6519
1 (800) 823-2357
(541) 737-6525 (fax)

Technische Universitat
Weihenstephan
Technische Universitat Munchen
Werwaltungsstelle
Weihenstephan
Freising 8050 Germany

United States Brewer's Academy
Siebel Institute of Technology
4055 W. Peterson
Chicago, IL 60646
(777) 279-0966
(773) 463-7688
http://www.siebel-institute.
com/welcome
siebelinstitute@worldnet.att.net

STARTING YOUR OWN BREWPUB

There is no denying the popularity of microbreweries and brewpubs. The more there are, the more people seem to show up and support them. And why not? Trying different beers and foods is a lot of fun. However, before you put a deposit on that vacant building you've been eyeing, there are some things to think about first.

Opening a brewpub, essentially a bar, is a very imposing (but rewarding) endeavor. You need to know what the state and local liquor laws are in your area. You also need to think about several key elements of your operation. Opening a brewpub is a capital-intensive prospect; i.e. it costs a lot of money! And one out of every six startup brewpubs or microbreweries fails. Not only do you have all the costs that a regular bar or restaurant require, such as cooking facilities, staff, equipment and supplies, tables, and chairs, but you'll need a liquor license (which will likely require lawyers' fees), insurance, a lease on a property, and—most importantly—brewing equipment. You can't lease this stuff; you have to buy it. For a brewpub of even a small size, you won't be able to get out without spending less than $30,000–40,000. And that's just for starters. That doesn't include the cost of raw materials, additional room and equipment for storage, etc. The only thing you won't need is a bottling machine.

You'll also need a brewmaster, and in all likelihood, it's not going to be you. Making good beer consistently is a time-consuming job. The reason you shouldn't be your own brewmaster is that you need to have someone who knows how to make a variety of beers. An experienced homebrewer may not have enough experience to brew in large quantities and be able to brew quickly. You need someone who makes great beer to open a successful brewpub.

While people will want to come for the beer, they'll more than likely want something to eat with it. This is not a small part of your business. Food is very important. Burgers and beer aren't going to get you by. Many brewpubs have upscaled their menus without increasing their prices dramatically. Some serve gourmet fare. You'll need an accomplished chef as well as a talented brewmaster who will be able to work together.

The other thing to remember is that the market is crowded with more microbreweries than ever before. The big brewers still run this market. Ten breweries control almost ninety-five percent of the market. Some industry analysts estimate that the microbrewers in America (now totaling around six hundred) are fighting over two to three percent of the entire beer market. The entire brewpub/microbrewery industry is valued at about $2.5 billion.

All that said, there is still plenty of money to be made in the brewpub business. Go to as many brewpubs as you can to get a better sense of how they market themselves and how they do their business. Talk to as many people as you can about the business, and don't skimp on sound business practices before getting involved. Once you establish a successful brewpub, you might want to consider having your beer either contract-brewed or bottling it yourself to sell. Of course, that requires more licenses and more capital.

The beer business has been one of the most entrepreneurial industries in the last five years and should continue to be so for some time. And with a whole new generation of Americans learning more and more about beer, there promises to be a very well-educated group of consumers looking for a quality product.

Resources

There are several published resources from which to draw upon to help you start a brewpub. The best known book on the subject is *Starting Your Own Bar* (McGraw-Hill). Hundreds of thousands of copies of this title have been sold—and with good reason. People have been using this book for years to help them establish their own businesses. It is the cheapest of all investments, and will give you a little insight into what goes into running a bar, not just in man-hours and common sense, but in dollars and cents.

How to Open a Brewpub or Microbrewery (260 pp; $7) by the American Brewers Guild, is an easy-to-read book on how to own and operate a microbrewery. As the Brewers Guild says, it can teach about everything "from grain to glass." At only $7 (plus $1.59

DID YOU KNOW . . .

- in Fairbanks, Alaska, the feeding of alcoholic beverages to a moose is strictly forbidden
- in Kentucky you can only be deemed sober until you "cannot hold onto the ground"
- drunkenness is an "inalienable right" in Missouri
- a bar owner in Nebraska cannot sell beer unless he is simultaneously cooking soup
- in the town of Nyala, Nevada, it is illegal for someone to buy drinks for more than three people
- it is illegal to sell beer and pretzels at the same time in any restaurant, bar, or club in North Dakota
- the entire *Encyclopedia Brittanica* could be banned in Texas because it contains the recipe to make beer
- in Wyoming, a woman who is not standing more than five feet from the bar while drinking could be arrested

shipping and handling), it's a tremendous return on investment. Buy this book! The ABG also offers a number of other publications available through the mail or via their 800 number.

Brewer Publications offers two books that are very practical. *Brewery Planner: A Guide to Opening and Running Your Own Small Brewery* (184 pp; $80) is an excellent book. Now in its second edition, many of the tips and stories included in the book come from established brewpub owners. The other book is the *North American Brewers Resource Guide* (448 pp; $100). This is one of the most comprehensive lists of resources ever gathered. From small homebrewing to microbrewing, this is the bible of supplies and equipment. Both books are very expensive, but for those who are truly considering opening a brewpub, they are worth it.

Brewers Resource Catalog is another comprehensive tome for the homebrewer and brewpub/mircobrewer wannabe. It's frequently revised so it's always up-to-date. Also check out *Brewpub Magazine*, which was developed by *Brew Your Own* magazine for the numerous brewpub owners and managers. It is a solid trade magazine.

The Brew Store is a manufacturer as well as a wholesaler of microbrewery equipment. They specialize in establishing U-Brews as well as brewpubs. They also sell bottling machinery and custom labels. Training comes with all of their systems. They have more than a dozen locations around the country. Call their 800 number for information and locations.

Micropub Systems International, Inc. is another supplier of brewery equipment for brewpubs. Their Micropub System is a fully automated system that provides excellent craft-brewed quality that reportedly does not require a brewmaster. You can view some of their information right through the Internet at the company's home page.

Another supplier who is well known among the brew-on-premises crowd is Custom Brew Beer Systems. They'll do anything you might need help with, including site selection, installation, training, operations, materials, and of course, equipment selection and purchasing.

American Brewers Guild
1107 Kennedy Place
Suite 3
Davis, CA 95616
(800) 636-1331

Brewers Market Guide
New Wine Press
P.O. Box 3222
Eugene, OR 97403-9917
(541) 687-2993
(541) 687-8534 (fax)
(800) 427-2993
http://www.BTcirc@aol.com

Brewer Publications
P.O. Box 1510
Boulder, CO 80306-1510
(303) 447-0816
(303) 447-2825 (fax)
http://www.order@aob.org OR
http//:beertown.org

Brewpub Magazine
P.O. Box 2473
Martinez, CA 94553-9932
(916) 758-4596
(916) 758-7477 (fax)
(800) 900-7594

Brewers Resource Catalog
409 Calle San Pablo
Suite 104
Camarillo, CA 93012
(800) 827-3983

OTHER BREWPUB AND MICROBREWERY RESOURCES

Bruce Brewing System
Brewery Builders
P.O. Box 61251
Denver, CO 80206
(303) 778-8574
(303) 778-0665 (fax)

Custom Brew Beer Systems (800)
363-4119

Micropub Systems International, Inc.
180 St. Paul Street
Rochester, NY 14604
(716) 454-2298
http://www..micropub@eznet.net

THE LAST WORD ON BEER

12

CHAPTER

BOTTLED BY
ADAMS MEDIA CORPORATION

BEER AND BREWING ASSOCIATIONS

There are many different beer and brewing associations. The difference between the two is that beer groups are aimed at consumers and brewing organizations are aimed at those in the beer business. These associations perform very useful tasks and will be more than happy to give you facts and figures, as well as invite you to become a member. Many have newsletters, brochures, magazines, and books that they publish themselves, aimed at their very targeted audiences. All of them provide a different window on the world of beer.

A little beer is divine medicine.

—PARACELSUS,
SIXTEENTH CENTURY PHYSICIAN

Professional and Consumer

American Society of Brewing
Chemists
3340 Pilot Knob Road
St. Paul, MN 55121
(612) 454-7250

American Brewers Guild
2110 Regis Drive #B
Davis, CA 95616
(916) 753-0497
(916) 753-0176 (fax)

American Beer Association and
Gourmet Beer Society
Box 1387
Temecula, CA 92593
(909) 676-2337

Association des Brasseurs de France
25 Boulevard Malesherbes
F-75008 Paris
France
011 41 01 42 66 29 27

Association des Brasseurs de Quebec
1981 Avenue McGill College
Montreal, Quebec H3A 2W9
Canada
(514) 284-9199

Association of Brewers
P.O. Box 1679
Boulder, CO 80306-1679
(303) 546-6514
(303) 447-2825 (fax)

Beer Drinkers of America
915 L Street
Suite C-414
Sacramento, CA 95814
(800) 441-BEER

The Beer Institute
1225 Eye Street NW
Washington, DC 20005

Brewer's Association of America
P.O. Box 65908
Washington, DC 20035-5908
(202) 467-6350

Brewer's Association of Japan
2-8-18 Kyobashi
Chuo-ku, Tokyo 104
Japan
011 81 03 3561 8386

Brewer's Guild
8 Ely Place
London EC1 N 6SD
England
011 44 0171 405 4565

Brewer's Society
42 Portman Square
London W1H 0BB
011 44 0171 486 4831

Brewing and Malting
Barley Research
206 167 Lombard Avenue
Winnipeg, Manitoba R3B OT6
Canada

Brewing Society of Japan
6-30 Takinogawa 2-Chome
Kita-ku, Tokyo 114
Japan

Bureau of Alcohol, Tobacco, and
Firearms
650 Massachusetts Avenue NW
Washington, DC 20001
(202) 927-7777

CAMRA (The Campaign for Real
Ale) Canada
1440 Ocean View Road
Victoria, British Columbia V8P 5K7
Canada
(604) 595-7728

CAMRA (The Campaign for Real
Ale) England
230 Hatfield Road
St. Albans, Hertfordshire AL1 4LW
United Kingdom
011 44 01727 867201
011 44 01727 867670 (fax)

Chicago Beer Society
P.O. Box 1057
LaGrange Park, IL 60526
(847) 692-BEER

Hop Growers of America
P.O. Box 9218
Yakima, WA 98909
(509) 248-7043
(509) 248-7044 (fax)

Institute for Brewing Studies
P.O. Box 1679
Boulder, CO 80306-1679
(303) 447-0816
(303) 447-2825 (fax)

Institute for Brewing (Australia)
P.O. Box 229
Brooklyn Park, South Australia 5032
Australia
011 61 08 356 0996

Institute for Brewing
33 Clarges Street
London W1Y 8EE
England
011 44 171 499 8144

Master Brewers Association of the
Americas
2421 North Mayfair Road
Suite 310
Milwaukee, WI 53226

National Association of
Beveragew Importers
1025 Vermont Avenue NW
#1025
Washington DC 20005
(202) 638-1617

National Beer Wholesalers
Association
1100 S Washington
Alexandria, VA 22314
(703) 683-4300

National Beverage Retailers
Association
5101 River Road #108
Bethesda, MD 20816
(301) 656-1494

National Licensed Beverages
Association
4114 King Street
Alexandria, VA 22302
(703) 671-7575

North American Guild of Beer
Writers
Reilly Road
La Grangeville, NY 12450
(914) 227-5520

Oregon Brewer's Guild
510 N.W. Third Avenue
Portland, OR 97209
(503) 295-1862

Saskatchewan Brewers Association
380 Dewdrey Avenue E
P.O. Box 3057
Regina, Saskatchewan S4P 3G7
Canada

Swiss Brewers Association
P.O. Box 6325
CH-8023 Zurich
Switzerland
011 41 01 221 2628

Homebrewing

American Homebrewers Association
P.O. Box 1679
739 Pearl Street
Boulder, CO 80306-1679
(303) 447-0816
(303) 447-2825 (fax)

Beernutz
c/o Brew & Grow
33523 W 8 Mile #F5
Livonia, MI 48152
(313) 442-7939

Bidal Society of Kenosha
7625 Sheridan Road
Kenosha, WI 53143
(414) 654-2211

Bloatarian Brewing League
7012 Mt. Vernon Avenue
Cincinnati, OH 45227
(513) 271-5298

Bluff City Brewers
8927 Magnolia Leaf Cove
Cordova, TN 38018
(901) 756-5298

Bock 'n'Ale-ians
7404 Hummmingbird Hill
San Antonio, TX 78255
(512) 695-2547

BOSS (Brewers of South Suburbia)
P.O. Box 461
Monee, IL 60449
(708) KEG-BEER

Boston Wort Processors
c/o John Dittman
P.O. Box 397198
Cambridge, MA 02139-7198
(617) 547-5113, ext. 900

Brew Free or Die
P.O. Box 1274
Merrimack, NH 03054-1274
(603) 778-1231

Brewers United for Real Potables
(aka BURP)
8912 Jandell Road
Lorton, VA 22079
(703) 339-8028

Capitol Beermakers Guild
405 Fairview Drive
Charleston, WV 25302
(304) 343-0350

Chicago Beer Society
P.O. Box 1057
LaGrange Park, IL 60526
(847) 692-BEER

Covert Hops Society
c/o David Feldman
5150 Vernon Springs Trail N
Atlanta, GA 30327
(404) 377-3024

Crescent City Homebrewers
2001 Neyrey Drive
Metairie, LA 70001
(504) 831-2026

Dukes of Ale
11524 Manitoba NE
Albuquerque, NM 87111
(505) 294-0302

Great Northern Brewers
3605 Arctic Boulevard #1204
Anchorage, AK 99503
(907) 337-9360

Green Mountain Mashers
10 School Street
Essex Junction, VT 05452
(802) 879-6462

Hudson Valley Homebrewers
P.O. Box 285
Hyde Park, NY 12538

Impaling Alers
7405 S 212 #103
Kent, WA 98032
(206) 872-6846

Kansas City Beer Meisters
8206 Bell Road
Lenexa, KS 66219
(913) 894-9131

The Keystone HOPS
Montgomery Farmers Market Route 63
Montgomeryville, PA 18936
(215) 614-HOPS

Madison Homebrewers & Tasters
Guild
P.O. Box 1365
Madison, WI 53701

Maine Ale & Lager Tasters
P.O. Box 464
Topsham, ME 04086
(207) 666-8888

Mid-Atlantic Sudsers and Hoppers
(aka MASH)
P.O. Box 105
Flagtown, NJ 08821
(908) 359-3235

Oregon Brew Crew
7260 S.W. 82nd Street
Portland, OR 97223
(503) 293-6120

San Andreas Malts
P.O. Box 884661
San Francisco, CA 94188
(415) 885-1878

Snowy Range Foamenters
810 S. 23rd Street
Laramie, WY 82070
(307) 742-1878

Society of Northeast Ohio Brewers
(aka SNOBS)
515 High Street
Wadsworth, OH 44281
(216) 336-9262

Sonoma Beerocrats
840 Piner Road #14
Santa Rosa, CA 95403
(707) 544-2520

South Florida Homebrewers
441 S. State Road 7
Margate, FL 33068
(305) 968-3709

St. Louis Brews
9 Adams Lane
Kirkwood, MO 63122
(314) 22-8039

Sultans of Swing
412 Lamarck Drive
Buffalo, NY 14225
(716) 837-7658

Three Rivers Alliance of Serious
Homebrewers
(aka TRASH)
3327 Allendorf Street
Pittsburgh, PA 15204
(412) 331-5645

The Underground Brewers of
Connecticut
(aka The YAHOOS —Yankee
Association of Homebrewers
Objecting to Organized Societies)
http://ourworld.compuserve.com/hom
epages/konamon/
homepage.htm
(203) 843-0800

The Unfermentables
c/o Chris Glavin
Wine and Hoops Shop
705 E. 6th Avenue
Denver, CO 80203
(303) 831-7229

Western Oregon Tasters Society
(aka WORTS)
2459 S.E. Taulatin Valley Highway
#167
Hillsboro, OR 97123

Zion Zymurgists Hops
(aka ZZ HOPS)
667 East 1200 North
Bountiful, UT 84010
(801) 298-4339

BREWERY WEBSITES

For those of you who are already Web-friendly and enjoy beer, you have probably gotten a taste of the variety of beer Websites out there. The following list is by no means complete, but the breweries' Websites listed are, like the breweries themselves, fun to visit. You will undoubtedly uncover your own favorites once you get surfing. Explore and enjoy.

AmBrew USA
Metairie, LA
http://www.Am-Brew.com/

Anderson Valley Brewing Co
Boonville, CA
http://catalog.com/avbc/home.html

Anheuser-Busch Companies Inc
St Louis, MO
http://budweiser.com

Arcadia Brewing Company
Bloomington, IN
http://kalamazoo.inetmi.com/
cities/kazoo/arcadia.html

Atlantic Coast Brewing Ltd.
Boston, MA
http:www.hnt.com/tremont

Aviator Ales Brewery/Seattle Brewing Co.
Woodinville, WA
http://www.aviatorales.com

Bad Frog Brewery Co.
Rose City, MI
http://www.badfrog.com/

Baltimore Brewing Company
DeGroen's Beers
Baltimore, MD
http://www.degroens.com/

Big Rock Brewery
Calgary, Alberta, Canada
http://www.bigrockbeer.com/

Blind Pig Brewing Co.
Temecula, CA
http://www.blindpig.com

Bloomington Brewing Co.
Bloomington, IN
http://bbc.bloomington.com/

Blue Hen Beer Company, Ltd.
Newark, DE
http://bluehen.com/

Blue Moon Brewing Co.
(subsidiary of Coors)
Golden, CO
http://www.moonme.com

Boston Beer Co.
Boston, MA
http://somadcms.com

Brew City/Brewers Guild Inc.
Walnut Creek, CA
http://www.brewcity.com

Brewery Atlantis
San Francisco, CA
http://www.hooked.net/users/
mcpdirt/atl5.html

Bristol Brewing Co.
Colorado Springs, CO
http://www.business1.com/webx/bris-
tolbrewery

Casco Bay Brewing Co.
Portland, ME
http://www.maine.com/brew/cbb

Celis Brewery Inc.
Austin, TX
http://www.celis.com

Elk Grove Brewing Co.
Elk Grove, CA
http://elkgrovebrewing.com/

Flying Fish Brewing Company
Cherry Hill, NJ
http://flyingfish.com/index.html

Frederick Brewing Co.
Frederick, MD
http://www.hempenale.com

Frio Brewing Co.
San Antonio, TX
http://www.frio-beer.com

The Great Northern Brewing Co.
Black Star Beer
Whitefish, MT
http://www.blackstarbeer.com/

Golden Gate Park Brewery
San Francisco, CA
http://goldengatepark.com/

Golden Prairie Brewing Co.
Chicago, IL
http://www.mcs.com/~nr706/
gp.html#story

Hale's Ales
Spokane and Seattle, WA
http://www.halesales.com/

Hart Breweries Inc.
Seattle, WA
http://www.HartBrew.com

Hoppy Brewing Co., Inc.
San Jose, CA
http://www.hoppy.com/

Labatt USA
http://www.labattblue.com/
home.html

Lakefront Brewery Inc.
Milwaukee, WI
http://www.lakefront-brewery.com

Left Hand Brewing Co.
Longmont, CO
http://www.lefthandbrewing.com

Long Island Brewing Co.
Jericho, NY
http://www.libc.com

McAulsan Brewing Co.
Montreal, Quebec Canada
http://www.mcaulsan.com

Massachusetts Bay Brewing Co.
Boston, MA
http://www.harpoonbrewery.com

Miller Brewing Company
Milwaukee, WI
http://www.mgdtaproom.com

Miller Lite
Milwaukee, WI
http://www.millerlite.com/
mlhome.html

North Coast Brewing
Fort Bragg, CA
http://www.ncoast-brewing.com

Nor'Wester Brewing Company
Seattle, WA
http://realbeer.com/portland/

Old Columbia Brewery/ Associated
San Diego, CA
http://goexplore.com/ads/ca/
so/kstrauss/home.htm

Oldenberg Brewing Co.
Fort Mitchell, KY
http://oldenberg.com/

Old Harbor Brewing Co. (The Pilgrim
Brewery)
Hudson, MA
http://www.pilgrimale.com

Owens Brewery/
Buffalo Bills Brewing Co.
Hayward, CA
http://www.ambrew.com

Pacific Hop Exchange
Novato, CA
http://www.wco.com./
wwmnsmrtr

Portland Brewing Company
Portland, OR
http://portlandbrew.com/

Pyramid Ales Brewery
Kalama, WA
http://www.PyramidBrew.com

Red Hook Ale Brewery
Seattle, WA
http://www.halcyon.com/rh/
rh.html

Riverside Brewing Co.
Riverside, CA
http://realbeer.com/riverside/

Rogue Ales/Oregon
Brewing Co.
Newport, OR
http://rogueales.com/

Routh Street Brewery
Dallas, TX
http://www.routhstreetbrewery.com/

Saint Arnold Brewing Co.
Houston, TX
http://www.saintarnold.com

San Andreas Brewing Co.
Hollister, CA
http://sanandreasbrewing.com

Samuel Adams
Boston, MA
http://samadams.com/

Shadow Mountain Brewing Co.
Temecula, CA
http://www.mcsintl.com

Shipyard Brewing Co.
Portland, ME
http://shipyard.com/shipyard

Spring Street Brewery/Wit Beers
New York, NY
http://plaza.interport.net/witbeer/

Stoudt Brewery
Adamstown, PA
http://www.beer/net.com/stoudts

Thomas Kemper Brewery/ Pyramid
Alehouse
Seattle, WA
http://www.ThomasKemper.com

Widmer Brothers Brewing
Portland, OR
http://www.widmer.com

Yakima Brewing and Malting Co.
Yakima, WA
http://www.grants.com

Yosemite Brewing Co./Yosemite
Beverage Co.
Mariposa, CA
http://www.yosemite-
brewingco.com

Yuengling
Pottsville, PA
http://www.yuengling.com/

Pottsville,
PAhttp://www.yuengling.com/

THE BEER BIBLIOGRAPHY: MAGAZINES, BOOKS, AND OTHER MEDIA

As beer has become more and more popular, so have magazines, newspapers, and newsletters about beer. There are magazines aimed specifically at brewers, homebrewers, beer fans, and everyone in general. If you haven't checked any of them out, the one thing you need to know is that they advertise in each other's periodicals all the time. Buy three or four of these magazines or newspapers at any one time, and you will invariably see at least one ad for each of the others.

Magazines (consumer)

All About Beer
1627 Marion Avenue
Durham, NC 27705-5808
(919) 490-0589
(800) 977-BEER
http://www.AllAbtBeer@aol.com

American Breweriana
P.O. Box 11157
Pueblo, CO 81001
(719) 544-9267

Bartender
P.O. Box 158
Liberty Corner, NJ 07938
(908) 766-6006/6007

Beer & Tavern Chronicle
244 Madison Avenue
Suite 164
New York, NY 10016

Beer Connoisseur
Adams Media Inc.
1180 Avenue of the Americas
New York, NY 10019
(212) 827-4700

Beer Drinkers International
P.O. Box 6402
Ocean Hills, CA 92056

Beer Marketer's Insights
51 Virginia Avenue
West Nyack, NY 10094
(914) 358-7751

Beer Statistics News
51 Virginia Avenue
West Nyack, NY 10094
(914) 358-7751

Beverage World
150 Great Neck Road
Great Neck, NY 11021

The Beverage Communicator
P.O. Box 43
Hartsdale, NY 10530

Beverage Media
161 Sixth Avenue
New York, NY 10014
(212) 620-0100

Brewer's Digest
4049 W. Patterson Avenue
Chicago, IL 60646
(312) 463-7484

Brewer's Bulletin
P.O. Box 677
Theinsville, WI 53092-0677

The Brewing Industry News
P.O. Box 27037
Riverdale, IL 60627

Brewing Techniques: The Art and Science of Small-Scale Brewing
New Wine Press
P.O. Box 3222
Eugene, OR 97403-9917
(541) 687-2993
(541) 687-8534 (fax)
(800) 427-2993
http://www.BTcirc@aol.com

Brew Magazine
Traveling America's Brewpubs and Microbreweries
All-American Publishing
1120 Mulberry Street
Des Moines, IA 50309
(515) 243-4929
(515) 243-4517 (fax)
(800) 340-4929
http://www.brewmag.com

Brew Your Own: The How-to-Homebrew Beer Magazine
P.O. Box 1504
Martinez, CA 94553-9932
(916) 758-4596
(916) 758-7477 (fax)
(800) 900-7594

Brewpub Magazine
P.O. Box 2473
Martinez, CA 94553-9932
(916) 758-4596
(916) 758-7477 (fax)
(800) 900-7594

Malt Advocate
3416 Oak Hill Road
Emmaus, PA 18049
(610) 967-1083
http://maltadvocate.com/
maltadvocate

Modern Brewery Age
50 Day Street
P.O. Box 5550
Norwalk, CT 06856
(203) 853-6015
(203) 852-8175 (fax)

The New Brewer
Institute for Brewing Studies
P.O. Box 1510
Boulder, CO 80306-1510
(303) 447-0816
(303) 447-2825 (fax)

Zymurgy for the homebrewer and beer lover
Association of Brewers
American Homebrews Association
P.O. Box 1679
Boulder, CO 80306-1679
(303) 546-6514
(303) 447-1815 (fax)
http://www.service@aob.org

Newspapers
Ale Street News
P.O. Box 1125
Maywood, NJ 07607
(800) 351-ALES
(201) 368-9100/9101

Barleycorn
P.O. Box 549
Frederick, MD 21705-0549
(301) 831-2759
(301) 831-6376 (fax)

Beer Traveler's Newsletter
P.O. Box 187
Washington, IL 61571
http://www.n-vision.com/
beertravelers

Celebrator Beer News
P.O. Box 375
Hayward, CA 94543
(800) 430-BEER
http://www.tdalldorf
@celebrator.com

Great Lakes Brewing News
214 Muegal Road
East Amherst, NY 14051

Midwest Beer Notes
339 Sixth Avenue
Clayton, WI 54004

Rocky Mountain Beer Notes
339 Sixth Avenue
Clayton, WI 54004

Southern Draft Brew News
P.O. Box 180425
Casselberry, FL 32718-0425
http//:realbeer.com/sodraft/

Southwest Brewing News
11405 Evening Star Drive
Austin, TX 78739
http//:www.swbrewing@aol.com

Yankee Brew News
P.O. Box 520250
Winthrop, MA 02152-0005

Newsletters
Alephenalia Beer News
140 Lakeside Avenue
Suite 300
Seattle, WA 98122

Books on Beer and the Beer Industry
The Ale Trail, by Roger Protz
Beer Blast: The Inside Story of the Brewing Industry's Bizarre Battles for Your Money, by Philip Van Munching
The Beer Taster's Log: A World Guide to More Than 6,000 Beers, by James D. Robertson
Encyclopedia of Beer, edited by Christine P. Rhodes
Secret Life of Beer: Legends, Lore & Little Known Facts, by Alan D. Eames
A Short, but Foamy, History of Beer, by William Paul Haiber and Robert Haiber
Simon & Schuster Pocket Guide to Beer, by Michael Jackson
A Taste for Beer, by Stephen Beaumont

Homebrewing
Brewing the World's Great Beers, by Dave Miller
Brew Ware, by Karl F. Lutzen and Mark Stevens
Great Beer from Kits, by Joe Fisher and Dennis Fisher
The Home Brewer's Companion, by Charlie Papazian
The New Complete Joy of Home Brewing, by Charlie Papazian

Cooking with Beer
Beer Navigator, by Doug Hexter
The Brewpub Cookbook, by Daria Labinsky and Stan Hieronymus
Cooking with Beer, by Lucy Saunders
Famous Chefs Cook with Beer, by W. Scott Griffiths and Christopher Finch
Jay Harlow's Beer Cuisine, by Jay Harlow

Beer CD-ROMs
The Brewer's Planner
Macintosh
Darryl Richman
15600 NE 8th Street
Suite B1-327A
Bellevue, WA 98008
(206) 641-5535

Brewer's Workshop 4.0
Windows 3.1 and Windows 95
TKO Software
1011 Pebble Brook Road
Cedar Park, TX 78613
(512) 918-9856

Cy-Beer CD-ROM: An Interactive Guide to Home Brewing
Interactive Video CD for Windows 95
Homebrews Outpost
(800) 450-9535

The Interactive Complete Joy of Homebrewing
Windows
by Charlie Papazian
Mediaright Technology
(212) 966-0333

Michael Jackson's World Beer Hunter: Search the World for The Perfect Beer
Windows 3.1 and 95 and Macintosh
Discovery Channel Multimedia
(800) 606-3331
http://www.beerhunter.com

RESPONSIBLE DRINKING:
MORE DOES NOT MAKE IT BETTER

The thirst-quenching embrace of a beer on a hot day, is a near perfect sensory experience. Link it with good friends, lovers, and favorite places and they capture life's truly satisfying moments. Alcohol enhances our lives.

But alcohol is a drug, pure and simple, and it is foolish not to be aware of its dangers. It affects our bodies and brains, our judgment, coordination, and perception. The amount of alcohol that brings on these impairments is entirely individual, depending on size and weight, metabolism and age, even on the variables of a single day.

The greater tragedy is that most traffic fatalities are not confined to the drinker. Drunk drivers are involved in nearly half of all American traffic fatalities and the innocent are often the victims. Over 20,000 people are killed in the United States each year because of drunk driving-related accidents. Awareness and responsibility are the only factors that will make a difference.

Enter law enforcement. The laws vary from state to state, but police are working hard to get drunk drivers off the road. Their primary weapon is the Breathalyzer, which can count your BAC, blood alcohol content—the percentage of alcohol in your blood. A BAC percentage as low as .05 has been found to increase the normal risk of accident by two to three times. So while you may not feel that your reflexes or judgment are impaired, if you are drinking you should not be driving. Period.

In most states a .10 BAC is considered evidence of driving under the influence of alcohol (DWI). In some states, the level is .08. The penalties range from a suspension of your driver's license for as little as a few days up to a year. Convictions include fines ranging from $100 to $500 and brief imprisonment—for the first offense. Punishment increases with repeated offenses. The BAC and the penalties are changing all the time, so check the laws of your state.

"Responsible drinking" is not an oxymoron. Moderation is the key to most pleasures. It is our responsibility as hosts, friends, and even citizens to keep people from driving drunk. In many states, it is our *legal* responsibility to do so.

To drink in moderation is not to have less fun, but to savor the drink we do have. We raise our glasses for so many joyous and solemn occasions—to the bride and groom, to the job well done, to the friend we have lost, and to the pure pleasure of the drink itself.

More does not make it better.

GLOSSARY OF BEER TERMS

Adam's ale. Water; another way of calling a beer watery or weak.

abbey, abbaye, abdj bier. For many years this meant a beer was made in an abbey or by monks. However, today it means that the beer is made in the Trappist tradition.

additives. Preservatives that some brewers sometimes add in order to lengthen shelf life or enzymes that produce an artificial head, to give their beer the appearance of having body. Mostly found in beers manufactured by larger brewers.

adjuncts. Adjuncts are added to the barley malt during brewing. This is done to create certain effects. Crafters use wheat and oats to gain special flavors. Many larger manufacturers add corn as a cheap substitute, or as a way to make their barley go a little further.

alcohol. Alcohol results in beer as part of the traditional brewing methods through the fermentation of grains. A beer does not have to contain alcohol to be called beer. Most beers contain four to five percent alcohol.

ale. A beer made with top-fermenting yeast, usually characterized by a fruitiness of flavor. Ales do not take much time to create from brewing to serving. A lager, for example, needs to be stored before serving, while an ale does not. According to some state laws, ale denotes a higher alcoholic content than a lager. The world brewing community does not see it this way. Ales range from bitter to sweet and vary greatly in their alcoholic content.

aleberry (alebrew, albrey, alebery). A spiced ale, dating from the Renaissance, that was brewed with sugar, spice, and bits of bread.

ale-conner. In England, an inspector of ale. Shakespeare's father was an ale-conner.

alecy. A decription of madness thought to be induced by beer.

alegar. Malt vinegar.

all barley. A beer brewed from only barley malt, with no other adjuncts, additives, grains, corn, rice, or sugars.

all malt. A beer brewed from only malted grains, with no other adjuncts, additives, corn, rice, or sugars.

alt. "Old" in German, as in altbier, meaning old beer.

altbier. Old beer in German; this is the type of brewing that preceded lagers.

barley. The central ingredient to brewing beer. By placing mature barley in a kiln and firing it, malt is created, which helps give beer its flavor and color.

barley wine. Not really a wine at all, but a very strong ale with alcohol usually twice that of strong beers. Barley wine is brewed in colorations ranging from pale to dark. The term is English, coming from the fact that its alcohol content was closer to that of wine.

barrel. One barrel equals thirty-one U.S. gallons of beer. Usually used to measure a brewery's output.

Bayriche. German for Bavarian.

beer. Any drink made from fermented grains and, more than likely, hops. Beer is the generic term for an entire family of beverages. Ales, lagers, porters, and stouts are all considered beer. In America, beer is usually meant to be lager, while the English tend to mean ale when they ask for a beer.

Belgian lace. The residue left on the inside of a glass after the head expires. Belgium has been famous for centuries for both its beers and its lace.

Berliner Weisse. Also known as a wheat beer. Known for its very low alcoholic content, this is a milky, white-ish beer that is highly carbonated.

bier. German for beer.

bière ordinaire. French for house beer.

bierworst. A German sausage flavored heavily with garlic. Usually dark.

bière de garde. A strong ale from France. Meant to be laid down or cellared.

bitter. An English ale brewed with high hop content. Designated as Special, Best, and Extra Special in order of alcohol content, with Special the lowest and Extra Special the highest, between five and six percent alcohol.

Black and tan. A mixture of stout or porter with golden ale or lager.

bock. German for billy goat, refers to a strong beer. A lager. In Germany a bock may be of many colors; however, outside of Germany it usually means a dark beer. Bock beer averages well above 6.25 percent alcohol by volume. It is usually served seasonally, once a year, depending upon which country you are in. There are many kinds of bocks, including Maibock, Doppelbock, and Weizenbock.

Bottle-conditioned. Usually an ale. Yeast is added to the beer right before bottling to further the fermentation process and increase carbonation. This usually refers to a craft beer that is unpasteurized. Known in the winemaking industry as méthode champenoise.

Bottom-fermented. How lager is brewed. Made with lager yeasts, the beer ferments at the bottom of the tun, resulting in a clearer brew than a top-fermented beer.

brewery. A place where beer is made in large quantity for sale, either retail or wholesale. The difference between a microbrewery and a brewery is that breweries produce more than 25,000 barrels of beer in any given year.

breweriana. Of or referring to beer memorabilia.

brewpub. A tavern, bar, or pub that brews its own beers. The beer is usually available on tap and, in some cases, is bottled for retail sale. Some people refer to these as microbreweries. The difference between a brewpub and a microbrewery is that a microbrewery sells larger amounts of beer, and sells its beer to beer retailers.

brewer's inch. The last inch of beer in a pot or vat; the lees.

brown ale. A dark, sweet ale, usually brewed in the south of England (sweet), in the northeast of England (less sweet, reddish), and in Flanders (brown, sour). Relatively low in alcohol.

burdock. An herb once used before hops for flavoring.

buttered ale. Ale served with sugar, butter, and cinnamon.

cask-conditioned. A draft beer usually brewed in the cellar of a pub. An unpasteurized beer that goes through a secondary fermentation in the cask in which it is sold.

cauliflower. The result of the brewing of ale; the top layer of yeast.

cream ale. An American ale brewed with both the bottom- and top-fermentation process at the same time. This produces a light pale ale, golden in color.

collar. Another name for the head on the beer.

contract brew. A beer brewed for a distributor by a brewery not owned by the distributor. Usually the distributor supplies the recipe. Bottling does not necessarily take place at the brewery. Some well-known small beers are made in this fashion.

coppery. The vessels, vats, or pots that beer is brewed in; usually made of stainless steel.

dark beer. A generic term. Usually refers to a dark lager.

decoction. Style of lager determined by the way in which the malt is mashed.

deglaze. To remove the remaining bits of sautéed meat or vegetables from a pan by adding a liquid (such as beer) and heating. Used to create the base for a sauce.

Diät Pils. A beer originally brewed for diabetics. By very careful fermentation, carbohydrates are eliminated, usually resulting in a very strong beer. Germany has laws now that require many brewers of this beer to reduce the alcohol content before finishing.

Doppelbock. German for double bock. Usually very dark and sweet. An extra-strong version of bock.

Dort. Short for Dortmunder, especially in the Netherlands and Belgium.

Dortmunder. A beer brewed in Dortmund, usually of the export style.

draft beer in a can. In an attempt to create the creaminess, richness, and foaminess of draft beer, nitrogen is added to the can during canning.

dry beer. Japanese name for Diät Pils, milder than the German original, and made even more mild in America. A dry beer in America has little taste and finish.

dry hopping. When fresh hops are added to a cask of beer.

dunkel. German for dark. Dark beers are sometimes referred to as dunkels.

eisbock. When a doppelbock beer that has been frozen and the ice is removed, the taste and alcohol level of the beverage left over is intensified.

export. A lager that usually has more body than a pilsner. The term in Germany refers to a lager that has less hops than most common pilsners. The beer is drier than a pilsner as well. Often classified as premium, which means little.

faro. A lambic beer that is sweetened by the addition of candy sugar.

festbier. Beer made for a festival. Refers to any beer. Most of these beers are high in alcoholic content.

fermentation. The chemical reaction whereby yeast organisms turn sugars into alcohol and carbon dioxide.

framboise (frambozen). A lambic made with raspberries.

fruit beer. Any lager or ale that has had fruit added to it during any stage of brewing.

genuine draft. A sterile, filtered, unpasteurized bottled or canned beer.

gueuze. A lambic beer that is a mixture, not necessarily in equal parts, of old and young lambic beers.

gravity. A weighing system used to judge the heaviness of a beer. When a beer is said to have gravity, it means that it has body and heft. In actuality, it judges the amount of hops in a beer.

grist. Barley that has been malted and milled. It is thrown in the mash tun and heated with hot water to produce the wort.

haute fermentation. French for top fermentation.

heavy. Term used in northern England to speak of the richness and gravity of a beer.

hefe. German for yeast. Often identifies the beer as either sedimented or that which has had yeast added to it just before bottling. See bottle-conditioned.

hell (or Helles). German for pale. Generally a golden color.

hops (humulus lupus). The female hops plant is used in full flower to add different flavors, bitterness, and aroma to beer. In earlier times it was thought to be a preservative.

ice beer. An attempt to emulate and market an Eisbock-like beer, beer is frozen either during the fermentation process or sometime after maturation during the storage period. The water is largely removed, and then the beer is reconstituted later.

imperial stout. A stout brewed in England for the Czars and sent to St. Petersburg. The alcoholic content was reportedly somewhere between seven and ten percent.

India pale ale. Originally a bitter beer brewed in Britain and exported to soldiers in India. It was made strong so that the beer would stand the long voyage and still be flavorful when opened halfway around the world. Today the moniker generally indicates a premium pale ale.

infusion. An English style of mashing.

kellerbier. A lager of low carbonation, very high in hops. An unfiltered beer.

kettle. Another name for the coppery, or vats, where beer is brewed.

kloster beer. German for cloister beer. Implies that the beer was originally or currently brewed in a convent or monastery.

Kölsch. A light ale from Cologne, Germany.

krausen. German for crown. This is the German term for bottle-conditioning, where yeast is added just before bottling so that a higher carbonation develops in the bottle.

kriek. A lambic beer made with cherries.

kruidenbier. Dutch for spiced beer.

kvass. A beverage very much like beer, made in Russia with rye bread.

lager. From the German word to store. Lagers are made with a bottom- or cold-fermentation and aged for a period of up to several months to complete the fermentation. Because of their longer fermentation process, lagers are generally smoother, crisper, and more subtle in taste than ales. Lagers are always served cold. While British lager tends to be golden in color, European lagers tend to be darker. In Germany and some Dutch-speaking countries it is the term for the house beer.

lambic beer. A wheat beer, most notably from Belgium, that is fermented with wild yeasts. Finishes almost like a cider.

lamb's wool. A concoction of ale, spices, and apples.

light ale. Not to be confused with the American version of light beer, this has nothing to do with calories. In England it is the opposite of a bitter beer, usually dark. Sometimes refers to an ale with less alcoholic content, but not necessarily.

light beer. A low-calorie, low-alcohol beer. A watery version of pilsner with little flavor or body. Usually between three and four percent alcohol by content.

Maibock. A lager made in the spring to celebrate the new season; usually light in color.

malt. The basic ingredient in almost every beer. Barley that has been soaked and begins to sprout. It is then fired in a kiln and ground down. This firing process determines the color and flavor of beer.

malt liquor. Often associated with cheap beers, these tend to be American ales that range up to 7.5 percent alcohol by content. More often than not they are sweet.

Märzen (or Märzenbier). German for March. A lager made in March for the Oktoberfest of the coming year. Usually a beer rich in malt flavors. Often amber-red in color.

mash tun. A large copper or stainless steel pot or vat.

microbrewery. A small brewery, sometimes referred to as a craft brewery. A microbrewery generally produces between 15,000 and 35,000 barrels of beer a year. Many of the small brewers that have grown recently have far exceeded that number but continue to be known as microbrewers.

mild. A beer light in hops. These are usually dark and not very high in alcoholic content.

Muenchener/Munchner. A beer-brewing style that is largely associated with Munich. These are dark lagers that are often spicy and generally not high in alcohol.

obergarig. German for top-fermenting.

Oktoberfest. A festival in Germany that takes place in the fall; millions come every year from all over the world to take part in the festivities. It is a celebration of German history and culture—and of beer. In ancient Germany the Märzenbier (the March beer) was made in March and was drunk in October to celebrate the harvests. The modern Oktoberfest lasts sixteen days, beginning in late September and ending in October. Oktoberfest found its roots in 1810 in an effort by Germans to celebrate the marriage of the crown prince of Bavaria. Smaller festivals around the world also coincide with this internationally renowned festival.

old. An English appellation given to dark beers. These beers tend to be dark and strong. They are not old in recipe or age.

oscura. Spanish for dark beer.

pale ale. A beer lighter in color. Generally not as bitter as India Pale Ale. Usually ranging from golden to reddish.

Pilsener/Pilsner/Pils. A lager or bottom-fermented beer, usually light in color. It draws its name from the town of Pilsen, in Bohemia in the Czech Republic. The original brewer of this beer was Frantisek Poupe, and the beer, first brewed and sold in 1842, was known as Pilsner Urquell. It is a dry beer and has a wonderful hoppiness about it. The Americanized pilsner is lighter in color, flavor, and hops.

porter. Almost black, porter is a bitter, dark lager. First brewed in England around the 1730s, it got its name from the carters and porters who tended to substitute it for a meal. Porter was largely forgotten until recently. Many American microbreweries were responsible for reviving this beer.

rauchbier. A lager largely brewed in Franconia and Hamburg. The style is achieved by using smoked malts. Other variations include smoking the malt with peat moss (Scottish style) or by throwing fire-heated rocks into the malt.

Reinheitsgebot. German laws that govern brewing in that country, originally known as the Bavarian Purity Law of 1516 and now called the German Beer Purity Law. The law states that beer can only be brewed from water, hops, barley malt, and yeast.

saison. A Belgian summer ale that is sometimes bottle-conditioned.

Scotch ale. A very dark, strong ale. Many are brewed in Scotland, hence its name. Some microbreweries have begun brewing this style of beer.

Schwarzbier. A beer made famous in Kostritz, Germany. A very, very dark beer.

shandy. A drink made of half beer and half lemonade.

steam beer. A product of the California Gold Rush, steam beer was America's first real addition to the craft of brewing. Using large shallow vats called clarifiers, lager yeast is used at high temperatures, as if one were brewing an ale. This produces a beer with the perplexities of both an ale and a lager. The only manufacturer in the world using this patented process is the Anchor Steam Brewing Company, San Francisco, California.

stout. A very dark, high hop content ale. The most famous brewer of stout, and the originator of this style, is Guinness, of Ireland. Stouts vary from dry to sweet, but all have sugar added to them at one stage or another. Guinness tends to be on the dry side and comes in a variety of alcoholic strengths.

top-fermented. The fermentation process used to make ale.

Trappist. A bottle-conditioned, sugar-added lager made by monks in only six breweries in the world (five in Belgium, one in Holland). While others might attempt a Trappist-style beer, only these monasteries are allowed to market their beers with this term on the label. Unusually high in alcoholic content, sometimes reaching twelve percent or more, they are fruity and some of the most highly prized beers in the world.

tripel. Dutch, meaning a brewer's strongest beer. Can be a lager, but most often is an ale.

trub. German for sediment.

Vienna. A reddish beer once made famous in Vienna, Austria. Also known as Vienna malt.

Ur-/Urquell. German for original source. A term that means the first or original brewer; i.e., Pilsner Urquell is the original source or brewer of pilsner: the original pilsner.

Weisse/Weissebier/Weizenbier. Wheat beer. Often served with lemon, this is an ale of extremely light color, mostly served during the summer. The beer is brewed with mainly wheat malt.

white. Another name for a wheat beer.

wiesen/wies'n. German for meadow. This is a beer especially brewed for an occasion or a festival, like Oktoberfest.

witbier. Dutch for white. Another name for white, wheat, or weisse beer.

wort. The stage in the brewing process before the addition of the yeast. The juices that result from the cooked barley.

yeast. A fungus or microorganism that causes fermentation, turning sugar into alcohol and carbon dioxide. Lager yeast is known as *Saccharommyces uvarum,* and ale yeast is known as *Saccharommces.*

zwickelbier. An unfiltered beer in Germany, usually characterless.

zymurgy. The science of brewing and fermentation, a branch of chemistry.

INDEX